Popular Buddhist Texts from Nepal

SUNY series in Buddhist Studies
Matthew Kapstein, Editor

Popular Buddhist Texts from Nepal

Narratives and Rituals of Newar Buddhism

Todd T. Lewis

Translations in Collaboration with
Subarna Man Tuladhar and
Labh Ratna Tuladhar

Foreword by Gregory Schopen

State University of New York Press

Published by
State University of New York Press, Albany

Printed in the United States of America

For information, address State University of New York Press,
State University Plaza, Albany, N.Y. 12246

Production by Diane Ganeles
Marketing by Patrick Durocher

Library of Congress Cataloging-in-Publication Data

Popular Buddhist texts from Nepal: narratives and rituals of Newar Buddhism/Todd T. Lewis; translations in collaboration with Subarna Man Tuladhar & Labh Ratna Tuladhar.
p.cm.—(SUNY series in Buddhist studies)
Includes index.
ISBN 0-7914-4611-5 (hc.: alk. paper)—ISBN 0-7914-4612-3 (pb.: alk. paper)
1. Buddhist literature—Nepal—History and criticism. 2. Buddhist literature, Sanskrit—History and criticism. 3. Mahayana Buddhism—Nepal. I. Lewis, Todd Thornton, 1952- II. Tuladhar, Subarna Man, 1940- Ratna, 1945-III. Tuladhar, Labh Ratna. IV. Series.

BQ1029.N352 M36 2000
294.3'85—dc21 99-045350
10 9 8 7 6 5 4 3 2 1

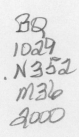

To Joy

Contents

Foreword

It is a curious fact that scholars interested in Mahāyāna Buddhism in India have paid so little attention to Nepal—indeed it may actually be perverse. It was Nepal, after all, that first revealed, and continued to supply, most of the Mahāyāna literature we have in Sanskrit. We have read, and continue to read, texts like the *Aṣṭasāhasrikā Prajñāpāramitā*, which have been judged significant, in editions based solely on manuscripts from Nepal. But we have *used* these texts—and here's the rub—in our own peculiar way: we have only *read* them (and that very selectively), as if this were the only thing they were for. We have not, moreover, approved—in fact likely seen as silly—what the Nepalese themselves did with these same texts: some, but very few, read them, too; most however, recited or had them recited (and recitation is not at all the same thing as our 'reading'), copied or had them copied when their mother died, worshipped them with aromatic powders, unguents, and pastes, or carried or saw them carried in procession. Such behavior implies a very different conception of the nature and function of sacred texts in a culture other than our own, but it is characteristic of South Asia. Mr. Edward Dimock, for example, in a delightful little book entitled *Mr. Dimock Explains the Mysteries of the East* (Chapel Hill, North Carolina: Algonquin Books, 1999), has recently described an amusing meeting between our values and those long held in South Asia. After repeated attempts to get access to (read: "capture") and old and therefore, for us, particularly valuable Bengali manuscript, this is what occurred at the moment of success:

> When they reached the village, there, sure enough, were the village headman and the communist official, all smiles and affability. They led the way to the temple, where the priest greeted them as if they were long-lost relatives and brought

> out the manuscript, in its cover of fine cloth (for it was a sacred object, deserving of care and respect), to have its picture taken. Such, in fact, was the veneration in which the manuscript was held that the top folios were unreadable, as it had for three centuries been smeared daily and reverently with the hands of the devout. As a matter of fact, of the 360 folios that the manuscript contained the top 359 were unreadable. The bottom one, with the colophon, was quite clear. (61–2)

But what Newars (and Bengalis) do with or to sacred texts is not just characteristic of South Asia. It is also the continuation of something very old: the Newar Buddhists who do what we do not approve of to *their* texts are doing precisely what these texts themselves explicitly say should be done. The *Aṣṭasāhasrikā*—to keep with the same example—has several long passages directing both monk and layman to worship books with aromatic powders, unguents, and paste, and detailing its great value. And this work is supposed to date back to the beginning of the common era. Here, then, 'late' Newar practice allows us to see clearly the enactment of 'early' Mahāyāna ideas in south Asian culture. To get a sense of how they would have looked, this otherwise would simply not be possible.

The Newar treatment of books, moreover, is not an isolated example. Some years ago I thought I was able to determine on the basis of canonical Mahāyāna texts that rebirth in *sukhāvatī* was a "generalized" religious goal for those who wrote and read these texts. But I had no idea of how this would play out in actual culture, or what it might have meant in practice, until I read Todd Lewis' "*Sukhāvatī* traditions in Newar Buddhism," (1996a) and then a whole range of possibilities opened up. There is, quite clearly, no substitute for living contexts and for Mahāyāna Buddhism in South Asia there is nothing else and nowhere better than the Newar communities of Nepal.

Ironically, while some students of the Mahāyāna have understood this, they have generally not looked in the most obvious places. One of the best of these has, for example, said: ". . . I find it extremely helpful to utilize the insights of Buddhist anthropology, the work of Buddhist culture on the group, as it were, especially in Southeast Asia. In this record I have profited greatly from the researches of Stanley Tambiah, Melford Spiro, Richard Gombrich, Gananath Obeyesekere, Sherry Ortner, Geoffrey Samuel, and various others . . ." [Paul Harrison, "Searching for the Origins of the

Mahayana: What are we Looking for?" *The Eastern Buddhist* (New Series), 28, 1995, 53) But where, one wonders, are the names of those who are working in an actual South Asian Mahāyāna culture—John Locke, David Gellner, and Todd Lewis? There is something rather strange here and it is time—indeed long overdue—that Newar Buddhism assume its rightful place in Buddhist studies. Todd Lewis' collection of both textual and ethnographic sources represents a major step in an important direction.

—Gregory Schopen, U.C.L.A.

Preface

A missionary religion originating in sixth-century B.C.E. India, Buddhism profoundly influenced the historical development of all major Asian civilizations. At the center of this tradition is a compelling spiritual vision and a path that leads to enlightenment; but underwriting Buddhism's pan-regional expansion over the millennia, was an equally compelling popular tradition that motivated householders to support the monastic elite and to commit themselves to taking refuge in the *Triratna* (Three jewels): the Buddha, the *dharma* (teachings), and the *saṃgha* (monastic order). Most Buddhists have been farmers, artisans, or merchants, not monks or intellectuals. While Buddhism attracted ascetics with myriad meditative regimens and philosophers with vast doctrinal discourse, Buddhism's mainstream traditions were those that cultivated the great majority of the population: exemplary stories that defined living rightly in the world and rituals designed to help householders realize the good and spiritual life.

The goal of this book is to help illustrate this assessment and, by so doing, to suggest correctives to the ahistorical and idealized portrayals of Buddhism that have been conveyed, often unintentionally, by both academic writers and modern exponents. To accomplish this, I utilize research among the Newar Buddhists of Nepal to explicate how five important vernacular texts have been incorporated into this community. These Newar case studies from a Himalayan oasis of Indic Buddhism yield several sets of data: they illumine how certain popular and ritual texts contributed to a Buddhist's religious life; they serve as paradigms regarding the pragmatic adaptation of the faith, particularly (but not limited to) societies adhering to Mahāyāna Buddhism; and finally, in highlighting a host of comparative or historical issues that arise, the discussion seeks to advance the understanding of Newar Buddhist history as well.

This book responds to the need for locality-specific research in religious studies. Scholarship on Buddhism has been dominated either by philological-textual studies that usually have left texts unrelated to their community context(s) *or* by ethnographic studies that have often neglected local literati and their domesticated vernacular literatures (Cabezon 1995; Gomez 1995b). The result has been either highly idealized portrayals of Buddhism based upon a small elite's philosophical definitions and disputations *or* more anthropological representations with cursory concern with a society's doctrinal awareness or textual culture.

The texts presented in this study arose from my earliest ethnographic fieldwork in Nepal (1979–82) when I attempted to collect and read many "working texts" published by local pandits pertinent to my much larger effort of researching modern Buddhism in the Kathmandu Valley. Hundreds were located and several have already been published either separately (e.g., Lewis 1989b 1994a) or as sources for thematic studies (e.g., 1993c 1996a). The five texts in this volume were among the many I worked through with my teachers and informants as I sought to learn Newari and to survey the labyrinth of surviving practices.

In pursuing the study of this vernacular literature on popular Buddhist narratives and rituals, I was finding the confluence of my own training in classical and Nepalese languages, the history of religions, and anthropology; in so doing, I came to realize the value of highlighting this vast and universal textual genre that has remained largely ignored by scholars specializing in the study of Buddhism. Over the last decade, the various disciplines comprising Buddhist studies (textual, historical, and anthropological) have converged in recognizing that the field needs to direct further attention to vernacular texts, ritual studies, and local expressions of devotion (e.g., Hallisey 1995b; Bowen 1995; Obeyesekere 1991; Strong 1992; Hoffman 1992). This book addresses the need for interdisciplinary scholarship, dialogue, and research in order to make progress in constructing Buddhist history with much more rigorous sociological and cultural imagination.

I have indicated that this book has been written in collaboration with two Newar men of letters from the Kathmandu Buddhist community, Labh Ratna and Subarna Man Tuladhar. These two individuals are distinguished members of the Urāy merchant community in which I have conducted most of my research. Both became friends and colleagues during my first year of fieldwork and their continuing association has enriched all of my subsequent investigations. Besides being learned about their own cultural heritage and authors of Newari short stories and religious poems, Subarna Man has been a decorated career civil servant and Labh Ratna has been a leading merchant.

We initially spent considerable periods of time reading through a variety of texts that they (and others) brought to my attention. Subarna Man and I initially read the texts in Chapters 2, 4, 5, and 6 and Labh Ratna read through the long *Simhalāvadāna* text with me. When I returned to these texts during a 1987 post-doctoral year in Nepal, I thoroughly revised these very rough translations and consulted with them again. I also made additional inquiries on the various ways in which these texts were utilized in community practice. Without their initial guidance, patience, and insight, I would not have been so wisely directed to these important sources or so expertly instructed in understanding them. To use Buddhist language, this book involves a large portion of Subarna Man and Labh Ratna's *karman* and I express here my immense gratitude to them as friends, scholars, and now as published collaborators. I must also note that the historical and analytical interpretations that I have wrapped around these texts are the responsibility of my own scholarship and authorship.

In assembling these case studies from the Newar community, I must point out that to do so often entails interpretative reconstructions of discrete Buddhist traditions. The fall of the Newar city-states in 1769 to the Shah dynasty of Gorkha, a military conquest that culminated in the creation of the modern state of Nepal, radically changed the patterns of local support for Buddhism and Hinduism. The latter, always a strong and roughly equal presence alongside Buddhism from the earliest known records of the valley (ca. 450 C.E.), became the object of almost exclusive patronage for the new dynasty. Other state acts included the seizing of lands endowed to support Buddhist institutions or festivals and new laws enacted to limit cultural performances. Many Newar groups wishing to assimilate with the new state's Hindu elite, especially the high-caste Shresthas, abandoned most of their connections to local Buddhist rituals and institutions. The loss of patronage and land endowments has slowly undermined the Newar householder *saṃgha* and internal factionalism has further weakened the tradition through the later decades of this century. All religious traditions now contend with the environmental and political crises engulfing a nation ranked among the poorest in the world; they must also compete with the myriad forms of modernization that draw people and their resources away from the older and increasingly fragmenting traditional practices.

The Kathmandu Valley's urban Hindu-Buddhist culture is one of the most remarkable and complex in Asia and this study admittedly takes a limited sample of it into consideration. Drawing upon texts still used in the modern period, I aim to reconstruct premodern observances from a chaotic pattern that simultaneously mixes archaic traditional continuities with modern elements of breakdown, revival, and transformation. There are many cultural case studies one might choose to highlight from this mid-Himalayan Valley; this is one of the most compelling for anyone interested in Buddhism's long Asian pilgrimage.

I would like to express my thanks for the compassion and understanding shown by many Nepali friends, for without them my studies in Nepal would not have been possible. The completion of my research in Nepal has been the greatest learning experience in my life and I thank every Newar for their contribution. For invitations to their households, for openness to my witnessing their religious observances with unfailing hospitality, for taking time from business and family life, and for sharing very personal thoughts, many women and men contributed to making my research richly blessed. Special mention goes, in addition to my two collaborators, to Nirmal Tuladhar and his family for their ever-generous support; to Nati Vajra Vajracarya, Hera Tuladhar, and their families for the far-ranging help emanating from my "second home" in Dagu Baha; and to Sumon Kamal, Dharma Ratna, Babu Ratna, and Pratyek Man Tuladhar for teaching me about doctrinal matters. Very special citations go to Sanu Vajracarya and Dolma Sherpa, my research assistant and *didī*, respectively; without their constant thoughtfulness, compassion, and energy, I could not have completed the range of studies that I began.

I also wish to express special acknowledgment to my teachers at Columbia University, particularly Ainslie Embree, Morton Klass, Fred Underwood, and Alex Wayman. I recall my indebtedness to the late Margaret Mead for hard-nosed practical fieldwork training and for the inspiration she imparted to everyone she taught. I also express special thanks to Stanley J. Tambiah both for his pathbreaking work on Buddhism and society and for his encouragement to pursue the interests represented in this volume. Finally, I also salute with affection the kind and insightful mentoring by Theodore Riccardi Jr. who pointed me toward such rich and challenging fieldwork and then patiently supported my scholarly development in every way.

I wish to acknowledge others who helped me in various ways through periods of fieldwork, writing, and scholarly survival: John Locke, Peter Burleigh, Kathy Krumhus, Kaye Wilson, Lynn Bennett, Chad and Linda Meyer, Brian and Judy Hollander, Ann and George Lewis, Richard English, David Smith, Steve and Sherry Culbertson, Tom Kelly, Steve Wilstein, Thornton and Dandy Lewis, David Sassoon, and Gerald Berreman.

I most gratefully acknowledge a Fulbright-Hays Dissertation Fellowship that supported my early fieldwork in Nepal (1979–82) and a Fulbright Faculty Postdoctoral Fellowship (1987) that allowed many kinds of follow-up studies. I also appreciate the support given by the staff of the United States Educational Foundation in Nepal, at the Center for Nepal and Asian Studies at Tribhuvan University, and the offices of His Majesty's Government of Nepal. More recent grants allowed short-term research excursions back to Nepal over the past six years and I thank the College of the Holy Cross, the American Philosophical Society, the American Academy of Religion, and the National Endowment for the Humanities for their support.

The chapters of this book evolved over the past ten years, some through their genesis as articles and book chapters,[1] others as translation projects. They have been improved through the beneficial and thoughtful editorial comments provided by Theodore Riccardi Jr., Robin Lewis, Grafton Nunes, Mani Gopal Jha, and anonymous manuscript reviewers. Thanks to James Giambrone for commissioning artists at Indigo Gallery, Kathmandu, to draw the five goddesses for chapter 6. I would especially like to thank Gregory Schopen for his general encouragement and for his many useful comments on possible historical connections between Newar traditions and those of ancient Indic Buddhism. The book also benefited from a thoroughgoing review and extensive comments made by

David N. Gellner. I dedicate any merit earned from insight conveyed by this volume to all who gave assistance, while bearing sole responsibility for any demerit resulting from my own ignorance or from other shortcomings manifested in the text.

Finally, I dedicate this work to Joy, who has supported me unstintingly throughout my academic career, shared many journeys while always sustaining the balance in our family despite the short and long absences that scholarship demands.

CHAPTER 1

Introduction: Buddhism as a Pragmatic Religious Tradition

Our approach to Religion can be called "vernacular" . . . [It is] concerned with the kinds of data that may, eventually, be able to give us some substantial insight into how religions have played their part in history, affecting people's ability to respond to environmental crises; to earthquakes, floods, famines, pandemics; as well as to social ills and civil wars. Besides these evils, there are the everyday difficulties and personal disasters we all face from time to time. Religions have played their part in keeping people sane and stable. . . . We thus see religions as an integral part of vernacular history, as a strand woven into lives of individuals, families, social groups, and whole societies. Religions are like technology in that respect: ever present and influential to people's ability to solve life's problems day by day.

Vernon Reynolds and Ralph Tanner,
The Social Ecology of Religion

The Buddhist faith expresses itself most authentically in the processions of statues through towns, the nocturnal illuminations in the streets and countryside. It is on such occasions that communion between the religious and laity takes place . . . without which the religion could be no more than an exercise of recluse monks.

Jacques Gernet,
Buddhism in Chinese Society: An Economic History from the Fifth to the Tenth Centuries

> Whosoever maintains that it is karma that injures beings, and besides it there is no other reason for pain, his proposition is false. . . .
>
> *Milindapañha* IV.I.62

Health, good luck, peace, and progeny have been the near-universal wishes of humanity. Buddhism, like all world religions, evolved to affect the human condition positively, utilizing its powers over the unseen forces that operate behind and beyond the mundane world. Since prosperity and security are optimum for both the individual and for the collective pursuit of spiritual goals, it was natural that Buddhism developed pragmatic means to achieve them. This "pragmatic ritual repertoire" included highly efficient donations to make good *karman* (*puṇya*) and to insure the regular recitation of the Buddha's words; it also featured the performance of rituals (*pūjā*) specified by Buddhas and bodhisattvas designed to project auspicious influences, to engage protective beings throughout the pantheon, and to repel all evil.

While textbooks rarely emphasize it, ritual has always defined the devout and active householder's adherence to Buddhism. The tradition's earliest stories recount the advantages of ritual actions that worked for individuals while also serving the important role of unifying Buddhist communities, both spiritually and socially.

This book provides a sample of the key rituals and narratives in one surviving Indic community's popular Mahāyāna observances. Each text focuses on the protective powers connected to the Buddhist *triratna* in order to spread well-being among the monks and nuns, among householders, and across the wider community, including the natural environment. Every Newar case study thus offers an example of how Mahāyāna masters extended their service to householders beyond instruction in salvation-oriented belief and practice so as to organize the performance of rituals. This "spiritual pragmatism" was one of the universal developments in the diaspora of successful Buddhist missions throughout Asia (e.g., Zurcher 1972; Yun-Hua 1977; Buswell 1990; Strickmann 1990).

Popular Narratives and their "Domestication" in Buddhist Communities

One attribute of Gautama Buddha as a "great teacher of gods and men" was doubtless his skillful turning of a story to demonstrate a doctrinal point, matching teaching to audience. Such parables are found in all canons compiled by the early schools. Hundreds of stories attributed to Shākyamuni are *karman*-retribution parables that illustrate the cause and effect of moral acts and ritual actions. Throughout Buddhism's first millennium, literati collected and redacted many such tales, called *avadāna* and *jātaka*s, and they are among the first identifiable genres of collected teachings (Law 1939). Many have pan-Indic elements, but were revised to conform to Buddhist doctrine, ethics, and hagiography. As indicated by its title, an *avadāna* (significant deed or adventure[1]) is a form of Buddhist literature that imparts simple religious instruction through the heroic actions of a bodhisattva (the future Shākyamuni or another), Buddha, or another spiritually advanced being.

Familiarity with these narratives and with their public recitation eventually became a recognized monastic avocation, as one text notes six such roles within the *saṃgha* that include folklorists (*tirascakathika*). The magnitude of the folklore collections is striking, as clearly this genre found a widespread audience among the laity through public storytelling.[2] The earliest examples of Buddhist art contain scenes from these stories and they remained a major thematic focus on later Buddhist monuments (e.g., Fontein 1981; Krairksh 1974; Grunwedel 1912; Mair 1997; Shih 1993). Among the earliest records of Buddhism in Nepal, a sixth-century inscription refers to a *stūpa* decorated with scenes from the *Kinnarī Jātaka* (Riccardi 1980: 273; Lienhard 1988: xiv).

It should not be assumed, however, that this literature was directed solely toward householders. Monks and nuns also collected these stories, but it seems that this was done just as much to explain the origins of prescriptions and proscriptions within the *saṃgha*s as for preaching to the laity (Schopen 1994a, 1994b). The Thai tradition (since the eleventh century) of artists sculpting scenes from *jātaka* stories on the *sima* stones (those used to mark the boundaries for *saṃgha* assemblies) also indicates this monastic-narrative connection within the archaeological record (Krairiksh 1974). Thus, by focusing on popular narratives, one is examining one of the earliest genres of Buddhist text, one that traveled everywhere Buddhism did, a literature that was the concern of all Buddhists, monastic and laity.

"Domestication" is a central concern in this study. I define it as the dialectical historical process by which a religious tradition is adapted to a region or ethnic group's socioeconomic and cultural life. While "Great traditions" supply a clear spiritual direction to followers who are close to the charismatic founders, including norms of orthodox adaptation and missionizing, religious traditions' historical survival has been related—often paradoxically—to their being "multivocalic" so that later devotees have a large spectrum of doctrine, rituals, situational instructions, and exemplary folktales to draw upon. In order to study "religious domestication" one seeks to demonstrate the underlying reasons for selectivity from the whole as the tradition evolves in specific places and times to the "logic of life" in a locality. As Charles Hallisey notes, this is one of the basic historical questions for locating and understanding the role of texts in any society:

> If the survival of any particular text is not self-explanatory, but in fact it is normally the case that texts fade in their significance as social change occurs, then we need to discover how these texts that do endure are maintained. (Hallisey 1995b: 51)

Buddhism became an expansive movement, then, as it successfully conveyed its teachings in forms that could reach beyond ascetics and logicians, that is, in vernacular narratives that could effectively and distinctively shape the lives of those comprising the wider society.[3] Through such domesticated stories, Buddhists grasped the significance of the religious teachings through example and exemplar, established their localities as sites of bodhisattva-related actions, and defined their moral duties and ethnic identities.

Stories reach deeply into a society's collective culture. They present, to use Clifford Geertz's terminology (1966), *models for* positive behavior and *images of* negative behavior, doing so with entertaining, multilayered plots that grip the individual's psyche (Amore and Shinn 1981). As such, as Stephen Crites points out, "[They] are the preconditions of experience to the extent that we move to their rhythms and they enter our dreams and ruminations, called to mind without our bidding, sometimes jarred into mind at unlikely moments by dramatically similar episodes in the broad daylight of our waking lives" (Crites 1975: 49).

The most influential Buddhist textual sources, then, cannot be equated with the entire canon that resides in the monastic libraries, but must feature the popular stories domesticated in vernacular tongues within given localities (Strong 1992: xi); their attraction was that they came to engender the community's familiarity such that, as Wendy Doniger O'Flaherty has noted, "Retelling the myths takes on the function of communion rather than communication. People listen to the stories not merely to learn something new (communication) but to relive, together, the stories that they already know, stories about themselves (communion)" (O'Flaherty 1989: 87).

The moral-ethical and utopian dimensions of Buddhist *jātaka*s and *avadāna*s will be explored in this volume. In their article on this topic, Hallisey and Anne Hansen define a three-dimensional field of meaning enabled by these narratives:

> *Prefiguration* (the effect of narratives in enlarging an agent's moral horizon), *configuration* (the power of narratives to expose the opaqueness of moral intention), and *refiguration* (the healing and transformative potential of narratives). (Hallisey and Hansen 1996: 308)

Buddhist stories also functioned via domestication to fix geographic and ethnic identification with the stories' places and characters. In the Indic hearth and out to the immediate Central Asian, northern, and southern frontiers, Buddhists identified places in the local topography where events described in these stories took place. (This "localization" is found in every Newar story.) They also in some cases claim as ethnic ancestors the protagonists found in a given story (as seen in chaps. 2 and 5). Literary "domestications" using such specific redactions of pan-Buddhist stories often have been done in the oral formulations in local dialects, as regional editors have "made a story their own."[4]

As Buddhism was constituted by myriad localizations without an overarching institutional authority, the doctrines and ethos of *avadāna*s and *jātaka*s provide invaluable insight about the missionary expansion of the faith, their becoming, in Arthur F. Wright's terms, "a treasure trove of legend" that "offered a new model for . . . the king who rules well and successfully through devotion to Buddha . . . and the related model of the munificent donor, the *Mahādānapati*. . . ." (Wright 1959: 170). In China, too, monks composed a class of illustrated vernacular texts called *pien-wen* from the eighth century onward in order to domesticate Buddhist ideas for popular audiences (Overmyer 1980: 170).

In modern Nepal, the Newar Buddhist *saṃgha's* role as translator and publicizer of the popular narratives also endures. "Folklorists" in the *saṃgha* still keep hand-copied personal story compilations that they use when invited by patrons to "tell stories" for an evening, a week, or a month. They still do so when they accompany disciples to Buddhist pilgrimage sites around the Kathmandu Valley. This recycling of tales from ancient texts by living teachers continues right into the modern period with the published editions featured in this book. The cultural process provides a Buddhist example of what A. K. Ramanujan so aptly describes as "The way texts do not simply go from one written form to another but get reworked through oral cycles that surround the written word" (Ramanujan 1990: 12). For, indeed, in modern Nepal the most popular stories are still told in public story recitations that attract hundreds.[5] Several of the texts in this volume represent a literary rendering of the most renowned performances of Buddhist storytellers from the local *saṃgha*.

The texts that are presented in chapters 2, 4, and 5 were compiled and published by Badri Bajracarya, modern Kathmandu's storyteller extraordinaire and respected scholar. Whether in one of the town's *vihāra*s or in the Kāṣṭamaṇḍapa, the great public assembly building from which Kathmandu derives its name, it was Badrī's sessions in the early 1980s that drew hundreds to hear his dramatic, multivocalic, and clearly elucidated doctrinal presentations as he read from, and expounded upon, popular *avadāna*s and *jātaka*s. The simple language of his stories employs repetitions to capture the storyteller's expository manner. In this continuance of ancient tradition, such Newar pandits conform to observations made in India fourteen centuries ago by the Chinese pilgrim I-Tsing: "The object of composing *jātaka*s in verse is to teach the doctrine of universal salvation in a beautiful style, agreeable to the popular mind and attractive to readers" (Takakasu 1896: 163).

What Newar tradition affords, then, is the chance to study literary redaction as part of the larger domestication of the Buddhist faith in the Kathmandu Valley. A useful question to ponder is this: among the many hundreds of *jātaka*s and *avadāna*s composed in the Buddhist world, most of which in their Sanskrit redactions were conveyed into Nepal, why were these few adopted, given local identification, and repeatedly recited within the local Buddhist community?[6] This study will attempt to formulate answers to this question for these five texts.[7] As it considers both popular Mahāyāna texts and rituals, another useful and recurring concern will be to consider how Buddhist rituals derived from these texts exemplify and express doctrinal views, a subject we must now introduce.

The Development of Buddhist Ritualism

Buddhist doctrine explains that all six realms of existence[8] are linked by causal contingencies and that the *dharma* affects all spheres universally.[9] Because the forces of the universe are connected to the unfolding actions associated with the *triratna*, the earth may quake (e.g., when a Buddha reaches enlightenment or reveals a *sūtra*) or rend apart (e.g., throwing Devadatta to Avici Hell), heavens can open (e.g., as part of a *sūtra* revelation), or "magical" transformations of outward appearances may occur (e.g., in response to an "Act of Truth" or when a householder realizes nirvaṇa and is instantly transformed into a monk/nun). All schools accept this nexus of causal contingency.

To evoke this fundamental cosmic power, the earliest tradition identified certain collections of the Buddha's words that had an extraordinary effect when carefully recited. In the Pali literature, there are passages in which Shākyamuni utters mantras to heal a woman who suffered a miscarriage, to remedy snake bites, to cure diseases, or to make rain fall (Bharati 1955: 104).[10] A *Dīgha Nikāya* passage states that the "Four World Lords" had given *mantra*s to the Buddha and promises certain protection to anyone chanting them (Thomas 1951: 186).[11] These short recitations were remembered and classified under *paritta* in the Pali tradition and as *rakṣā* in Sanskrit texts (Skilling 1992). Such spells were regarded as efficacious for promoting longevity, for alleviating suffering from a variety of crises, and for creating a sort of radiant auspiciousness permeating individuals and/or localities (Gombrich 1971; Prebish 1975b: 168). Such *mantra* recitations are elements in all of the Newar texts considered in this study. (Further discussion of this subject is found in chap. 6.)

The presence of such recitation traditions in all schools underlines the important early doctrine that not all phenomena are caused by karmic contingencies. This teaching is forcefully expressed in the Theravādin *Milindapañha* through the Monk Nāgasena's explanation of how the Buddha Shākyamuni had been subject to pain and disease throughout his lifetime:

> . . . It is not all suffering that has its root in karma. There are eight causes by which sufferings arise, by which many beings suffer pain. . . . Superabundance of wind and of bile, and of phlegm, the union of these humors, [seasonal] variations in temperature, the avoiding of dissimilarities, external agency, and karma. . . .
>
> And there is the act that has karma as its fruit, and the pain so brought about arising from the act done. So what arises as the fruit of karma is much less than that which arises from other causes. And the ignorant go too far when they say that every pain is produced by karma.
>
> No one without a Buddha's insight can fix the extent of the action of karma.
>
> (Rhys-Davids 1963: 191–93)

Since most of still-unenlightened humanity cannot "fix the extent of the action of *karman*," it is always apt to chant *mantra*s that can harness both the powers of the Buddha and his teachings to affect both karmic and nonkarmic contingencies. This core Buddhist understanding of the multifaceted causalities affecting human destiny was no doubt the foundation for the later elaboration of Buddhist ritualism—in all lineages—directed toward the devotee's search for health, prosperity, long life, and good rebirth.[12]

Thus, it became the ubiquitous goal of Buddhists to sustain and to nurture the monks and laity—the *pariṣad*—as this constitutes the central "project" of any Buddhist community. In exchange for the material donations (*dāna*) that have housed, clothed, and fed them, monks and nuns from the earliest days were instructed to serve the world through their example of renunciation and through meditation (Wijayaratna 1990), by performing rituals (Gombrich 1971: 201ff; Carrithers 1990: 149), and by providing medical service (Zysk 1991). All Buddhist rituals stem from this compassionate occupation, expressing devotion to the *triratna* and asserting their interrelationship: on the authority of the Buddha, the *saṃgha* acts to utilize the *dharma* to create mundane and supramundane blessings.[13] Domesticated Buddhisms across Asia developed many avenues whereby monastic leaders adapted their lineage's resources as a "Triple Jewel" to remain a compelling refuge.[14]

The Ritual Innovations of Mahāyāna Buddhism

For those who adopted the Mahāyāna bodhisattva ethos, serving the lay community was their compassionate duty and an important channel for this was ritual. It was doubtless *saṃgha* specialists who applied the Mahāyāna doctrines on emptiness, mind, and Buddha nature to articulate myriad efficacious actions and utterances[15]—*mantra*s and *dhāraṇī*s—to mitigate suffering and to cultivate spiritual insight.

To tap the often invisible but always-enduring Buddha/bodhisattva connection to the human world and to express their aspiration for compassionate service, Mahāyāna practitioners sanctioned an immense ritual agenda to enhance their society's well-being and to make the laity's spiritual journey easier (Miller 1962: 430; Strickmann 1990; Lewis 1993c). Michael Pye has noted the doctrinal basis of this development:

> The main focal point of Buddhist devotions from earliest times . . . [must be seen in] the context of the thought of skillful means [*upāya*]. It is not only doctrinal concepts which are understood as skillful means but also ritual practice. . . . The Mahāyāna articulation of Buddhism as a working religion along these lines is altogether controlled by the concept of skillful means. (Pye 1978: 58–59)

The evolution of Mahāyāna Buddhist ritualism must also be understood in relation to other developments in Buddhist history. The growth of popular devotion to celestial bodhisattvas such as Avalokiteshvara and Tārā fostered ritual elaborations. Indic Mahāyāna *bhakti* texts directed Buddhists to take refuge in these divinities that occupied a similar, competing niche alongside the great *deva*s of the Brahmanical pantheon. Popular texts recount these bodhisattvas' rescuing devotees, bestowing boons, and controlling nature. The establishment of Buddhist temples to these saviors created the need for attending ritualists and for the development of proper ritual procedures for daily, lunar monthly, and yearly observances. For this reason, the great texts of the later tradition, for instance, the *Saddharmapuṇḍarīka* and the *Bodhicaryāvatāra,* all contain chapters concerned with Buddhist *pūjā* and its rewards. A host of ritual guidebooks were also composed in this later Buddhist era.

As an extension of Mahāyāna Buddhism, the Vajrayāna tradition that grew in importance from the fifth century C.E. onward in South Asia furthered these ritualistic tendencies (Snellgrove 1987: 456), representing both a critique and a fulfillment of early Mahāyāna praxis (Gomez 1987). The chief *tantra*-path exponents and exemplars, the *siddhas*, developed *sādhana* traditions outside of the scholarly monastic circles and rejected the prevalent multi-lifetime, slow approximation bodhisattva approach to enlightenment. These yogins introduced the means to cultivate *prajñā* (insight) by visualizations from *shūnyatā* (emptiness) and by directly associating with the Buddha's three "secrets": Body (*mudrā*), Speech (*mantra*), and Mind (*samādhi*) (Wayman 1971: 443). Through a host of innovative techniques, the Vajrayāna masters showed the immediate possibility of harnessing the experience of *shūnyatā* in order to attain enlightenment.

As a corollary to their soteriological discoveries, the *siddhas* also composed rituals that applied a master's power to accomplish both supramundane and mundane goals. The later scholars who eventually organized and domesticated the *sādhana* practices fashioned a Mahāyāna-Vajrayāna Buddhist culture that emphasized *pūjā* (ritual performance) and *vrata* (devotional rites to a chosen deity, as in chaps. 4 and 5). It is likely that both were originally designed for use as intensive practices on the two *uposadha* days each month and on the two *aṣṭamī* days. At the root of advanced Vajrayāna practice was *abhiṣekha* (esoteric initiation) and ritual performances that constitute an important part of most tantric texts (Snellgrove 1987: 456); pilgrimage was also emphasized in the religious life-style (Bharati 1955).

This shift in religious emphases was also accompanied by adaptations within the *saṃghas*. Mahāyāna monks who adopted the bodhisattva ethos viewed serving the lay community as their chief duty, and ritual was a principal medium. As Robert J. Miller has noted:

> This responsibility may be thought of as community service. Thus, the . . . monk . . . rejects complete release from the cycle of existence, choosing instead to return again and again in the world in order to aid others in attaining release. This new duty is added to the old one of achieving personal enlightenment through the performance of the regular

> prayers and observances. . . . Since the layman is unable to pursue enlightenment directly, the *saṃgha* . . . is obliged to find a means by which he can pursue it indirectly. (Miller 1962: 430)

Thus, by establishing many levels of legitimate religious practice for layfolk and for many areas in which the *saṃgha* served society, the Mahāyāna tradition sought to inspire and to unite a large community. Farmers, traders, and artisans had a place in the spiritual hierarchy, as ritual offerings linked householders to temple-dwelling celestial bodhisattvas as well as to their ritualists and teachers in the *saṃgha*. By the Pāla period in northeast India (ca. 750–950), this sort of Mahāyāna-Vajrayāna culture flowered (Dutt 1962: 389); it clearly shaped the emergence of Buddhism in the Kathmandu Valley, located just north of Bihar in the Himalayan foothills, as it did the successful domestication of Buddhism in East Asia and Tibet. Before proceeding further in this area, we must finally introduce the community of contextual reference, the Newars of Nepal.

Nepal and Newar Buddhism

Any scholar who has worked with Indic Mahāyāna texts or with later Buddhist iconography knows of the plenitude of Sanskrit manuscripts preserved in the Buddhist and state libraries of the Kathmandu Valley. The discovery of these Nepalese manuscripts in the nineteenth century was a landmark in modern Buddhist studies; sent out to Calcutta, Paris, and London by the indefatigable collector Brian H. Hodgson, the British Resident from 1820 to 1843, these texts gave European scholars their first complete overview of northern Buddhism's vast Indic literary heritage (Hunter 1896). Since Nepal was largely sealed off from the outside world until 1951, only recently have scholars recognized the value of Sylvain Levi's long-ago assertion (1905, 1: 28) that other aspects of Buddhist culture there *besides Sanskrit texts* might provide case studies for garnering insight on the faith's later Indic history.

"Nepal" until the modern state's formation (1769) referred only to a roughly three-hundred-square-mile valley in the central Himalayan foothills. The mountainous topography shaped Nepal's destiny to remain as an independent petty state and its predominantly Indicized civilization developed relatively unmolested by outside states. The fertility of valley soils allowed for intensive rice and for other crop cultivation; more lucrative were the earnings from trans-Himalayan trade, as merchants centered in the valley could control the movement of goods from the Gangetic plains to the Tibetan plateau using the valley as an entrepôt (Lewis 1993b). The wealth from trade allowed the peoples of the Kathmandu Valley to import, domesticate, and reproduce many traditions in a distinctive urban civilization organized on caste principles and around both Hinduism and Buddhism. There have been Sanskrit *paṇḍitas* in Nepal for over fifteen hundred years; equally long-established were Hindu temples and *ashrams*, Buddhist monasteries and *stūpas,* and wealthy aristocrat and merchant patrons.

"Newār" derives from the place name "Nepāl." There has also been a diaspora of Newars to market towns throughout Nepal, the eastern Himalayan hills, to Tibet, and across South Asia (Gellner 1986; Lewis and Shakya 1988; Lewis 1993b). "Newari" is a modern English neologism for the Tibeto-Burman language spoken in the Kathmandu Valley. There are two emic terms preferred by Newars: the colloquial *Newa: Bhāy* or the Sanskritized *Nepāl Bhāṣa* that also expresses the old pre-Shah (before 1769) boundary of "Nepāl" as the Kathmandu Valley.

The Newars also proved themselves exceptionally able artisans, adapting and domesticating Indic ideals into quite beautiful expressions of lost wax metal icons, stone and wood sculpture, multistory wooden architecture, and painting. Over the past millennium, Newar artisans were employed across Tibet and their workshops in the valley supplied the needs of the "devotional goods market" that accompanied the expansion of Buddhism across the Tibetan plateau (Vitali 1990; Bue 1985,1986).

Three city-states—Bhaktapur, Kathmandu, and Lalitpur—came to dominate the valley, although smaller towns and villages have given the polity a broad variation in settlement types (Gellner and Quigley 1995). After conquest by a Kshatriya dynasty from Gorkha in 1769, state policies favoring Hinduism precipitated the decline of Buddhist traditions, although a great wealth of both devotional and cultural observance remain. Today, with Kathmandu the capital of the modern state and a center of contact with the outside world, there are still many surviving archaic cultural traditions. A Mahāyāna-Vajrayāna Buddhist culture is among the most unique of them.

Buddhism has existed in Nepal since at least the Gupta era. Throughout the centuries of political autonomy, the Kathmandu Valley remained accessible to migrants, monks, and traders. Newar

Buddhism has always been predominantly "Indic," and through Nepal later Indic Mahāyāna traditions were conveyed to Tibet; at times, too, Tibetan Buddhist influences have been strong (Lewis 1989c, 1996d; Lewis and Jamspal 1988). In at least the last four centuries, Nepalese Buddhism has shared much in common with the domesticated forms of Mahāyāna Buddhism in modern Tibet and Japan, notably with a householder *saṃgha,* special emphasis on death ritualism, and most preeminent devotion shown to great regional *stūpa*s and to the celestial bodhisattva Avalokiteshvara.

Despite Newar Buddhism's slow decline, over three hundred Buddhist *vihāra*s (monasteries) still exist (Locke 1985) as do *vajrācārya* ritualists, bodhisattva temples, *stūpas,* Mahāyāna festivals, tantric meditation passed on through *dikṣā* lineages, and *avadāna*-related pilgrimage traditions. Devout Buddhists still form a large proportion of the valley's urban population and being Buddhist remains a vital marker of group identity (Gellner 1992; Lewis 1989b, 1995a, 1996c). This rich cultural survival disproves the often-repeated assertion that Indic Buddhism ever completely died: the Newars in their small but vibrant oasis of tradition continue to practice Indic Mahāyāna-Vajrayāna Buddhism (Lienhard 1984) alongside a Hindu majority. In fact, Buddhism has survived in Nepal by adapting to the logic of caste society, by incorporating the pollution/purity ethos of Brahmanical *dharmashastra* law codes, and by supporting Hindu kingship while continuing to articulate an alternative counter-(Hindu)-culture where Mahāyāna practices, deities, and tantric initiations were considered superior.

The Buddhism of most Newars is exoteric Mahāyāna devotionalism, as they direct their devotions to *caitya*s in their courtyards and neighborhoods and to the great *stūpa*s such as Svayambhū (Locke 1986, Lewis 1984: 86–120, Gutschow 1997). Mahāyāna adherents also express strong devotion for the celestial bodhisattvas and make regular offerings at temples and shrines dedicated to them, especially to Avalokiteshvara and Mahākāla, among others. Newar Buddhists participate periodically in special observances dedicated to these divinities—a host of *pūjā*s and *jātra*s—which hold the promise of transforming their worldly and spiritual destinies (Locke 1987, Lewis 1989a). Most laity also worship other Indic deities: Gaṇesha, Bhīmsen, Shiva, Viṣṇu, Devī in many guises, *nāgas,* and so forth. One strong belief is that worshiping all local deities is the Mahāyāna ideal (Gellner 1992: 75,82).

The Newar Buddhist *saṃgha* is one of the "householder monks" now limited to only two endogamous caste groups having the surnames *Vajrācārya* and *Shākya*. These *saṃgha*s still dwell in courtyards referred to as *vihāra* (New.: *bāhā*) and undergo first (in local parlance) *shrāvaka*-styled celibate ordination, then (usually just a few days later) Mahāyāna-styled initiation into the householder bodhisattva *saṃgha* (Locke 1975; Gellner 1988). Like married Tibetan lamas of the Nyingmapa order, they then serve the community's ritual needs, with some among them specializing in textual study, medicine, astrology, and meditation. David N. Gellner has aptly characterized modern Newar Buddhism as a religion in which "the good Buddhist" is one who conforms to prescribed ritual practices (Gellner 1992: 3, 134); local Buddhist intellectual culture today does not emphasize any singular doctrinal formulation of Mahāyāna Buddhism.

The lay majority in the Newar Buddhist community understands basic Mahāyāna doctrines as conveyed by *avadāna* and *jātaka* stories that feature bodhisattvas, their spiritual virtues (*pāramitās*), and related practices (e.g., Lienhard 1963). In addition to compiling many recensions of these tales and telling them in public sessions, the *vajrācārya*s also perform for their community dozens of highly sophisticated Buddhist life-cycle rites (Lewis 1994a), healing ceremonies, and many other rituals adapted for local festivals and pilgrimages.

Newar Buddhism also has an esoteric level: Vajrayāna initiations (Skt.: *dīkṣa* or *abhiṣeka;* New.: *dekka*) that direct meditation and ritual to tantric deities such as Saṃvara, Hevajra, and their consorts (*yoginīs*). It is the *vajrācārya* spiritual elite that also passes on these Vajrayāna initiations to members of other high castes, including merchants and artisans; this training in tantric meditation and ritual forms the basis for the authority of their ritual service for the community (Stablein 1976c). Newar laity support the local *vajrācārya saṃgha* that helps them, in return, to look after their spiritual destiny in this world and beyond. In their maintenance of this exchange and out of concern for *puṇya,* most Newars very closely resemble lay Buddhists in other countries. We now turn to the central interest of this study, the pragmatic ritual and narrative traditions incorporated into the Mahāyāna-Vajrayāna culture of the Kathmandu Valley.

Fig 1.1. Sculpture Illustrating the Three Paths of the Newar Buddhist Tradition

Judging by the central Sanskrit texts, icons, and rituals still utilized by Vajrācāryas and Shākyas of the Newar *saṃgha,* it is clear that for roughly the last one thousand years Kathmandu Valley Buddhists have roughly extended the cultural developments that coalesced in the Pala regions of northeast India.[16] The Newars, as with most Buddhists across Asia, seem to have closed the door on core formulations of doctrine; perhaps influenced by teachings of the *dharma*'s decline (Williams 1989: 10; Nattier 1991), and possibly overwhelmed by the sheer diversity of alternative doctrinal formulations, new emphasis, and high priority shifted toward "preserving Buddha tradition."

One could surmise that certainly by 1200 Mahāyāna devotees in Nepal regarded the basic religious questions as solved: the bodhisattva ideal became the predominant religious standard and the philosophical understanding of the universe—for those concerned with intellectual subtleties—was rooted in Nāgārjuna's Mādhyamaka dialectic or in Yogācāra idealism (Willis 1979; Mus 1964). Householders inclined to more immediate accomplishments could proceed upon any among dozens of Vajrayāna paths that held the promise of attaining quick spiritual progress toward enlightenment. The status of Mahāyāna-Vajrayāna texts as they evolved in the early modern Newar tradition is expressed in the set of Nine Texts (*Navadharma* or *Nava Grantha*) arranged in the *dharma maṇḍala* and used in the *vrata* rituals (discussed in chaps. 4 and 5):

Prajñāpāramitā
Saddharmapuṇḍarīka
Lalitavistara
Subvarṇaprabhāsa
Laṃkāvatāra
Dashabhūmika
Gaṇḍhavyūha
Saṃādhirājā
Guhyasamāja Tantra

Since so many manuscripts and tantric praxis traditions were brought to the Kathmandu Valley after the Muslim conquest of polities across the Gangetic plains, the Newar *saṃgha*'s major areas of religious focus turned to perfecting ritual expressions of the doctrine within society and preserving the *dharma* via manuscript copying. For this reason, Nepal for the centuries since then became a center for the copying of Buddhist manuscripts, and this specialization in the Newar *saṃgha* was a source of both merit and a lucrative scribal occupation (Lienhard 1988: xvi). The scale of this reproduction was so great in medieval Nepal that, since the time of the British resident Hodgson (1820–40), modern scholars have found that Sanskrit texts from Kathmandu *vihāra*s have been extensive and invaluable, a resource that Tibetans had recognized and utilized for centuries before (Lewis 1989b; Lewis and Jamspal 1988). This has been so despite the uneven quality of the manuscript copying (Brough 1954). As with acquiring tantric initiations, to get a copy of a text required payment; as in China, too (Gernet 1995), there developed a commoditization of the later Mahāyāna traditions.

Even in modern Nepal, one finds the continuity of the "cult of the book" (Schopen 1975) in the popular Buddhist festivals that involve the display of gold leaf manuscripts. This distinctly Mahāyāna form of ritual, which many texts hail as highly beneficial for those who copy, worship, or recite the Mahāyāna *sūtra*s, doubtless contributed to the strong copying tradition among the Newar Buddhist elite. The long-standing Newar practice of copying manuscripts has given way since 1909 to the printing press, with the community showing great piety and energy in producing over a thousand Buddhist publications like those featured in this book.[17]

In this case, modern technology has *expanded* the opportunities for authors and patrons to express their *traditional* spiritual goals: spreading the *dharma* and benefiting sentient beings. Both of these ideals are usually stated in the printed texts.

Ritual priests in medieval Nepal also devoted themselves to adapting Mahāyāna/Vajrayāna religious understandings in ritual terms. We have already noted how this was done in a most thoroughgoing manner. Lifelong ritual relations tie householders to a family priest among *vajrācārya*s in the *saṃgha,* and their services include Buddhist versions of Indic *dharmashāstra saṃskāra*s (Lewis 1994a), *homa pūjā*s (Gellner 1992), the *nitya pūjās* for temple-residing bodhisattvas (Locke 1980), and their *ratha jātra*s (Owens 1989, 1993). Based upon the Mahāyāna householder bodhisattva ideology and tantric practice,[18] the Newar *saṃgha* members still justify their Buddhist occupation, continuing to use monastic designations and claiming to be worthy of merit-making *dāna* from others. Layfolk and the *saṃgha* exchange material support for ritual protection and merit accumulation. For Newar *upāsaka*s (devout layfolk), their expression of distinct Buddhist identity became adherence to this ritually-centered life-style, patronage to the *vajrācārya saṃgha,* devotion to Mahāyāna savior deities, and faith in the *siddha*s and *yoginī*s who discovered the tantric paths.

This pattern of development can help explain why Newar Buddhist tradition seems to lack a strong philosophical/scholastic dimension. What *is* carefully elaborated is the ritualism that expresses and interjects the Mahāyāna-Vajrayāna worldview into every conceivable juncture: relating to deities, celebrating festivals, progressing through one's lifetime, and seeking nirvāṇa. Lacking a strong elite tradition of philosophical inquiry, the "genius" of Newar Buddhism lies in its pervasive orchestration of Vajrayāna rituals and teachings that channel blessings, well-being, and—for those willing to practice in the tantric path—accelerated movement toward enlightenment. In this respect, Newar Buddhism carries on the evolutionary patterns of ritual practice and the lay ideals of later Indic Buddhism.[19]

The Context and Paradoxes of Modernity

The discussion and utilization of contemporary traditions of Newar Buddhism in this book should not obscure the fact that in the modern setting the faith is in decline and what follows is, at times, a scholarly reconstruction of the recent past when belief and practice were more vibrant. Buddhism in the Kathmandu Valley has declined throughout the modern period's transitions: from a polity of isolated medieval city-states, the Kathmandu Valley has become the capital region of the modern Nepalese nation. Far-reaching changes in many spheres have accelerated, with the medieval Newar preoccupation of celebrating the rich and elaborate cumulative religious traditions the cultural domain that has suffered the most precipitous decline.

Today there is no widespread understanding of the doctrinal concepts underlying the most common rituals still performed. Few *vajrācārya*s grasp the underlying philosophical assumptions or relate to the rituals beyond the procedural level of proper order and *mantra* recitations (Lewis 1984: 569–73). Nonetheless, these traditions are so deeply embedded in Newar life that they survive in many families, castes, and courtyards. Even though so many observances have been lost in the last century, the vast cumulative tradition of Mahāyāna-Vajrayāna ritual remains one of the most distinctive characteristics of Newar culture.

Suffering declining patronage, Hindu state discrimination, and anti-Mahāyāna missionizing by the revivalist Theravādin monks (Kloppenberg 1977; Tewari 1983; Lewis 1984: 494–513), the Newar Buddhist *saṃgha* has struggled to survive over the last century. The authors who have redacted and compiled the modern printed works in this study are all Kathmandu *vajrācārya*s by birth and religious training, and they have been prominent leaders seeking to overcome these circumstances by establishing a school for training young Vajrācārya men, by giving public lectures, and by organizing a host of traditional ritual programs in *vihāra*s and in other pilgrimage sites, including Vajrayāna initiations. Despite their anomalous social organization as a Buddhist caste, the Newar *saṃgha* has done what Buddhist leaders have always done to revive the faith: preach the *dharma* in society and encourage the performance of rituals, both to support their *saṃgha* and for the good of all donor-practitioners.

As already indicated, the ability to use the printing press has enabled Buddhist revivalists to use modern technology to work for cultural survival. But as with the addition of all new media, especially in a rapidly modernizing environment, the results have not been so simple to assess: while the urge "to spread the *dharma*" that has motivated over a thousand Buddhist publications is traditional, their effect still has not stopped the decline of traditional Mahāyāna culture. Susan S. Wadley has noted the same situation in modern Hinduism:

> While an explanation for this growing popularity cannot be explicitly stated, several factors clearly are important. Increasing literacy allows thousands to use texts where once they had relied solely on oral traditions. . . . Finally, texts are valued in Hinduism in part because of their traditional inaccessibility: to many newly literate persons, reading a pamphlet is more authentic and prestigious than reciting the stories of their elders. The stories of the elders had themselves taken the place of the teaching of *guru*s, to whom people had little access. Currently, then, written texts are replacing the elders and act as a stand-in for the traditions of the *guru*. (Wadley 1983:150)

Thus, despite the modern period's remarkable record of having numerous Mahāyāna *sūtra*s translated into, and published in, modern Newari, and even with the publication of hundreds of ritual guidebooks and traditional stories, the modern "cult of the book" has been overtaken by the "cult of the T.V." and other mass media, especially for younger adults.[20]

Finally, a few notes to introduce the organization of this book. Each chapter has a consistent order of presentation: a discussion of the Newari text's Indic background and an introduction to its subject matter. Then follows the ritual or narrative text in translation. In rendering these translations, I have retained the modern authors' terse shorthand style and I have also inserted only minimal explanatory glosses parenthetically. Most divisions in the originals have also been retained. A third section in each discusses the text's use or "domestication" in local Buddhist traditions in the Kathmandu Valley.[21] Every chapter ends with a discussion about how this text, its content, and related traditions might refine or revise the historical understanding of Buddhism. These observations are directed both to the general reader as he or she places the particular work in the wider context of understanding Mahāyāna Buddhism and to the more specialized audience of historians of Buddhism. The final chapter builds upon each of these final sections to reach some further conclusions and speculations regarding our assessment of Buddhism as a world religion.

CHAPTER 2

*Stūpa*s and Spouses: The *Shṛṇgabherī Avadāna*

The priests and laymen in India make *caitya*s or images with earth, or impress the Buddha's image on silk or paper, and worship it with offerings wherever they go. Sometimes they build *stūpa*s of the Buddha by making a pile and surrounding it with bricks. . . . This is the reason why the *sūtra*s praise in parables the merit of making images or *caitya*s as unspeakable . . . as limitless as the seven seas, and good rewards will last as long as the coming four births.

I-Tsing
(J. Takakasu, *A Record of the Buddhist Religion*)

For those who are capable of being saved by a woman, housewife, officer's wife, or a Brahman woman, the bodhisattva appears as a woman, housewife, officer's wife, or a brahman woman to teach the Dharma.

Lotus Sūtra, chapter 24
(Diana Y. Paul, *Women in Buddhism: Images of the Feminine in the Mahāyāna Tradition*)

If both. . . .
Living as the *dhamma* bids, use loving words
One to the other—manifold the blessings
That come to a husband and wife, and to them
The blessing of a pleasant life is born;

Anguttara Nikāya II, 54
(F. L. Woodward, *The Book of the Gradual Sayings*)

The making and ritual veneration of *stūpa*s began with the death of Shākyamuni Buddha and up to the present day remains the chief means by which the laity seek the good *karman* needed to advance toward nirvāṇa. In the Kathmandu Valley, many traditions link meritorious *stūpa*-related practices to humanity's most common social bonds: those to parents[1] and, as explored in this chapter, to spouses.

Background

Stūpa / Caitya Veneration

For all Buddhist schools, the *stūpa* was the focal point and singular spiritual landmark denoting the tradition's presence (Dallapiccola 1980; Harvey 1984; Snodgrass 1985). Early texts indicated the best site for these *stūpa*s: either on a hilltop or at a crossroads where four highways meet (Dutt 1945: 250); in Nepal these are typical locations, as are monastic courtyards.

From antiquity, *stūpa* and *caitya* were often used as synonyms in Buddhist inscriptions and literature. But definitions on usage varied: as L. de La Vallee Poussin (1937: 284) noted, a Dharmagupta *Vinaya* commentary suggested the existence of a technical distinction between shrines with relics (*stūpa*) and shrines without them (*caitya*). The Chinese pilgrim I-Tsing in 700 C.E. indicates yet another Buddhist definition: "Again, when the people make images and *caitya*s which consist of gold, silver, copper, iron, earth, lacquer, bricks, and stone, or when they heap up the snowy sand, they put into the images or *caitya*s two kinds of *sarīra*s: 1. The relics of the Great Teacher; 2. The *Gāthā* of the chain of causation."[2]

Early texts and epigraphy link *stūpa* worship with the Shākyamuni Buddha's life and especially to the key venues in his religious career. The tradition eventually recognized a standard "Eight Great *Caitya*s" for pilgrimage and veneration (Tucci 1988), a point the Newar publication alludes to. *Stūpa* or *caitya* worship thus became the chief focus of Buddhist ritual activity linking veneration of the Buddha's "sacred traces" (Falk 1977) to an individual's attention to managing *karman* destiny and mundane well-being.

Throughout history, Buddhist writers have advanced many explanations of *stūpa* veneration. First, a *stūpa* is a site that marks supernatural celestial events associated with a Tathāgata and for remembering him through joyful devotional celebration. The Pali *Mahāparinibbāna Sutta* describes the origins of the first veneration directed to Shākyamuni's relics:

> And when the body of the Exalted One had been burnt up, there came down streams of water from the sky and extinguished the funeral pyre . . . and there burst forth streams of water from the storehouse of waters [beneath the earth], and extinguished the funeral pyre. . . . The Mallas of Kushinara also brought water scented with all kinds of perfumes . . . surrounded the bones of the Exalted One in their council hall with a lattice work of spears, and with a rampart of bows; and there for seven days they paid honor, and reverence, and respect, and homage to them with dance, and song, and music, and with garlands and perfumes. . . . (Rhys-Davids 1969: 130–31)

A prominent Nikāya theme is the celestial wonders visible at *caityas*. As Nagasena explains in the *Milindapañha* (IV,8,51):

> Some woman or some man of believing heart, able, intelligent, wise, endowed with insight, may deliberately take perfumes, or a garland, or a cloth, and place it on a *caitya*, making the resolve: "May such and such a wonder take place!" Thus is it that wonders take place at the *caitya* of one entirely set free. (Rhys-Davids 1963: 2:175).

The Newar's *Shṛṇgabherī Avadāna* is of this textual genre.

The subsequent elaborations on *stūpa* ritualism in Buddhist history are extensive: a "power place" tapping the relic's Buddha presence (Schopen 1987a: 196) and healing power; a site to earn merit through veneration (Lamotte 1988: 415); and a monument marking the conversion and control of *nāgas* and *yakṣas* (Bloss 1973: 48–49). Only the Theravāda *Vinaya* omits instructions to monks on how to construct and to make offerings at *stūpas* (Bareau 1962; cf. Schopen 1989), and the archaeological record shows that *stūpas* were frequently built in the center of *vihāra* courtyards (Seckel 1964: 132–34), often by monks themselves (Snellgrove 1973: 410), a custom still ubiquitous in Nepal. I-Tsing's account from ca. 690 C.E. illustrates the monastic focus on *stūpas* in the *saṃgha*'s communal life:

> In India priests perform the worship of a *caitya* and ordinary service late in the afternoon or at the evening twilight. All the assembled priests come out of the gate of their monastery, and walk three times around a *stūpa*, offering incense and flowers. They all kneel down, and one of them who sings well begins to chant hymns describing the virtues of the Great Teacher . . . [and] in succession returns to the place in the monastery where they usually assemble.
>
> (Takakasu 1982: 152)

In the Mahāyāna schools, the *stūpa* came to symbolize yet other ideas: of the Buddhahood's omnipresence;[3] a center of *sūtra* revelation (Schopen 1975); a worship center guaranteeing rebirth in Sukhāvatī (Williams 1989); and a form showing the unity of the five elements with Buddha nature (Rimpoche 1990; Seckel 1964). A passage from the *Pañcarakṣā* (in chap. 6) states that those worshiping relic *caityas* and chanting *dhāraṇīs* will make themselves immune from diseases of all kinds. Later Buddhists identified *stūpas* as the physical representation of the *dharmakāya* in the *trikāya* schema[4] and expanded the possible *sacra* deposited to include his words in textual form (*sūtra*, *dhāranī*, and *mantra*) (Seckel 1964: 103; cf. Scherrer-Schaub 1994; Bentor 1995), and the remains of exemplary human *bodhisattvas* (Mumford 1989).

The popular Mahāyāna *sūtra*, the *Saddharmapuṇḍarīka*, explicitly states that relic worship itself is linked to the great skillful manifestation (*upāya*) of the Buddha's dying: by seeming to pass away, he induces spiritual self-examination on the part of the living (Pye 1978: 58). Relic veneration at *stūpas* maintains for the devout a continued connection with that compassionate action and its effect:

> By skillful means I manifest nirvāṇa
> Though I am really not extinct. . . .
> They all look on me as extinct
> And everywhere worship my relics,
> All cherishing tender emotions
> As their hearts begin to thirst with hope.
>
> (Quoted in Pye 1978: 58)

Gregory Schopen has shown that the *stūpa/caitya* cult was well established by the time of the Mahāyāna's emergence. The first Mahāyāna *sūtras* (e.g., *Saddharmapuṇḍarīka* and *Prajñāpāramitā*) clearly seek to redefine and reinterpret the *caitya*'s origin and "higher" meaning. What characterizes the key difference between Nikāya and emerging Mahāyāna lineages was the loyalty that was demanded of devotees, respectively, to either *stūpas* enshrining the Buddha's bodily relics or *stūpas* marking sites where *sūtras* were taught or venerated (Schopen 1975: 168–69). It is the latter that for the Mahāyāna is the most prestigious and most potent for earning the greatest merit.[5]

The *Saddharmapuṇḍarīka* also places great emphasis on developing and venerating *caityas*. Its exalted, utopian vision of Buddhist civilization features a landscape dominated by these monuments:

> There are also bodhisattvas
> Who, after the Buddha's passage into extinction,
> Shall make offerings to his relics.
> Further, I see sons of the Buddhas
> Making *stūpa* shrines
> As numberless as Ganges' sands,
> With which to adorn the realms and their territories,
> Jeweled *stūpa* to the lovely height, . . .
> Every individual stūpa shrine
> Having on it a thousand banners, . . .
> So that the realms and their territories. . . .
> Are of a most refined beauty.
>
> (Hurvitz 1976: 10)

The *Lotus* also exalts gem-encrusted *stūpas*, *stūpas* of immense size, and musical veneration at the monuments (ibid., 39). The most valued *stūpa* is one encasing the *Lotus* itself and those in this category should be decorated with, and called, a Seven-Jeweled *Stūpa*. The *Shṛṇgabherī Avadāna* echoes the Lotus's assertion that all who make *stūpas* achieve the Buddha Path (ibid., 39) and that those who worship the "Seven-Jeweled" are close to complete enlightenment (*anuttarasamyakasaṃbodhi*).[6]

One final and recently noted dimension to *stūpa* veneration was a votive/mortuary aspect (Schopen 1987a): certain Buddhists, and especially monks (1989a), apparently had their own ashes deposited in small votive *caityas*, often arranged close to a Buddha relic *stūpa* (1991a, 1991b; 1992a). These structures perhaps established a means for perpetual *puṇya*-generation for the deceased. The *caitya* creation in the *Shṛṇgabherī Avadāna* may perhaps be related to this custom and to other Tibetan Buddhist mortuary traditions using cremation ash and bone.[7]

Rooted in the doctrine of *upāya*, Mahāyāna Buddhism thus cultivated inclusive symbolic multivalence at *stūpa*s. Asanga's *Bodhisattvabhūmi*, for example, lists ten progressive ritual practices at *caitya*s.[8] The Khotanese *Book of Zambasta* links *stūpa* veneration to the cultivation of *pāramitā*s (Emmerick 1968: 157). The Vajrayāna tradition also utilized the *stūpa* as a *maṇḍala* and as a model for visualization meditation. In the Nepalese-Tibetan Vajrayāna traditions, these directional points also have esoteric correlates in the human body itself.

Thus, it is with these myriad understandings that Buddhist virtuosi as well as others at all levels of aspiration have circumambulated *stūpa*s. Our Mahāyāna text from Nepal indicates yet another reason why individuals were drawn to these centers of the Buddhist faith: to aid their kin, the topic to which we must now turn our attention.

Fig 2.1. Newar *Stūpa* Veneration

Gender Relations in Buddhist Texts

The early Buddhist canons share with the *jātaka*s many stories that emphasize how the householder's life, and especially the burden of a spouse, obstructs the quest for nirvāṇa. These are consistent with the more philosophical teachings that argue for a radical individualism in karmic operation and in its reckoning. In justifying the superiority of the renunciatory life-style over that of the domestic householder, and despite passages noting the possibility of women being enlightened,[9] there is no shortage of textual advice on viewing wives as loathsome and as certain obstacles to spiritual progress. Among the 547 Pali *jātaka*s,[10] for example, over 35 contain explicit teachings on the evil that women may do to destroy a man's spiritual development. The *Kaṇḍina Jātaka*, for example, concludes with these lines:

> Cursed be the dart that works men pain!
> Cursed be the land where women rule supreme!
> And cursed the fool that bows to woman's ways.
>
> (#13, 1: 43)

Likewise, the *Asātamanta Jātaka* ends with this observation:

> "So you see, Brother [monk]," said the Master, "how lustful, vile, and woēbringing are women." And after declaring the wickedness of women, he preached the Four Truths.
>
> (#61, 1: 150)

This kind of discourse is found in all of the early narrative traditions, and it is no doubt explicable by the fact that it was largely monks vowed to celibacy under *Vinaya* rules who redacted the discourses and who directed them to other male renunciants. The *Mahāvastu* collection also has many passages like this one regarding women:

> Seers should keep them at a distance, for they are a stumbling block to those who would live chastely. Have nothing to do with them. They are like snakes, like poisonous leaves, like charcoal pits. (Jones 1956, 3:144)

The author of the *Shikṣāsamuccaya* has collected the "wife derision" side of the tradition and summarized it:

> The Bodhisattva in the presence of his wife must realize three thoughts. . . . She is my companion for passion and dalliance, but not for the next world; my companion at meat and drink, but not for the fruition of the maturing of my acts. She is the companion of my pleasure, not of my pain. . . . Three other thoughts are these: that a wife must be regarded as an obstacle to virtue, meditation, and to wisdom. And yet three more: she is like a thief, a murderer, or a guardian of hell. (Bendall and Rouse 1971: 83)

But the *Shṛṇgabherī* joins other early narratives in offering a competing, opposing Buddhist position, one that I suspect was far more commonly voiced in Buddhist monastic preaching on fortnightly *uposaḍha* days and on other gatherings of householders: rather than threatening a man's quest for salvation, a good wife is essential for moving toward it. We will examine these issues in the last section of this chapter, as we must now turn to the Newari recension of the story and consider its domestication.

Translation

Notes on Language, Textual Publication and Translation

The twenty-four-page printed text is written in simply constructed modern Newari, with Sanskrit used sparingly for Buddhist terms. Not surprisingly, the style is that of a storyteller, with intermittent resort to requoting dialogue, a device that enhances the dramatic oral effect. The following translation aims to capture the storyteller's effect; the paragraph breaks in the translation generally match those in the book.

The compiler, Badri Bajrācārya, notes in his introduction that his source is the Sanskrit *Citraviṃsati Avadāna*, one of the popular collections of Mahāyāna-style stories preserved in Kathmandu Valley *vihāra* libraries (Mitra 1971; Takaoka 1981: 2). Separate texts containing this story alone exist in Newar collections, and the versions show plot and character variations (Novak 1986).

Finally noted must be the insertion of two short devotional additions to the printed work. The first is a one-page Sanskrit poem, "*Stotra* in Praise of the Eight *Caityas*," which reveres the usual eight relic *caityas* of ancient India (Tucci 1988: 23) as well as *dhātu caitya* sites. The second is the one-page insertion of a devotional hymn that can be sung by a musical procession. Although Bajrācārya's introduction does not refer to either, both are clearly appended to assist devotees wishing to use the book as they perform their rituals at the Svayambhū *stūpa*.

Shṛṇga Bherī Avadāna
(The Buffalo Horn-blowing Tale)
Kathmandu, Nepal: Smrti Press, 1979

> So I have heard: Once Lord Shākyamuni was dwelling on Mount Gṛddhakūṭa in Rājagṛha city accompanied by 1300 fellow *bhikṣus*, *bodhisattvas* and *mahāsattvas*.
>
> At that time the gods and human beings also gathered there to listen intently to the discourses delivered by the sage of the Shākya clan, Lord of the world.
>
> From the audience, Shāriputra arose and went close to the Tathāgata, then knelt down before him with folded hands and said, "O Lord! Kindly tell me about those who were liberated through *caitya* worship accompanied by the playing of musical instruments, including the buffalo horn."
>
> Upon hearing this, Tathāgata Shākyamuni said to Shāriputra within the hearing of all the gods and human beings in the audience, "Verily, Verily, O Shāriputra! Emancipation obtained through *caitya* worship that is accompanied by the blowing of buffalo horns, is illustrated in the following story:
>
> In the distant past, the King Suvarṇaketu and his queen Hiraṇyavatī lived happily in the city of Suvarṇavati. The king had five sons from his queen Hiraṇyavatī, namely: 1. Puṣpaketu 2. Ratnaketu 3. Shuryaketu 4. Dīpaketu 5. Chandraketu. The oldest son Puṣpaketu once went to his parents, paid them compliments, and asked for permission to go to Bandhumati city for listening to the discourses being

delivered by Vipashvī Buddha. With their permission, he left Svarṇavati city for Bandhumati city.

Upon reaching Bandhumati city, Prince Puṣpaketu went to see Vipashvī Tathāgata at a monastery. Kneeling down before Vipashvī Buddha, Prince Puṣpaketu said, 'O Lord! Please tell me of those who were liberated through *caitya* worship performed while playing musical instruments, including the buffalo horn.'

Hearing the prince's request, the Buddha said, 'The month of Shrāvaṇa is considered holy for *caitya* worship accompanied by music. For this, the month of Kārtik is equally holy. During these two months, after ritual bathing in the morning, if one circumambulates *caitya*s or *vihāra*s playing drums, cymbals and blowing horns, one will accumulate good fortune and religious merit here in this life and be reborn hereafter in a noble family. If one circumambulates the *caitya* blowing horns and then offers gifts in the name of the dead, that one will avoid bad destinies and be reborn in a family of noble birth. And anyone seated in front of a *caitya* who seeks refuge in the *Triratna* with a purified mind will attain supreme enlightenment or be reborn hereafter in heaven to attain the title of Indra, King of Gods. Similarly if one whitewashes a *caitya* with lime, decorates it with flags and garlands, and worships with a fivefold offering (*pañcopacāra pūjā*), that one will accumulate a great deal of religious merit. O Prince! Please be attentive and let me now proceed to tell you how once one person was liberated through buffalo horn playing.

Once there was a king named Siṃhaketu who ruled the city of Shashīpaṭṭana. The King there had no consideration for the lives of other living beings and every day visited the forest to hunt. With his bow and arrow, he killed many different wild birds and beasts such as deer, tigers, and bears.

Unable to bear the daily sight of her husband taking the lives of wild birds and beasts in the forest, Queen Sūrakṣaṇī said to her husband one day, "O my Lord! I must make an urgent request: Please give up hunting the wild birds and beasts in the forest. Listen! The demerit of taking the lives of living beings will subject you to a great deal of suffering in your future births. [She quoted the verses:]

Ahiṃsā is the best among knowledges,
The greatest of all teachings.
Ahiṃsā is the best among virtues,
The greatest of all meditations.

[Sūrakṣaṇī continued:] If men say they earnestly seek salvation, they should be non-violent in body, speech and mind, toward all living beings. O my Lord! If you so wish, you may pronounce the names of the *Triratna* seeking refuge, worship a *caitya* while saying prayers and circumambulating, give liberally to the *bhikṣu*s, the *brāhmaṇ*s, the *ācārya*s, and show compassion to many suffering ones. By so doing, your happiness here and in the hereafter will be assured."

Hearing this, the king replied, "Darling! What's this you are saying? Don't you know that a son born in a royal family can take his pleasure in hunting wild birds and beasts in the forest?"

Having discerned the king's attitude, the queen still tried her best to change his mind but could not stop him from hunting in the forest.

After a certain time, the king passed away and Sūrakṣaṇī was so upset at his death that she immolated herself on her husband's funeral pyre. His wicked hunting of the wild birds and beasts in the forest caused the king to be was consigned to purgatory and afterwards be reincarnated as a buffalo in the same city of Shashīpaṭṭana. But Queen Sūrakṣaṇī, as a result of her meritorious deeds, including sparing the lives of living beings and being chaste and faithful to her husband, was reincarnated as a woman in a certain *brāhmaṇ* family in the same city of Shashīpaṭṭana.

The *brāhmaṇ* couple became very glad when she was born to them. They celebrated the name-giving ceremony of the baby girl in accordance with their custom. The name of Rūpavatī [Beautiful One] was given to the child because she was very beautiful. The baby was brought up with proper care and gradually grew up like a lotus in a pond. When Rūpavatī became a mature girl, her father gave her the job of tending a buffalo in the forest.

Rūpavatī every day tended her buffalo, cleaned his shed, and took great care of him.

Because Rūpavatī was beautiful, many people came to propose marriage. Her parents discussed this and eventually broached the subject, "O Rūpavatī! Now you have come of age. People have come to us asking for you in marriage. Do you want to marry?"

The daughter answered her parents, "Dear Father and Mother, I do not want to be married. Please do not insist on it. I prefer staying unmarried and devoting myself to you here. I will not marry."

Hearing this, the parents gave up the idea of giving their only daughter in marriage and she remained at home.

One day Rūpavatī was in the forest as usual tending her buffalo. While she was sitting under a tree looking at the many-hued blossoms, listening to the sweet birdsongs, and smelling many colorful sweet-scented flowers, a bodhisattva named Supāraga, emanating brilliant light from his body, descended from the sky and stood before her. He said, "O Rūpavatī! The buffalo you are tending was your husband in a previous birth. In his former existence, he hunted many birds and beasts in the forest. As a result of this, he is now reborn as a buffalo. For his past wicked deeds, the buffalo will be killed and devoured by the birds and beasts of the forest. O Rūpavatī! If you wish to assist the husband of your previous birth to attain a good destiny, collect the mortal remains of the buffalo after it is killed and devoured, then deposit them inside a sand *caitya*. One of the two horns of the buffalo may be used for offering water to the *caitya* and the other horn may be used as a trumpet at the time of circumambulating it." Having said this to Rūpavatī, Supāraga Bodhisattva disappeared miraculously.

Then Rūpavatī also remembered the facts of her previous birth and took even greater care of the buffalo by taking it to the forest and feeding it nutritious grasses.

One day as usual, Rūpavatī was sitting under a tree while tending her buffalo. After eating grass nearby the buffalo wandered off to drink water from a stream in the forest. In an instant, tigers and lions attacked the buffalo and tortured it to death. Then they and bears, vultures and other birds devoured its flesh, leaving only bones and the two horns behind.

[At just this same time] Rūpavatī heard a strange sound made by the buffalo and it did not come back as usual from the stream. Very much agitated, she went to the stream looking for the buffalo but did not find it. Instead, she saw only the dead animal's bones and two horns left behind. At the sight of the buffalo's bones and horns, Rūpavatī wept. Taking them affectionately in her arms, she said to herself, "What bodhisattva Supāraga prophesied has come true." She then returned home crying and related to her parents all that had happened to her in the forest that day.

Upon hearing Rūpavatī's story, her parents comforted her, saying, "Enough, enough! Do not mourn the death of one buffalo very much. We will buy another."

In response to her parents, the daughter cried out, "Oh Mother and Father! No buffalo can be like the one that has been killed. You may buy a new buffalo but the new one cannot bring me peace and consolation." The parents retorted, "Grieve no more over a dead animal. It is of no use because the dead cannot be brought back to life. Get a hold of yourself!"

Then Rūpavatī went again to the streamside, collected all the pieces of bone, and buried them in a sand *caitya*, all as advised by Supāraga Bodhisattva. She next used one of the two horns of the buffalo for offering water to the *caitya* and the other for playing while circumambulating and performing a *pañcopacāra pūjā*. She worshipped the *caitya* in this way daily. One day during her *caitya* worship, while Rūpavatī was offering water with one of the horns and blowing the other, a bejeweled *caitya* appeared in the sky emitting radiant light in all directions. She was surprised and with folded hands looked skyward in great reverence.

Then the *caitya* that appeared in the sky descended to the earth and merged into the sand *caitya* in which the bones of the buffalo were buried. When the bejeweled *caitya* did so, the sand *caitya* was absorbed into it.

Because of the presence of the *caitya* there, stone walls and other masonry constructions came into sight by themselves around the *caitya* to make a high-walled courtyard. Doorways and festoons also appeared, just as plants possessing different flowers and fruits started growing all around.

This is not all. From the horn of the buffalo that was used for blowing, a person came out who grew instantly into a young man. At that sight of the individual springing from the horn, Rūpavatī became very surprised and said, "Who are you and where did you come from?"

Turning to the brāhmaṇ lady, the person who emerged from the horn said, "How could you not recognize me, O faithful woman! You liberated your husband through your conjugal fidelity and pious charitable acts. O Rūpavatī! I have been able to come out of the horn, liberated on this day. It is all due to your accumulation of *puṇya*. Do you not know that in our former existences I was the king of this city and you were my queen Sūrakṣaṇī? Although you tried to prevent me from going to the forest to hunt birds and beasts, I insisted upon doing so. As a result of these wicked deeds, I was consigned to purgatory, subjected to great suffering. Ultimately I was reborn as a buffalo. Now I am liberated through your pious meritorious *caitya* worship accompanied by buffalo horn playing."

Upon hearing this from the person emanating from the horn, Rūpavatī, said, "Oh! How fortunate I have been! As a result of the pious act of this *caitya* worship I have been able to end the separation and rejoin my husband." Jubilant, they both circumambulated the *caitya*. Then the person emanating from the horn chanted the goddess Tārā's name and remained seated before the *caitya*. He recited prayers from a holy text while blowing on the horn. The whole of Shashīpaṭṭana city echoed with the sound produced by the horn. Once the citizens of Shashīpaṭṭana city heard the pleasant sound of the horn, they gathered there.

All those who assembled around the *caitya* were taken aback to see Rūpavatī seated beside a handsome person and so they asked her who he was. At that time and within the hearing of all, Rūpavatī related the whole story of how

Fig 2.2. Line Drawing of the Miraculous Appearance of the Former Husband from the Buffalo Horn

Supāraga Bodhisattva had prophesied strange events, how they had lived in their previous births as King Siṃhaketu and Queen Sūrakṣaṇī in Shashīpaṭṭana, and what had happened in front of the sand *caitya*.

The people assembled there were gladdened after hearing this and realized that the person emanating from the horn and the *brāhmaṇ* lady were formerly their king and queen. Both of them were taken to the city in an elaborate, joyful procession. Then the person emanating from the horn was given the name of Bhadra Shṛṇga and was enthroned as king.

Then King Bhadra Shṛṇga and Queen Rūpavatī ruled over the city of Shashīpaṭṭana happily. One day King Bhadra Shṛṇga invited the citizens to his palace to tell them the story of how his queen delivered him from his sufferings in purgatory by her pious and charitable devotional actions and how he eventually succeeded in ascending to the throne of Shashīpaṭṭana for the well-being of the people.

King Bhadra Shṛṇga and Queen Rūpavatī lived happily for many years. King Bhadra Shṛṇga made it widely known to his countrymen how his wife delivered him from his sufferings in purgatory. He preached and propagated the significance and sanctity of *caitya* worship and reigned happily over the country.

This is what was told to Prince Puṣpaketu by Vipashvī Buddha. After hearing this from Vipashvī Buddha, Prince Pushpaketu returned to Suvarṇapura and relayed to his parents the same story. Upon hearing the story from his son, King Suvarṇaketu happily ruled over the country and performed the proper worship of *caitya*s. And this was told to Bhikṣu Shāriputra by Lord Shākyamuni on Mount Gṛddhakūṭa.

The Domestication of the Text

The Mahāyāna Mythological Framework of Nepal's Buddhist Sites

To introduce his recension of the *Shṛṇgabherī Avadāna*, the modern Newar redactor in his introduction first recounts the basic creation narrative of the *Svayambhū Purāna*, a local text describing the origin of the Kathmandu Valley itself as a Mahāyāna Buddhist hierophany. While this *Purāna* represents itself as spoken by Shākyamuni Buddha, its content reaches back to earlier world ages and to a succession of previous Buddhas: his summary ends by recounting how Newar civilization itself began under the tutelage of the Bodhisattva Mañjushrī. The compiler merely outlines this sequence to show that the Svayambhū *stūpa* (the enduring site of this hierophany), like the distinctive musical veneration described in the text, both date from an earlier world era, the time of Newar—and simultaneously Mahāyāna—origins. This is Buddhist domestication par excellence on the cosmological scale, although historically this story itself was likely imported from Khotan (Brough 1948).

*Ritual at Svayambhū and Other Valley Stūpa*s

The Mahāyāna *purāṇa*'s history of Nepal, claiming origins in earlier *yuga*s, also centers on the valley's great *stūpa*s. Texts recount the Svayambhū *stūpa*'s origins—and the entire Nepal Valley's establishment—as the product of Mahāyāna hierophany and the compassionate actions of the Bodhisattva Mañjushrī. The epigraphic evidence is that "Svayambhū Mahācaitya" was founded in the Licchavi period (400–879 A.D.) in the early fifth century (Slusser 1982: 174; Riccardi 1980). Today, this hilltop *stūpa* over eighty feet in diameter is surrounded by three monasteries and is linked to the Buddhist festival year of Kathmandu City (Lewis 1984; 1993c) and to all Buddhists in the Kathmandu Valley and in surrounding regions. Svayambhū once had extensive land endowments traditionally dedicated to its upkeep (Shakya 1977) and in many respects the history of regional Buddhism is embedded in the layers of this *stūpa*'s successive iconography, patronage, and restoration. As noted in the next section, specific rituals connected to the *avadāna* are performed at Svayambhū.

In the Kathmandu Valley, other *stūpas* exist in great numbers and they remain the main venues for daily public Buddhist observances. There are large directional *stūpas* that mark the old urban boundaries of Lalitpur and Kathmandu. In courtyards, at riverside *tīrthas*, and around temples in most Newar settlements, there are also thousands of more modest family votive *caityas* (Gutschow 1997). The ubiquity of *caityas* here can be illustrated by the Asan Tol neighborhood in Kathmandu, where a survey of all free-standing religious shrines (numbering over three hundred) revealed that half were *caityas* (Lewis 1984: 116).

There has been a succession of *caitya* styles in Nepalese history. *Stūpas* dated to the Licchavi period (e.g., those published by Pratapaditya Pal [1974: 16] from Dhwāka Bāhā, Kathmandu) depict standing *buddhas* and *bodhisattvas* surmounted by small *stūpas*, indicating early Mahāyāna influences. Since the nineteenth century, the commonly preferred design features seated directional Buddhas surmounted by a *stūpa*, with some also adding the particular *bodhisattva* "sons" standing beneath. (Chapter 6 will discuss Newar cast-metal *stūpas*.)

Still other Newar *caityas* are small and usually impermanent in nature. There are sand *caityas* that layfolk mold by riversides to make merit, most commonly for certain *shraddha pūjās*, but also at the time of eclipses, and during the special Newar month of Guṃlā. Another ephemeral Newar *caitya* is made of clay that layfolk fashion using special molds. These miniature clay images can be used for building the interiors of permanent monuments as well as for disposal by the riverside. This practice, called *dyaḥthāyegu* (New.: making the deity), requires the use of special black clay; observed during Guṃlā, the final votive assemblage must be empowered by special rites of merit dedication (Lewis 1993c). The *Shṛṅgabherī Avadāna* can be read aloud as part of these observances.

Finally, Newar Buddhists can make evanescent *basma caitya*s with relic ashes at riverside *tīrtha*s following the cremation rites (cf. Dargyay 1986: 182–85). Vajrācārya ritualists also make a *durgati-parisodhana caitya* to fix in place the *dhāranī* in a Buddhist *piṇḍa* ritual of mourning, symbolizing the text's presence as witness. The relic tradition connected with the *Shṛṅgabherī Avadāna* perhaps can be related to the already-cited ancient tradition of merging cremation relics with molded sand or miniature clay *caitya*s and clay-inscribed *dhāraṇī*s, a custom once ubiquitous in South Asia (Schopen 1985, 1987b: 198ff) and still practiced in modern Tibet, Nepal, and Thailand (Lester 1987: 116–17).

Living the Text's Promise: Stūpa Rituals during Mourning

The modern Newar pandit asserts in the printed text's introduction that the old custom was for devotees to venerate all *stūpa*s in the Kathmandu Valley with buffalo horn-playing *bājan*s for a full month twice each year. These months are the midsummer Guṃlā and the fall Kacchalā. The Buddhist community in the former capital Bhaktapur still organizes morning Guṃlā musical processions led by devotees blowing buffalo horns who visit all *stūpa*s within the town.

Today, the *avadāna*-related horn-blowing practice in Kathmandu is sponsored mainly by families in the first year of mourning and usually by widows. The regular performance of this *caitya* veneration is now done by a special *vihāra goṣthi* located at Svayambhū: a team of young men from the Shākya caste *saṃgha* circumambulate the Svayambhū *stūpa* complex each morning during Guṃlā. Their service is usually contracted by families at the start of the month. It seems likely that some Buddhists in Patan participate in the Matayā Festival in connection with this text (Bajracarya 1990)

Newar Buddhists have been influenced by the text in other, optional observances. Like the heroine in the story, Newar devotees also mold sand *caitya*s at riverside *tīrtha*s to make merit, most commonly for certain *shraddha pūjā*s, but also at the time of eclipses, and during Guṃlā. Although modern families making postmortem *basma caitya*s may not articulate the relationship, this widespread practice doubtless reflects *Shṛṅgabherī* textual influences.

Our text has an explicit connection with the custom of *upāsaka*s fashioning clay *caitya*s using special molds. Several Newar *vrata*s require the manufacturing of these images. The *avadāna* is linked to some versions of the popular *Lakṣacaitya Vrata*: as the title implies, families mold a hundred thousand or more miniature *caityas* over a given period and celebrate the completion with a special ritual that includes the reading of the *Shṛṇgabherī Avadāna*. A *Buddhacarita* appendix written early in the nineteenth century confirms that this association likely has a long local history (Cowell 1969: 199).

Observations on the History of Practical Buddhism

Patronage

At the outset, it is important to identify the context of the modern *Shṛṇgabherī* text's production, that is, as a product of patronage: the pundit-compiler thanks his patrons, a Newar farming family with the surname Maharjan, who sponsored publication in memory of the husband's parents. The deceased father's portrait, blowing on his wooden flute (suggesting his devout musical skills), adorns the first page. Even though this recension is a modern one, it nonetheless illustrates the typical scenario of lay memorial merit-making underwriting the creation of a new recension of a Buddhist text.

Fig 2.3. Sand *Caitya* Making by the Riverside

Fig 2.4. The Svayambhū Horn *Bājan*

*Stūpa*s *as Centers of Buddhist Communities*

Symbiotically, great regional *stūpa*s were pivotal in the social history of Buddhism: these monuments became magnets attracting *vihāra* building and votive construction, for local *pūjā* and pilgrimage. The economics of Buddhist devotionalism at these centers generated income for local *saṃgha*s, artisans, and merchants (Liu 1988), an alliance that was an integral component of Buddhism throughout its history (Dehejia 1972; Lewis 1994c). Thus, *stūpa* veneration was the most important activity that unified entire Buddhist communities, especially on full moon and eighth lunar days. Around the monument, then, diverse devotional exertions, textual/doctrinal studies, and devotees' mercantile pursuits could all prosper in synergistic style. Such shrines could in fact serve as actual places where the unifying vision of the *Saddharmapuṇḍarīka*—of all Buddhists following one vehicle (the *ekayāna*)—could be manifest through rituals. For over the past fifty years, the harmonious merging of Tibetan Buddhists with Nepalese Theravāda, Mahāyāna, and Vajrayāna devotees has been visible at Svayambhū, the great hilltop *stūpa*. The importance that tradition accorded to such complexes is reflected in the extreme *karman* penalties incurred from disrespecting, damaging, or destroying *stūpa*s (Schopen 1987a: 208).

The regional *Mahācaitya* complexes, with their interlinked components—*vihāras* with land endowments, votive/pilgrimage centers, amulet markets, state support, and so forth—represent central fixtures in Buddhist civilization.[11] Our text contributes yet another of the centripetal forces that drew Buddhists toward such *caityas*' sacred precincts.

The Practical Fruits of Mahāyāna Bhakti

The opening lines of the *Shṛṇgabherī Avadāna* set forth the text's clear message: veneration of *caityas* employing a musical procession yields a good destiny for oneself (fortune in this life and next rebirth in a noble family) and for departed relatives. No evil destinies will befall the deceased if the rite is done in their name(s). The text also asserts that going for refuge at a *caitya* leads to a purified mind, attaining *bodhi*, and securing rebirth as Indra; the building and maintenance of *stūpas* yields even greater merit.

One special significance of this story is the series of linkages asserted between the Mahāyāna *bhakti* orientation and *caitya* veneration: the *karman* forces released are especially amplified. More striking still is the display of powers by the celestial *bodhisattvas* (Tārā and Supāraga) in connection with *caitya* veneration. A curious feature of the *avadāna* is that the relics interred in the *stūpa* are those of a mere buffalo, not a saint; but even these, when shaped into the archetypal Buddhist form and worshiped, yield a wondrous hierophany and miraculous individual destiny.

Buddhist Husbands and Wives

The chief social ideal conveyed to householders in this *avadāna* is that a wife should take responsibility for the rebirth destiny of her husband. The *Shṛṇgabherī* text focuses upon the possibilities of generating grace from the ritual and from the *bodhisattvas* to insure the best rebirth for the husband. Any evil destinies due to *karman* retribution that might befall the deceased can be eliminated and the power of Tārā supports the practice, as the *bodhisattva*'s grace seems to amplify the good results of a wife's *caitya* veneration.

The *Shṛṇgabherī* story presents the king as willful and violent, blind to the reality of karmic retribution. As a husband he pays no heed to his wife, dismisses her objections to his hunting fixation, and ignores her when she urges him to engage in alternative Buddhist activities. His fall into purgatory, then into the animal world, is due to the man not taking his wife's moral criticism seriously. Yet when they are reunited in their next lives, as herder-girl and buffalo, the *karman* of attraction and affinity endures:[12] the wife-herder refuses marriage to human suitors and mourns excessively for the slain buffalo. Her "rescue" of the husband is driven by this *karman* along with her devotion to the *bodhisattva* who advises her to perform the *caitya* rituals.

The good queen's self-immolation (*satī*), a practice that comes up again in the Tārā *vratakathā* (chap. 4), should be highlighted. This practice that is mentioned in a Buddhist text seems to be anomalous, especially so soon after an eloquent statement on *ahiṃsā*. Yet one quite unavoidably must point out that this *avadāna* supports the logic of widow immolation: without the queen committing *satī*, the entire transformation and miraculous *bodhisattva* revelation cannot take place. Other examples from the later *avadāna* literatures must be surveyed in order to evaluate this aspect of Mahāyāna Buddhism's domestication in later Indian society. There were apparently opposing opinions regarding suicide across the Mahāyāna literature, with *avadāna*s illustrating both views (Ku 1991: 157ff; Yun-hua 1965; cf. Wiltshire 1983).

In the following two sections, I show how the *Shṛṇgabherī* story connects with a minority current of pro-spouse discourse, texts that speak about a proper Buddhist attitude toward married life and that allude to an ideal of conjugal relations conflicting with the "misogynist ascetic" perspective.

A Buddhist Defense of Marriage

Existing alongside the wealth of pejorative portrayals of women in the early canonical passages are other discourses that value the spouse and illustrate how a compassionate and spiritually minded wife or husband can be a valued ally both in this life and over a series of lifetimes. In the Pali *Sigālovāda Sutta*'s classic definition,[13] husband and wife should see themselves as best engaged in one of life's pivotal and reciprocal exchanges:

> In five ways, young householder, should a wife as the west be administered to by a husband:
>
> i. being courteous to her
> ii. not despising her
> iii. by being faithful to her
> iv. by handing over authority to her,
> v. by providing her with ornaments.

The wife thus ministered to as the west by the husband shows her compassion to her husband in five ways:

i. she performs her duties well,
ii. she is hospitable to relations and friends,
iii. she is faithful
iv. she protects what he brings
v. she is skilled and industrious in her duties.

The *paritta* called the *Mahāmaṇgala Sutta*, perhaps the most often chanted verses in the modern Theravāda world, likewise counsels husbands to "cherish wife and children." The *Mahāvastu* asserts that if this exchange is entered into, a man's trust will be rewarded: "When a man is successful, his wife is the cause of it" (Jones 1956, 3: 403).

Though less numerous than the aforementioned stories condemning women, there are a number of Pali *jātaka*s that allude to marriage in positive terms. In the *Kakkaṭa Jātaka*, for example, a devout elephant-wife saves her husband from a deadly giant crab, saying:

> Leave you? Never! I will never go,
> Noble Husband, with you all these years three score.
> All the Four Quarters of the earth can show
> None so dear as thou hast been of yore.
>
> (#267, 1: 236)

The *Anguttara Nikāya* (3:96) finds Shākyamuni in one situation saying, "It has been your good gain . . . in having had the good wife . . . full of compassion and desire for your weal, as a counselor, as a teacher" (Hare 1988: 214). The Mahāyānist *Sūtra on Upāsaka Precepts* likewise connects ethical practice with the karmic reward of "being loved by wife, children, parents, brothers" (Shih 1993: 75ff).

The most extensive discussion of wives in the Pali *jātaka*s is found in the frame narrative to the *Sujāta Jātaka* (#269), a story in which the Buddha chides a haughty wife and describes the "seven types of wives" as follows:

> One is bad-hearted, nor compassionates
> The good; loves others, but her lord she hates.
> Destroying all that her lord's wealth obtains,
> This wife the title of Destroyer gains.

Whatever the husband gets for her by trade,
Or skilled profession, or the farmer's spade,
She tries to filch a little out of it.
For such a wife the title Thief is fit.

Careless of duty, lazy, passionate,
Greedy, foul-mouthed, and full of wrath and hate,
Tyrannical to all her underlings—
All this the title High and Mighty brings.

Who evermore compassionates the good,
Cares for her husband as a mother would,
Guards all the wealth her husband may obtain—
This the title Motherly will gain.

She who respects her husband in the way
Young sisters reverence elders pay,
Modest, obedient to her husband's will,
The Sisterly is this wife's title still.

She whom her husband's sight will always please
As friend that friend after long absence sees,
High-bred and virtuous, giving up her life
To him—this one is called the Friendly wife.

Calm when abused, afraid of violence,
No passion, full of dogged patience,
True-hearted, bending to her husband's will,
Slave is the title given to her still.

(2:239–40)

The text also indicates that the first three go to purgatory while the last four go to heaven.

A recurring Buddhist view in the pro-marriage narratives is that the extended family should foster compassionate and generous deeds, with love of children and parents seen as far more important than the love of a spouse since strengthening the latter will counterproductively enhance the force of sexual desire. (See, e.g., the Pali *Kaṇhadīpāyana Jātaka*, #444.) Stories such as the *Suruci Jātaka* (Pali #489) promise earthly and heavenly rewards to the good wife who treats her husband, his parents, cowives, servants, and mendicants compassionately (cf. Schopen 1985).

Another type of discourse valorizing marriage is found in scattered stories that specify how to live best with a spouse. Although passages providing advice to men on how to live with wives far outnumber those directed to women regarding their husbands, "the bad husband" is a subject treated. The *Kuṇāla Jātaka* (Pali #536) gives eight grounds for a woman that justifies "despising" her husband: "For poverty, for sickness, for old age, for drunkenness, for stupidity, for carelessness, for attending to every kind of business, for neglecting every duty towards her" (Cowell 1969, 5:232).

Many *jātaka*s and *avadāna*s, then, do give a sense that householders could and should make their marriage and family life conform as much as possible to the teachings of the Buddha. This duty was incumbent upon both husbands and wives. Although the texts are emphatically inclined toward a model of the husband dominating the wife, with both limiting their carnal desire as much as possible, there is still evidence that the teachings held both men and women responsible for the moral quality and outcomes of their relationships. The multivocalic quality of Buddhist narrative literature suggests that for seeking advanced spiritual attainment, it was best to renounce the world, to join the *saṃgha*, and to practice celibacy. But most Buddhists did not do so. So barring this, Buddhist social life simply could not have been based upon consistent monastic invective directed against householders living in the married state.

The Buddhist Ideal of Recurring Conjugal Reunion

The *Shṛṇgabherī Avadāna* and its related Newar observances assert that the celestial *bodhisattva*s' powers are available to reunite husbands and wives in their *saṃsāra* destiny. But this continued reunion motif is not unique to the Mahāyāna:[14] its source in all early canons is none other than Shākyamuni Buddha. In fact, many *jātaka*s chart the lifetimes of alliance (and dalliance) shared by the future Shākyamuni and Yasodharā.

Among such highly authoritative accounts, perhaps the most striking is found in the *Divyāvadāna*, where their original union is amply developed. In this work, the connection between future Buddha and future Yasodharā goes all the way back to the lifetime when the thought of Buddhahood was awakened as he encountered Dīpaṃkara Buddha. The story has him reject a maiden given among the rewards granted by a king for his learning; as a result, this prized lady becomes "a devotee of the gods" who again encounters the *bodhisattva* when he goes to meet Dīpaṃkara. In fact, it is her lotus flowers that the *bodhisattva* offers to this Buddha, but she gives them with conditions attached:

> But I will give you these lotuses on one condition: if you, at the time of your offering them to the Buddha, make a formal, earnest wish to have me as your wife in life after life, saying, "May she become my spouse in repeated existences." (Strong 1995: 21)

The *bodhisattva* takes this vow. After he receives Dīpaṃkara's prediction of Buddhahood, undergoes a host of magical transformations, and finds many householders then also wishing to be his future disciples, the woman seals their bond with a similar vow, "When you fulfill your resolve to become a Buddha, a guide, then I would be your wife, your constant companion in the Dharma" (ibid.: 22).

Thus, in many *jātaka* stories in the various collections, it is the future Yasodharā who reunites with the *bodhisattva*. For example, she is identified as the doe who rescues her deer husband, the *bodhisattva* (Pali #359), and she is the wife given away in the most well-known *Vessantara Jātaka* (Pali #547). The *Mahāvastu*'s *Nalinī Jātaka* notes that this long-term liaison did in fact bind both individuals powerfully:[15]

> By living together in the past and by kindness in the present, so is this love born, as a lotus is born in water.
>
> When it enters the mind and the heart becomes glad, the understanding man will be assured, saying, "She was happy with me in the past."
>
> For a long time in the course of recurrent lives, a thousand *koti*s of births, the two had intercourse together as wife and husband.

Of course, it is not only the future Yasodharā who shares *saṃsāra* reunions with the *bodhisattva*: the leading Arhats, other struggling disciples, and even enemies (most prominently, Devadatta) do so as well.

Other instances of multilifetime conjugality found in the texts include well-known figures such as the Buddha's parents Queen Maya and King Suddhodana (Pali #340) as well as more ordinary folk. One discourse supporting disciples who wanted this same future conjugal union is found in the *Anguttara Nikāya* (2:61), where an elderly husband named Nakul Pitā addresses Shākyamuni in a speech that meets with the Buddha's approval:

> Blessed one, when my wife was brought to my house, she was a mere girl, and I was only a boy. I cannot recall having been unfaithful to her, not even in thought. Blessed One, we both want to live together in this way, in this life and in our future lives. (Wijayaratna 1990: 169)

The wife expresses the same opinions.

Knowing the thread of connection preserved in the popular narratives, it is not surprising that this same view of husband-wife alliance in Buddhist devotion is expressed by Yasodharā[16] herself in the *Buddhacarita*:

> He does not see that husband and wife are both consecrated in sacrifices, and both purified by the performance of the rites . . . and both destined to enjoy the same results afterwards. . . .
>
> I have no such longing for the joy of heaven, nor is that hard even for common people to win if they are resolute; but my one desire is how he my beloved may never leave me either in this world or the next. . . . (Cowell 1969: 88)

The *Shṛṇgabherī Avadāna* and the associated practices suggest that this Newar wish for continuing alliances in future existences was not a local innovation but more widespread, another aspiration that motivated devout Buddhist householders—husbands, wives, and children—to build *stūpas*, to venerate them joyfully, and to perform rituals dedicated to the celestial *bodhisattvas*.

It is here that we must underline the multivocality of Buddhist doctrinal tradition and highlight the problematic historical method of relying on the voices of ascetic monks and nuns to understand how the faith informed an ethos of living in the world as a "good Buddhist." Although many philosophical texts establish the radical individualism of karmic operation and the superiority of the renunciatory life-style over the domestic householder, this *avadāna* joins other pragmatic texts in suggesting that through ritual and through the powers of the celestial *bodhisattvas*, Buddhists can enhance the interlocking destinies of others. Is this a misunderstanding of the *dharma* or a proper social application of the law of dependent origination?

The Sociological Context of Vajrayāna Buddhism's Evolution

Finally, this examination of Buddhist views regarding spouses has indicated that a discernible minority voice in the texts, one contradicting the dominant expressions of monastic misogyny, instructs householders to make their familial relationships as fully in conformity with the *dharma* as possible. In many cases, as with future Buddha Shākyamuni and others in the *jātakas*, spouses are reunited in *saṃsāra* due to a common *karman* that disposes them to rekindle desire while continuing (in most cases) to move in a positive spiritual direction. For embodied beings destined to live married and precept-observing in the realm of desire, the good spouse—rather than threatening salvation—was essential for each party eventually moving along the path toward nirvāṇa. The popular textual tradition here *inverts* the monkish values.

Scholars who have speculated about the emergence of, and acceptance of, the Vajrayāna tradition should consult the popular narratives in Nepal and consider the domestication of Buddhist tantra among married Newar householders. Here, in Newar tantric circles, a man's dependence on the wife for advanced spiritual practice is made explicit (Gellner 1992).[17] My suggestion looking across these fields is that the Vajrayāna found its most receptive audience within the communities of *upāsaka/upāsikās* who found misogyny dissonant with their experience and valued (even cultivated) in their spouses a kindred spirit, a partner who mutually wanted every sphere of life to be connected to Buddhist practice.

CHAPTER 3

Merchants, Demonesses, and Missionary Faith: The *Siṃhalasārthabāhu Avadāna*

O monks, if you desire Enlightenment
You should walk steadily in the Dharma
With a resolute heart and with courage
You should be fearless in whatever environment
you may happen to be in and destroy every
evil influence that you may come across,
For thus will you reach the goal.

Sūtra of the 42 Chapters

The reason people like to hear stories, however, is not transparent to them. People need a context to help them relate what they heard to what they already know. We understand events in terms of events we have already understood. . . . People who fail to couch what they have heard in memorable stories will have their rules fall on deaf ears despite their best intentions and despite the best intentions of their listeners.

Roger C. Schank, *Tell Me a Story*

"L'enfer, c'est les autres."

Sartre, *No Exit*

Presenting a popular adventure narrative known from early Indic traditions that in Nepal was titled the *Siṃhalasārthabāhu Avadāna*, "The Story of Caravan Leader Simhala," this chapter illustrates how the narrative elements were integrated within the Buddhist mercantile community of Kathmandu, for whom long-distance trade with Tibet was an important undertaking throughout the last millennium. Before delving into the distinctively redacted text itself, the ancient affinity of merchants with Buddhism must first be described, followed by further aspects of Nepal's relations with Tibet and with the Hindu-Buddhist culture of the Kathmandu Valley.

Background

Buddhism and Trade

It has long been recognized that Buddhism spread across India and Asia following the trade routes[1] and that the mercantile sector of the Buddhist community has underwritten the faith's diaspora.[2] The "merchant class" in South Asia included caravan leaders, bankers, and great and petty traders of a particular locality. It should not be surprising, then, that this group is often featured in Buddhist popular literature in all canons.[3] Further, in all early Buddhist literatures, wealthy merchants are both extolled and cultivated as exemplary donors.[4] In the Sarvāstivādin *Vinaya*, for example, the first humans converted by Shākyamuni Buddha after his enlightenment were not ascetics but Bactrian traders. (They were from Burma and they returned to build the first *stūpa*, the Shwedagon, according to Burmese sources.[5])

One measure of who comprised the early *saṃgha* itself suggests that about 30 percent were *vaishya*s (Gokhale 1965: 395) and inscriptions at early monastic centers show that individual merchants and artisans, as well as their collective communities (*goṣṭhi*) or guilds (*shrenī*), vied with kings to act as principle supporters (Dehejia 1972; Heitzman 1984: 121). This relationship spanned the earliest sectarian divisions within the greater Buddhist community, with strong evidence from both Hīnayāna and Mahāyāna literatures as well as in the epigraphic sources.[6]

The tradition supported merchants in a multitude of areas, beginning with natural doctrinal affinities: Buddhist teachings undermined the ideology of birth-determined socio-spiritual privilege of *brāhmana*s and *kṣatriya*s, for whom the *vaishya*s were an inferior caste. The duty of giving (*dāna*)—to *buddha*s, *bodhisattva*s, saints, or the *saṃgha*—is presented as the best investment for making maximum *puṇya*. The Buddha's teachings on lay life also instructed *upāsaka*s in an early Pali *sutta* to avoid trade in weapons, animals, meat, wine, and poison (*Anguttara Nikāya*, 1). A Pali *jātaka* also lists "the four honest trades: tillage, trade, lending, and gleaning" (Rhys-Davids 1901: 881). Such declarations by the Buddha surely encouraged followers to move into these occupations, a tendency (and similar preference) especially pronounced in the history of Jainism. In addition to encouraging nonviolent occupations, early Mahāyāna texts also emphasize the norms of mercantile honesty (standing by quoted prices and measuring accurately), sobriety, and disciplined investment.[7]

Wealth, though not the *summum bonum*, is ubiquitously held up as the reward for moral uprightness and pious generosity. If acquired dishonestly, it leads to later torments in one of the hells.[8] But rightly acquired and properly invested wealth is called a bliss (*sukha*, one of four, along with "ownership [of property]", debtlessness, and blamelessness) that provides the "capital" for certain spiritual success.[9]

Many later texts continue this promise of worldly blessings to the laity in return for adhering to Buddhist norms. This affinity meshes with descriptions of an ideal Buddhist kingdom ruled by a *cakravartin*: among traits listed in the *Mahāvastu* is "thriving in wealth"[10]. Rightly acquired wealth, if donated as *dāna*, will beget even greater future wealth, encouraging the merchants to redistribute their riches back into society:[11] material wealth cannot be "taken with you"; but turned into *puṇya* through *dāna*, one can seek to reacquire the circumstances of wealth beyond this life in human form or in heavenly rebirth. In practice, then, Buddhist merit-making provided the means by which to "cheat death" in two key areas of life: *puṇya* can unite couples after death and reunite the donor with his or her wealth! The juxtaposition of accumulating wealth and achieving advanced spiritual progress is one of the great paradoxes of Buddhist tradition, embodied in the life of Shākyamuni in his last and former lives.

This same value attributed to wealth continues in the Mahāyāna texts as it is the means for satisfying the first perfection (*pāramitā*) of giving (*dāna*). Closely mirroring the passages from Pali, the *Ugraparipṛccha* extols becoming wealthy as a legitimate—even necessary—vocation, allowing for a *bodhisattva* to become a protector of his own household and kin, a community leader, who "take[s] responsibility for the physical and spiritual well-being of all who live in his land, giving Dharma as well as material goods" (Barnes 1993: 3).

Later Buddhist texts often speak in the language of the bazaar: the *Mahālaṃkāra Shāstra* compares the *dharma* to a "great market where the goods are sold to all."[12] The *Saddharmapuṇḍarīka* calls

Amitābha "Caravan Chief of Living Beings" (Hurvitz 1976: 407). One Mahāyāna text explicitly promises success in overseas trade as a reward for meritorious service to one's parents.[13]

Other Buddhist traditions designated certain Buddhas, *bodhisattvas*, and allied *devas* as protectors of pious Buddhist merchants. Across the maritime communities of medieval South and Southeast Asian traders worshiped the former Buddha Dīpaṃkara as "Calmer of Waters," an association we'll return to in the Newar context.[14] There is also pan-regional evidence for "Buddhist deities" that gave assistance to devotees seeking wealth and trade: Pañcika and Pāṇḍuka enjoyed popularity in the Northwest and in Khotan[15]; in Tibet and Java it was Jambhala;[16] in the Pali *jātakas* there is also the sea goddess Maṇimekhala who fills this role.[17]

Mahāyāna texts that extol *bodhisattva bhakti* specifically mention their services to merchants. For example, in Ajanta and in other early cave sites on trade routes, there is a standard rock sculpture depicting Avalokiteshvara as Savior against the "Eight Dreaded Things," potential dangers that might befall merchants.[18]

From the scattered travel journals from antiquity, we know that monks traveled with the caravans, allied with artisans and merchants plying the trade networks. By the Gupta era, many Buddhist monasteries were granted land and also had extensive economic ties with their surrounding communities. The administrative practices of monastic officials—for instance, lending money at interest and warehousing goods[19]—created symbiotic relationships with traders (Ray 1986: 87-89). Given the common fact of *vaishyas* becoming monks, the regular income from *dāna*, and the attested role that merchant *upāsakas* played in administering the *vihāras*' practical affairs, the economic evolution of Buddhist institutions as endowed, financially sound concerns seems to be an intelligible historical convergence (Schopen 1994b; Gernet 1995). The early missionary success of Buddhist monasticism must therefore be linked to the devoted patronage and service of the mercantile class and to alliances with the dynamic political-economic sectors of prospering Indic empires.

The spread of Buddhist tradition itself motivated transregional trade; the alliances and wealth generated affected the entire Indo-Sinic region. Across the trade routes leaving South Asia—northward on the international silk route, across the Himalayas, via Tibet and Yunnan, and eastward via maritime trade—the network of marts, ports, and oases defined a web of Buddhist monasticism.[20] Gernet points to the pan-Asian pattern from his studies of the faith in early China: "Buddhism, in other words, was good for business, and invigorated a whole sector of the Chinese economy" (Gernet 1995: 167). Thus, the logic of Buddhism's diasporas, domestications, and historical survival conformed, in large part, to the interdependent exigencies of trade, the expansion of monastic wealth, and the patronage of merchants.[21] This was certainly so in the Himalayas.

Newars in Himalayan Trade

In the central trans-Himalayan region by the time of our text's early local redactions (1400 C.E.), this ancient relationship between merchants and Buddhism endured. Highland salt, gold, silver, musk, and yak tails were valuable commodities in the plains, and a wide variety of diaspora trade networks existed to exchange products for them.[22] Prominent Kashmiri, Bengali, Marwari, and Tibetan traders figure prominently in the region's history alongside Newar and other Nepalese traders (Thakali, Sherpa, and Manangi) (Furer-Haimendorf 1975). In the Kathmandu Valley and environs, however, the dominant merchants were Newar Buddhists. It is to their text and traditions that we now turn.

The important role of Newar merchants and of the trans-Himalayan Buddhist trade network must be emphasized in the histories of both Nepalese and Tibetan civilizations (Lewis 1989c). Newars for at least a thousand years were highly sought artisans across Tibet[23] and since 1500 C.E. lamas were called to Kathmandu to supervise major renovations of Svayambhū and Bauddha (Lewis and Jamspal 1988). For over five centuries, Newars desiring the classical celibate monastic discipline could take ordination in the local Tibetan *vihāra*s. As we have seen, this trade/art connection likely represents an ancient transregional pattern.

In many domains, Newar Lhasa traders have exerted a strong effect on their own core tradition. In addition to transplanting lamas and highland monasteries into the Kathmandu Valley, the often great mercantile profits returned to contribute to Kathmandu's economy, primarily through religious patronage. Local inscriptions and records amply document the fact that in this century Lhasa traders restored and made additions to all major indigenous Buddhist shrines. In addition, they sponsored the majority of extraordinary patronage events to the Newar *saṃgha* in this century. Thus, we cannot fully understand Buddhist history in the central Himalayan region or the *Siṃhalasārthabāhu Avadāna*'s role in the Kathmandu Valley without taking into account the transregional relationships that diaspora Newar merchants sustained across the

Indo-Tibetan Himalayan frontier (Lewis 1993b). We now turn to one text that helped define this Newar connection. (While this overview establishes the basic setting of the *avadāna*, additional specific details of the regional context will be added after the translation to aid in comprehending the domestication of the text.)

The Siṃhala Narrative's Indic Genealogy

This narrative adventure, one of the most famous of the many Buddhist stories, has ancient origins: there are partial versions in the Pali *jātaka*s and in an extant Jain Prakrit version. It also appears in two recensions in one of the most disseminated collections of Buddhist stories, the Sanskrit *Divyāvadāna* (Heavenly stories)[24]. Following this genealogy, the Siṃhala story reached nearly all Asian Buddhist communities.[25] Siegfried Lienhard has established the fact that the modern Newari recension likely derives from the early *Divyāvadāna* that subsequently inspired a longer Mahāyāna-styled revision in the *Kāraṇḍavyūha*, a text that dates back to 620 C.E. when it was translated into Tibetan. The Nepali Buddhist narrative draws upon the *Kāraṇḍavyūha*-derived *Guṇakāraṇḍavyūha*, a Sanskrit text in verse form devoted to Avalokiteshvara[26] that Lienhard dates as late as the sixteenth century (Lienhard 1993: 93), but shows yet another stage of redaction into Newari, especially through its innovative plot turns and attention to certain geographic and material culture details.

Translation

Notes on the Published Text

The Newari version of this text used is that published by Bhikshu Sudarshan in 1967. This modern vernacular Newari version likely developed through the local storytelling of the *Guṇakāraṇḍavyūha*, another instance of the oral-written travels of *jātaka* narratives.

The Story of Caravan Leader Siṃhala

In the town Siṃhalakalpa ruled by Siṃhakeshara, a son named Siṃhalasārthabāhu was born to Siṃhasārthabāha. Once he grew up, the son thought that he should leave the traditional family jewelry business and said to his parents,

"O Mother and Father, we should not give up our family business. I shall go across the Ratnākar sea to trade."

Having heard the son say, "Bid me farewell!" both parents felt distressed and replied, "O son Siṃhalasārthabāhu, we are now old. We already possess innumerable properties. You should be content; stay here and enjoy the riches we already possess. Why are you so eager to abandon gold, gems, and other wealth to risk great misery? Why go to this Ratnākar? The troubles along the way to Ratnākar are so many: after passing through many villages and countries, you will reach a great forest. In that forest there is danger from many lions, tigers, wild animals, and also from thieves. In some places you must tolerate great cold and high temperatures. Furthermore, since you are an immature young man, your body is still delicate. O son, please do not talk about going to Ratnākar."

Having listened to his parents' objections, Siṃhalasārthabāhu replied respectfully, "O Mother and Father, the effects of the *karman* written on the forehead will unfold in the world, no matter where I go. How can you regard me as an accomplished man if I merely enjoy my parental wealth? How can I become an accomplished man if I do not earn a living from my own labor? How can I perform the duty of meritorious giving (*dāna*)? For this additional reason I must go. Please, both of you, do not worry. In undertaking a mission of *dharma*, certainly no troubles will befall me. Give me your blessings and let me be off!" After doing *nāmaskāra* to his mother and father, he touched their lotuslike feet; and having taken leave with their auspicious blessings, he assembled five hundred less one attendants who speedily prepared elephants, horses, donkeys, camels, and so on, loaded the luggage, then departed in the northern direction, toward Ratnapura.

Later, however, they committed the evil deed of destroying *caitya*s along the way, and Saturn intervened. Despite Saturn's intervention, having crossed many villages, towns, rivers, and mountains, they eventually reached the shore of the Brahmaputra River. From the result of destroying *caitya*s at that time, Siṃhalasārthabāhu, having seen the oceanlike Brahmaputra river, cautiously restrained the 499 and called out and hired a boatman named Karṇadhāra; after doing *nāmaskār* to the broad Brahmaputra, Siṃhalasārthabāhu and his attendants embarked in his boat and started to cross the mighty river.

When they reached the middle of the river, a very terrible wind arose and began to capsize the boat. Seeing the danger of sinking with the boat and fearing their possible deaths, the 500 attendants[27] addressed their leader: "O Siṃhalasārthabāhu, we 500 attendants along with you are about to go to our deaths in the middle of this very river! Here and now is there any means by which [we can] be rescued? Please tell us immediately!" Siṃhalasārthabāhu quickly replied, "O attendants! In times of the greatest trouble, the only one capable of rescuing [us] is the glorious *Triratna*; there is no other in the world. Take refuge in the *Triratna*!" But due to the demerit (*pāp*) of destroying *caitya*s along the road, they could not concentrate their minds, or even pronounce the name of the *Triratna*; they could only pronounce the name of their own family protector deities (*kula devatā*s). As a result, Siṃhalasārthabāhu and the 499 attendants fell into the sea as the boat broke into small pieces. At that time, by the strength of their own limbs, they crossed the great river and reached an island shore [where] they laid under *campaka* trees, making great lamentations, crying and weeping loudly. Remembering their love of their own country again, they sighed out sadly.

At that time, the *rākṣasī*s from the town of Ratnapura on Tāmradvīpa island saw the 499 attendants who had fallen into the river and who had climbed up on the banks with their own hands and who were making lamentations beneath *campaka* trees. Delighted, the *rākṣasī*s of Ratnapura joined together to appear as maidens possessing the spotless beauty of 16-year-olds looking like [goddess of desire, Kāma's wife] the youthful beautiful Ratidevī. Having become immensely alluring, they reached the place where Siṃhalasārthabāhu and the 499 attendants were resting beneath the *campaka* trees. All of the *rākṣasī*s were delighted; with smiles and expressions captivating to look at, they spoke sweet charming words to Siṃhalasārthabāhu and to the rest, and proposed, "O Masters, having overcome disaster in the great river, why do you have such gloomy faces, anxious minds, and uncertainty? For what reason is this so? What country have you come from? What trouble [occurred] such that you are in this place by the river? Tell us the details." Saying "O Master," they inquired of Siṃhalasārthabāhu, showing great affection.

Having listened thus to the *rākṣasīs*' speech and feeling spellbound, Siṃhalasārthabāhu responded, "O Beautiful Ones! I am no other than Siṃhalasārthabāhu the Merchant, son of Siṃhalasārthabāha from the town of Siṃhakalpa in Jambudvīpa. Including me, there are five hundred in all. Carrying loads of different kinds of trade goods, we were unable to cross the broad river: when our boat reached the middle a very terrible wind came from the opposite direction and broke up the boat. We and our goods fell into the river and everything was washed away. We ourselves by our own strength made it here. And so sitting under these *campaka* trees, we are remembering our families at home. We feel great sorrow, O Beautiful Ones."

So having heard his speech, the *rākṣasīs* in their beautiful female forms made a request, "O Masters, how great is our fortune to hear this! Since we have come to live in the country called Ratnapura, we have been lacking men as sexual

Fig 3.1. Shipwrecked Merchants Coming Ashore to *Rākṣasīs*

Fig 3.2. Merchants and *Rākṣasīs* at Home

partners although we are now fully mature and beautiful. By our good luck we have taken sight of you." They implored them, "Please come live in to our Ratnapura and make love to us[28] who are happily in our adolescence. Do make love to us in all the different ways."

Having been persuaded, Siṃhalasārthabāhu and the other attendants each escorted one woman and carried her to her own dwelling. Having fed them with different divine foods, given them many types of gold, jewels, and ornaments, at night the *rākṣasīs* made love to them and kept them there every night. After seven days of enjoying lovemaking and all love sports, the *rākṣasīs* in the form of beautiful women happened to fall asleep.

Now at that time, Shrī Shrī Shrī Ārya Avalokiteshvara—[the celestial bodhisattva] who lends assistance with compassion to poor suffering men in the world—saw Siṃhalasārthabāhu and his entourage deluded and imprisoned in the grip of the *rākṣasīs* in Ratnapura on Tāmradvīpa island. Feeling compassion, Avalokiteshvara thought, "My miserable children are imprisoned in the grip of the evil-souled man-eating *rākṣasīs* of Tāmradvīpa." Vowing to help these people, Shrī Shrī Shrī Ārya Avalokiteshvara immediately entered the lamp placed in the room of Siṃhalasārthabāhu on Tāmradvīpa for the purpose of discoursing with him and so made the lamp flicker. Having seen the lamp flicker, Siṃhalasārthabāhu was surprised and focused on the lamp alone. For a second time, Avalokiteshvara made the lamp flicker. Having seen the lamp flicker yet again, Siṃhalasārthabāhu asked, "O lamp! Why do you flicker? Who is it who has come into the lamp? What is your purpose in coming? Please tell me the reason!" Shrī Avalokiteshvara answered, "O Siṃhalasārthabāhu! How little do you know! They are not really beautiful women: they are evil-souled ones and man-eating *rākṣasīs* as well. These *rākṣasīs* will most certainly devour all of you. You must escape as soon as possible."

Having heard these words and feeling terrified, he prayed respectfully again [to the lamp] and said, "O Lord of the Lamp, how have you come to know this? Is it really true?" and then he respectfully saluted the lamp. Shrī Lokeshvara replied, "O Siṃhalasārthabāhu, if you do not believe me, go and look in the cell called Āyasha in the southern direction."

Following this advice, that very night Siṃhalasārthabāhu went out alone in the southern direction, holding his sword.

Having arrived at the Āyasha cell, he saw a house without doors or windows. He also heard peoples' voices only. Feeling great surprise, he climbed a tree and looked in. Having heard the cries again, he climbed higher up the *campaka* tree and asked, "O people! Who are you and why are you living here?"

They responded, "O sir, having come for Ratnākar trade, while we were crossing the Brahmaputra a terrible wind blew and broke up our boat, and we fell into the river. And when we emerged from the water, we fell into the grip of *rākṣasīs* from Ratnapura. We had sex and love play with them, but then they came to know of other traders on the road. They threw us down into this Āyasha cell and come to eat us every day." They also added, "What is to be done, O Great Man, and who are you?"

Fig 3.3. Avalokiteshvara Speaks in the Wick Lamp

Fig. 3.4. Siṃhala Discovers the Prison of Former Traders

Siṃhalasārthabāhu listened to them and replied, "O people, I am none other than the son of Siṃhalasārthabāha called Siṃhalasārthabāhu from Jambudvīpa. I also came to trade in Ratnākar. I have come to see who you are here and what things there are. I have come to investigate." Having replied in this way and heard as much as he needed to, he returned.

After returning to his own room, Siṃhalasārthabāhu saluted the still-burning lamp with joined palms and addressed the deity, "O Lamp, O Divine One! By your grace I have looked into the Āyasha cell. Guide us [to know] how we can be saved. You must protect us!" He ended his petition with a *nāmaskāra*.

Dwelling in the lamp, Shrī Avalokiteshvara replied, "O Siṃhalasārthabāhu! If you are determined to return to Jambudvīpa, I will show you how. Listen: the means of crossing the Brahmaputra River is there on the bank of the river. It is a compassionate soul living there called Shrī Vārāhaka, a great horse. This one living there [will be] eating white medicinal herbs and rubbing his back on the gold sand bank. This one will call upon you and what will he say? 'Who is willing to go across the river? I will send you across.' At that time all of you must go before him, make three circumambulations around him with joined hands, touch your heads to his lotus-like feet, and make this request: 'O Protector! O Lord! O Vārāhaka! O Noble Horse who is a store of compassion: please take us across the broad river.' And at that time, having aroused the compassion of the supreme lord, he will transport you across the ocean." After instructing him, Shrī Ārya Avalokiteshvara vanished in an instant.

Afterwards, Siṃhalasārthabāhu climbed into bed in order to sleep alongside the *rākṣasī*. At that time, she awoke and asked, "O Master! Where have you been? Your body feels very cold." Siṃhalasārthabāhu replied, "My dear beauty, I had to go out to answer a call of nature. For this reason my body became very cold." Saying this, he convinced the *rākṣasī* by his lie. After that, Siṃhalasārthabāhu felt disgust at having slept with the *rākṣasī* who appeared beautiful. And so the night passed. Once dawn came, Siṃhalasārthabāhu met the 499 attendants outside the town in a grove after finishing the daily routine of ablutions and *pūjā*s. He addressed them, "O Attendants! I will make a speech on one topic. Listen! If you say 'What is this about?', [it concerns] your beloved ones here, your very own wives. How much do they love you? How much do they care? What do they feed you? You must tell me the details in all honesty."

Having heard this, the leader among Siṃhalasārthabāhu's attendants smiled and answered merrily, "O Leader! O Brave One! Master! By your grace and by the influence of your great and good fortune we have come to enjoy such sensual pleasures with the beautiful ones of Ratnapura. Another one [from the group] said, "O Brave One! To have had the chance to enjoy such sex and lovemaking, how fortunate we are to have been so divinely blessed! We have no desire at all to leave this, our own great fortune, and return to Jambudvīpa." Another said, "O leader, my beloved wife, having put on different jewels and ornaments, honored me happily and allowed me such delightful sexual dalliance with her." And yet another said, "O Siṃhalasārthabāhu! My wife, having put on clothes and special royal robes of different types, allowed me to enjoy the sexual pleasure of her tender body." And another, "O Brave One! By the fruit of what *puṇya* have we enjoyed the pleasures of the *apsarā*s of Ratnapura? We have certainly settled here happily and received the greatest respect. Such kinds of pleasure, even for those kings living in the Three Realms, must be rare. Again, in Amarāvatī heaven, even with Indrāyanī does Indra rarely obtain such pleasure. In this world, the illusion of love prevails. Again, it is rare for Shrī Kṛṣṇa with Rādhikā to enjoy such sexual pleasures. O Leader! For this reason, if we were to return to Jambudvīpa, we would not obtain such pleasures. We will stay here and do not ever want to return."

Other attendants made similar statements, narrating their own many pleasures. Having heard the remarks of his attendants, Siṃhalasārthabāhu told them, "O Companions! Although they seem to be beloved ones, only if you do not tell this secret to your own wives can our own lives be saved. Listen and I will explain. And how is this? We have left our own country and homeland, including family, wealth, property, friends, and neighbors and have come to this Ratnapura. If you wish to return and see these faces ever again, I will tell you how." Shocked at hearing this, they inquired, "O Siṃhalasārthabāhu! What happened? What is it? Even though we love them, we will not tell them. O Master, please answer us."

Siṃhalasārthabāhu replied, "All these women are not who they appear to be. They are, in fact, man-eating *rākṣasīs* of Tāmradvīpa. They are not human. You must not be deceived, even though they give you all sorts of sensual pleasure, jeweled goods, endless delight, and say "My Own Master." Undoubtedly they will devour us. This is absolutely certain. For this reason and for the good of everyone, you must keep it a secret."

Having listened again and felt the horrifying fear of death, they joined their hands and touched their heads to Siṃhalasārthabāhu's feet and pleaded with him, "O Protector! How did you come to know that these women are the *rākṣasīs* of Tāmradvīpa? Can it be true? How can we rescue ourselves? Have we arrived at death's door? Is there any means of saving us from death? You must give us instructions on how to cross the river and go back to Jambudvīpa." Having answered him with great urgency, they sighed deeply.

After their speech, again Siṃhalasārthabāhu spoke, "You should not panic, O attendants! Be patient. Patience in the face of misery is called for and all of you must do exactly as I say. On the shore of the Brahmaputra River, on a gold sand beach is a Compassionate One, King of Horses, called Vārāhaka, who will convey us across." Having given all the instructions, Siṃhalasārthabāhu and all the attendants went to their places with their own beautiful ones.

And later, after returning to their own houses and having enjoyed different foods, at night they enjoyed and made love to their beautiful wives. At that time, the beautiful ones asked their own men, "O Master, in the daytime today where did you go for amusement? Have you been out to see gardens of different types? Have you brought [us] different types of flowers, fruits, and vegetables?"

Responding to their wives' queries, they answered, "O beautiful ones, we did not see any of these things. After four days we will go to see [them]. [Now] prepare and give us some flattened rice and food."

Having heard their answer, the wives replied teasingly, "O Masters! Where did you really go? How is it that you did not see any gardens, flowers, fruits, and so forth?" Later on, those attendants, while sitting in their own places, remembering the danger of death, sat deeply sighing. And so the women, seeing them taking deep breaths, asked them, "O Masters! Why are you now and then sighing so? What trouble has arisen? Please tell us."

At that time, Siṃhalasārthabāhu and the 499 attendants told their own beautiful ones, "O, dear beloved ones, there is no other reason for our heavy sighs than having remembered our mothers, fathers, sons, daughters, wives, relatives, and friends from our homeland. Feeling attachment for them, we have passed a long time absent from our own country." Having answered in this way, even though worried, they tried to brighten their faces as much as possible.

At that time, the *rākṣasī*s, looking at the faces of their own men and smiling, enticed them; revealing the youthful curves of their bodies, they spoke tenderly to them and asked, "O Masters! O greatly beloved Ones! Why are you frequently sighing after remembering your wives, sons, etc. in your own country, Jambudvīpa? Here in the city of Ratnapur Nagar in Tāmradvīpa, isn't there everything? Living here are many different cows, buffalo, horses, elephants, camels, she goats, sheep, deer, stags, yaks, musk deer, etc. and all species. There are also all varieties of fruits and vegetables. All kinds of flowers are here: fragrant, night-blooming, etc. There are all sorts of scented things, too, such as musk, camphor, saffron, sandalwood, herbs, cardamom, cloves, nutmeg, betel nut and betel leaf, etc. And again there are all sorts of delightful places such as gardens, stone fountains, pleasure groves, etc. And there are birds of every variety such as peacocks, swans, *bubil*s, *cakora*, as well as butterflies all with sweet voices that are lovely to listen to. So delightful is this place! Why do you long for your own country in spite of the charms of Ratnapura? You are in command of all of this and of our beautiful adolescence, so enjoy yourselves," they said clearly.

Having listened to the *rākṣasīs*' words, though worried about the danger of death, the men [still] enjoyed their *rākṣasīs* sexually in the night and fell asleep. Feeling very worried and anxious, just as a hungry one longs for food, a sick one for a doctor's face, a devotee for the deity, a *cakora* bird for the moon, so they waited for the four days to pass.

Thereupon after four days passed, they went about the daily rituals and had their own women prepare their meals. On the evening of the fourth day, they went to sleep.

At dawn on the next day, in their own houses they recalled the deities in their daily *pūjā*s. After eating and having gathered up their equipment and food, they went off after making a pretense of seeing the pavilions and ponds to mislead them. Having said good-bye to their wives, they remembered their own *kula devatā*s. After this, Siṃhalasārthabāhu and the 499 attendants arrived outside the town. And at that time, all of them gathered together and hastily went to the Brahmaputra shore with the golden sand. Then the black-eared King of Horses Vārāhaka arrived nearby. When he saw Siṃhalasārthabāhu and the merchants arrive, he stood up from the golden sand, shook his body three times, and called out, "I will carry all those wishing to cross the river to Jambudvīpa."

Having heard the horse's words, they circumambulated him three times, touched their heads to his feet, and greeted him reverentially. Then Siṃhalasārthabāhu addressed him, "O Noble King of Horses, you must protect us who are living in the grip of the evil *rākṣasīs* of Ratnapur Nagar in Tāmradvīpa. If you do not protect us, surely they will devour us. O Compassionate One, for this reason we have come for refuge to your feet. Please look upon us compassionately and send us across the Brahmaputra." This all the men repeated with tears falling from their eyes.

Having heard this request and feeling compassion, the horse again spoke, "O five hundred merchants, if you have the wish to go across the river to Jambudvīpa, I will send you across. Until you reach the other side, you must remember the *Triratna* and not look back. If you can obey, I will deliver all of you to the other side."

Fig. 3.5. Meeting with the Divine Horse Vārāhaka

They listened and again touched the horse's feet with their heads and said respectfully, "O Parameshvara, King of Horses, we will certainly not cease reciting the names of Shrī Buddha, Dharma, and Saṃgha. Nor will we look back. We are poised at the mouth of death, so please send us across the river."

Having heard their plea, the glorious horse became large and said, "O Siṃhalasārthabāhu and you 499 attendants! All of you get on my body and pronounce the names of the *Triratna.*" Having heard this instruction, they touched their heads to his feet and got on the horse's back, remembering their own *kula devatā*s.

Making the sound "Hu-nu-num," the horse then accelerated like the wind and soon reached the middle of the great river. But noticing the noise, the *rākṣasī*s realized that Siṃhalasārthabāhu and the rest were crossing the river and one called out, "O sisters! The 500 traders we have taken as husbands are all escaping across the ocean. Now let us go and devour them." They called to one another as they revealed their true forms and produced the wild crying sound *kilikila*. Lighting up the sky in many ways, they came flying through the air.

Flying up close to them, the *rākṣasīs* made lamentations to elicit sympathy and used endearing, lovely words which created the illusion of enchantment and love. From behind them, they cried, "O Masters! Where are you going? Are you leaving us with youthful figures, whose longings you have satisfied in Ratnapura? Where are you going? Why are you disgracing us? What misery has arisen! O Masters! Why are you going, abandoning your royal robes and sensual pleasures, forgetting the virtues of heaven-like Ratnapura, forsaking our love? O Husbands, Beloved Ones, Lords of Life! Being unable to subdue the longing for enjoyment and the various ways of sex, we have followed after you. Let us accompany you to your country. If you will not do so, then just look back a little, show us just a little glimpse of your faces. How can you abandon our love and not give us even a glimpse of your faces? We will be helpless! Because of you, we will die! We never thought that you could be so cruel!" They cried on and on with these and other love-inducing words, speaking to them as they followed behind, flying across the sky.

Fig. 3.6. Siṃhala and the Merchants Pursued by the *Rākṣasīs*

Remembering the sensual pleasure and enjoyments, each and every attendant was unable to ignore his *rākṣasī*'s endearing words. One by one, each looked back at them. From the evil *karman* of destroying the *caitya*s along the road, those who glanced back fell into the river. And right after each fell down, his *rākṣasī* swooped over her own husband, plucked him from the sea by the hair, and took him to the bank. Back on the shore they devoured each and every one of them.

But due to the compassion of Ārya Avalokiteshvara, Shrī Shrī Shrī Karuṇāmaya, from the effect of performing the *Aṣṭamī Vrata*, and from having taken refuge in the noble *Triratna*, it was Siṃhalasārthabāhu alone who still held on to the mane of the horse Ashvarāja [with one hand] so that he could embrace the neck [with the other]. He alone crossed the great river.

Having reached the other shore and climbed down from the horse's body, he went around the horse three times, touched the horses feet, joined his hands, and said respectfully, "O Karuṇāmaya, King of Horses! I am the only one who has had good fortune. Although I dangled just beyond the mouths of the *rākṣasī*s, due to your grace and the grace of the *Triratna*, I have crossed this great river. I have reached Jambudvīpa. You must always protect me!"

The horse replied, "O Siṃhalasārthabāhu! For the merit of taking the name of the *Triratna* you were protected from the *rākṣasī*s. Now go to the town called Siṃhakalpa in Jambudvīpa and have sight of your parents' own feet. Always take refuge in the *Triratna*. Perform the *Aṣṭamī Vrata*. Whenever you are in danger, I will protect you. In the future, you will be the king of Siṃhakalpa. And having given him different blessings and after he handed over the kingdom of Siṃhakalpa to Siṃhalasārthabāhu, the King of Horses immediately vanished, giving a divine sighting [*darshan*] of Shrī Avalokiteshvara in the sky.

And so after the King of Horses gave these instructions, Shrī Avalokiteshvara made his own luminous flame go up into the sky like a fire and then he [too] disappeared. Feeling awe for that deity, Siṃhalasārthabāhu joined his hands for as long as he could see, then did an eightfold salutation.

Then, grasping his sword called *candraprabha*, he started off alone toward Jambudvīpa and came upon a dense forest.

At that moment, all the *rākṣasīs* of Tāmradvīpa circled around their leader who was Siṃhalasārthabāhu's wife and said to her, "We have just finished eating our own husbands who fell back into the river. Yet you alone let your husband escape and he was not eaten. That one will go to Jambudvīpa and tell this news to everyone. If others hear his tale, who else will come to our place? There will be no food in the future. If you do not go and devour that Siṃhalasārthabāhu, we will eat you."

Once she heard their ultimatum, the head *rākṣasī* felt afraid and said, "O younger sisters! Please do not say that you will devour me. It is certain that I will return after having eaten that husband Siṃhalasārthabāhu." After convincing them, the head *rākṣasīs* flew into the sky. Having assumed her beautiful form, she appeared in front of Siṃhalasārthabāhu, frightening him. But Siṃhalasārthabāhu, seeing the *rākṣasī* before him, quickly took his special sword in hand and when he started to chop at her, the *rākṣasī* ran away in fear.

Soon the *rākṣasī* saw other traders who had come there from many countries. She assumed her beautiful form and went nearby. After seeing such a beautiful one and feeling amazed at seeing the woman's face, they said, "O Younger sister! Who are you? Why are you living alone in this unpleasant dense forest?" She answered, "O elder brother traders! For one trying to escape great danger, there is nothing other than the *Triratna* so I have come for refuge in the *Triratna*. O Brothers! What can I do feeling such great misery?" After saying this, she took deep breaths like those of the male and female *nāgas*, made a gloomy face, and then sighed deeply again. Then the merchants said, "O Younger sister! Where have you come from? What evil has befallen you? Whose daughter are you? Who are your friends? You must tell us in detail."

After she heard the traders' request, she produced tears in her eyes, joined her hands, and spoke politely, "O traders, what to do? I was a princess in the Ratnapura kingdom of Tāmradvīpa. My father gave me in marriage to Siṃhalasārthabāhu when he was trading [there]. Now this Siṃhalasārthabāhu, after having enjoyed marital bliss with me for several months in my parents' country, announced [one day] to my father, 'Now I am returning to my own country. Farewell!' and brought me here. Then we were shipwrecked and we barely crossed the river by our own strength. All the wealth given by my parents—gifts, jewels, and so on—was washed away. After this, Siṃhalasārthabāhu scolded me and said, 'O evil woman, having crossed the river with you, I was almost lost. With such an unlucky woman I will not go anywhere. If I do go on with you who has such bad luck, I will surely die. You must not come along with me. Wherever you wish to go, be off! And I will be off to where I please.' [After he said this] I tried many means of changing his mind, but I could not. Today I have been left alone in this dense forest. What to do? Thus, traders, you must see my husband for me and convince him to love me again."

After hearing her request, they said, "All right, we will do so," and soon they came upon Siṃhalasārthabāhu and addressed him. After making perfunctory conversation, they [finally] said, "O Siṃhalasārthabāhu! Regarding the king's daughter of Ratnapura: after choosing her and bringing her to this dense forest, why did you abandon her? It is rare to find a woman who does not make a mistake and they are powerless. You must forgive her and take her along." So having heard the traders' speech, Siṃhalasārthabāhu replied, "O Traders and Friends! This woman is no princess nor did I bring her along. This very woman is in fact a *rākṣasī* who feeds upon men living in Tāmradvīpa."

Having heard Siṃhalasārthabāhu's response, the traders again spoke, "O Siṃhalasārthabāhu, O Friend! How did you come to come to learn that in fact this woman is a *rākṣasī*? From whom did you hear this? Is it really true? You must tell us truthfully." Siṃhalasārthabāhu replied, "O friends, this woman is really a *rākṣasī*," and he started then to tell the story in detail. After hearing this tale, the traders were very frightened and they quickly returned to their own countries.

Then, Siṃhalasārthabāhu took his sword in hand and set off alone toward his country Siṃhalakalpa in Jambudvīpa.

After reaching his own house, he touched the feet of his parents, and after exchanging formalities, he cried out, "O Mother and Father, all of the goods and properties you gave to me—they all are lost. Also, the 499 attendants sent with me, they fell into the hands of the Tāmradvīpa *rākṣasīs* and died. I have come home safely due to your virtue and the influence of the glorious *Triratna*. What to do?" After saying this, he respectfully related the tale in detail.

Both mother and father listened to this, sobbed, breathed deeply, and looked anxious. Peering into their son's face, they replied, "O Son, O Jewel of the Family! It is our good fortune to have the opportunity to see you again. Beset by such trouble, you have escaped great misfortune. O Son! Of what consideration is the lost property? Although the goods we gave are all gone, do not worry at all! In our house, there remains a great portion of wealth that we have earned. Having command over this property, take pleasure in making meritorious gifts (*puṇya dāna*). O Son, although some wealth was lost, there is the ability to make it back again. If a son like you is lost, what can be recovered thereafter? At the time when we are old, a son is like a walking stick; when the eyes cannot see, he is like a guide; at the time of death, he is the one to light the cremation fire; and he is the one to do the *piṇḍa dāna* [ritual] that sends [us] to a heavenly abode. So, dear son, do not worry and be content."

Soon afterward, the *rākṣasī* who was driven off in the Tāmradvīpa forest entered Siṃhakalpa city with a beautiful baby whose face and traits resembled Siṃhalasārthabāhu, though he was not real [lit. "made with *māyā*"]. At that time, she went about asking in every neighborhood of the country, "O people! Where is the house of Siṃhalasārthabāhu." The people then escorted her to his house. While staying near the house door, she placed the magically-produced baby in her lap, sat silently and cried so as to elicit sympathy from the others.

The people wanted to know who the beautiful woman was and asked, "O Beautiful Sister, where are you from? Who are you? Who is the father of this baby? What sorrows have befallen you?" She responded, "O People, having wondered about whose son this might be, please look!" Hearing this, the people replied, "O beautiful woman, looking at this baby's appearance, he resembles Siṃhalasārthabāhu, son of Siṃhalasārthabāha. It is his son, is it not? Or else is it another's son? Why are you staying here?"

The *rākṣasī* replied, "O people! I am the princess of Ratnapura, a kingdom of Tāmradvīpa. Not long ago, Siṃhalasārthabāhu traded in Ratnapura and my father gave me to him in marriage. After we lived several months in my father's country, I was brought by him to his own country. But once we reached the river bank and began to cross the water, the boat sank and by our own strength we reached the shore. After that, having said I was an evil one, he left me in the forest. What could I do? For the sake of this very child, I have come to this place, inquiring all along the way, facing great troubles. O people, having put myself in your graces, speak to my husband and convince him to love me."

Having listened to her account, the people went to Siṃhalasārthabāhu. After relating what the woman had said, they told him, "O Siṃhalasārthabāhu! Having married this woman who seems to be a heaven nymph [*gandharva*], a blameless woman of Tāmradvīpa, why did you abandon her in the forest? Even if blameworthy, forgive her. Welcome this princess who has a son and please keep her inside your home." Siṃhalasārthabāhu replied, "O Beloved Friends and Fellows! This very woman is not a Tāmradvīpa princess. I never married her nor is this child mine. This one is in fact made from *māyā*. This very woman is a *rākṣasī* from Tāmradvīpa." This he told to the people.

After they heard his answer, the people, unable to convince Siṃhalasārthabāhu, went to his father Siṃhalasārthabāha and said, "O Siṃhalasārthabāha! You are famous among the people as a virtuous man. Your son Siṃhalasārthabāhu, after marrying a Tāmradvīpa princess and fathering a son, then accompanied both but later abandoned them in the forest. Together with the baby, this princess is knocking at your door. After hearing her request to convince him, we tried but failed to persuade your son. You must convince your son to take this princess into your house. Hearing the people's words and coming to believe them, Siṃhalasārthabāha called on and counseled his son, "O Son Siṃhalasārthabāhu!

Having married a princess of Tāmradvīpa and fathered a son, why did you abandon them in the forest? Where will a blameless woman go? Therefore, forgive all her mistakes, admit them together into the house, and love her."

Having listened to his father's words, Siṃhalasārthabāhu touched his father's feet and said, "O Father! I never married this woman, nor is she a princess from Tāmradvīpa, nor is this child mine. This woman is undoubtedly a *rākṣasī* and this child has been created by her *māyā*. This very *rākṣasī*, having completely eaten all of our attendants, has returned to eat me as well. Hearing this response, both the mother and father responded, "O Son, all women are *rākṣasī*s. Therefore, after forgiving her faults, you must love her." Hearing their command, Siṃhalasārthabāhu replied angrily, "O Mother and Father! If you do not believe me, then you may love her. If you insist that this woman will be kept in this house, I will go away from here. Go ahead then and accept her in this house!"

Noting the son's anger, the parents replied, "O Son, having driven out a son, what is the use of a daughter-in-law? After you recover, there can be many brides." And so they came down from the house, held the girl by the neck, pushed her away from near the door, and cast her out.

Having been driven off by Siṃhalasārthabāhu's parents, she took her child and reached the gate of King Siṃhakeshara's palace, while sobbing and making great lamentations. She then placed the child on her lap and made her appearance fascinatingly beautiful for the people. At that moment, many people, including the ministers who were coming to see the king, saw this beautiful woman; feeling greatly surprised and deluded, they quickly went up to King Siṃhaḳeshara and made a request, "O King Siṃhakeshara, on this very day, a beautiful, youthful woman with child is staying at your door. Whether she is a heavenly maiden, a *nāga* beauty, or else a *gandharva*, we don't know. Please consider her case."

At that time, therefore, the king listened to their account and responded, "O Ministers, admit this beautiful one. I will consider her case." And so the ministers escorted the woman before the king. Once King Siṃhakeshara saw the beautiful one, he was overcome by lust and remained silent for an instant.

Having looked at the beautiful one's face, the king responded in a soft and pleasant voice, "O Beautiful one! Where do you come from? And whose son is this? Why have you come to stay at the palace door? What trouble has befallen you? You must explain everything in detail." Then with tears in her eyes, the beautiful *rākṣasī* made whimpering sounds in her throat that aroused compassion at the mere sight of her. She then touched the king's feet and spoke in a voice inspiring compassion, "O King Siṃhakeshara, what to do? My suffering is just as I say: I am an unfortunate princess of Tāmradvīpa. At the time when Siṃhalasārthabāhu went to trade in Ratnapura, my father gave me to him in marriage. Therefore, having brought me along on the way to cross the river, our boat sunk and then we fell into the water. Saying, 'How unlucky is this woman I have brought, who has made us fall into the river,' he left me. Then I gave birth in the forest and together with this son I went to find Siṃhalasārthabāhu's house. There his father and mother both grabbed me by the neck and threw me out. O Great King! I have come to you for refuge. You must make my husband love me."

Having heard the beautiful one's story, the King called for his chief police officer and said, "O Chief of Police, go and bring Siṃhalasārthabāhu here." He did as he was commanded.

Seeing Siṃhalasārthabāhu before him, the king spoke, "O Siṃhalasārthabāhu! Having married this princess of Tāmradvīpa, and after fathering this child, why did you abandon them in the forest? Do not treat women such as this unjustly. Although she may have faults, forgive her as you must love and accept her." Siṃhalasārthabāhu replied, "O King Siṃhakeshara! I did not take this woman in marriage. She is not a Tāmradvīpa princess nor is this child my son. This one before you is a *rākṣasī* and she has produced this child through *māyā*; having come from Tāmradvīpa, she intends to eat me also." This is how he answered the king respectfully, giving a detailed account.

Caught by his desire, the king replied, "O Siṃhalasārthabāhu! All women are *rākṣasī*s. Having forgiven them, love them. But if you do not really like her, then turn her over to me. Relegate her to me and I will keep her." Hearing this, Siṃhalasārthabāhu replied, "O King, this woman here is without doubt a *rākṣasī*. I cannot turn her over to you. Having considered this statement, go ahead and do [what you wish]." The king, having heard Siṃhalasārthabāhu's warning, but feeling desire for the beautiful pubescent one, carried her to his private quarters.

After going home, Siṃhalasārthabāhu dwelt happily and enjoyed himself. King Siṃhakeshara, having enjoyed sensual pleasures with the beautiful one, felt the delusion of happiness. Once the *rākṣasī* satisfied the wishes and desires of the king, she covered him with a net of delusion and ensnared him more deeply with each passing day.

But one night, after completely satisfying the king's desire for pleasure, the *rākṣasī* made the king, all his family, and the people living in the private quarters fall into a deep sleep. In the night she flew up into the sky, returned to Tāmradvīpa, went to the place where her *rākṣasī* friends were dwelling and said, "O Younger Sisters! After eating just Siṃhalasārthabāhu, is that enough? In Siṃhakalpa town, I have made King Siṃhakeshara and all of the people in the royal family fall into a deep sleep. Let us go and devour the king and all the others." And after all the *rākṣasī* friends flew and reached the king's palace, they devoured all the people there, including King Siṃhakeshara. After finishing, all the *rākṣasī*s flew off.

Once dawn broke, many vultures, kites, and crows were circling in the sky around and above the royal palace. At this time, the chief police officer and ministers came to have *darshan* of the king and royal officials. They then noticed that the palace doors were closed. Seeing the birds circling above, they asked, "What has happened in the royal palace?" They cried out with all the people. After Siṃhalasārthabāhu heard the news, he came out of his house holding the sword in his hands and went to the place where all the ministers and courtiers were assembled at the palace. "O Ministers," he said, "Here in the palace [I fear] the king and all of the rest of the people have been completely eaten. Go quickly and bring a ladder. We will go and look. Hurry up!" After hearing this speech, the ministers and police raised a commotion; crying and sobbing, they brought a ladder and leaned it against the palace wall.

Then Siṃhalasārthabāhu with sword in hand climbed the ladder, went up to the balcony, and cursed the *rākṣasīs*, driving away those remaining. Once they saw the glint of Siṃhalasārthabāhu's sword, the *rākṣasīs* felt terrified and flew up and away to Tāmradvīpa. Siṃhalasārthabāhu and all the others then went inside the palace and unlocked the doors. There they saw the slaughtered king, queen, and all the people who had lived in the palace. The ministers and police were upset and made lamentations. They mourned, cleaned up the palace, and ritually purified it.

After some days, the ministers called upon all the country's *pandits*, astrologers, and the senior men and women to assemble. On that occasion, they held a discussion and the chief minister said, "O Subjects! Our king and queens were eaten by *rākṣasīs* and killed. And so there is no natural successor. How to proceed? Without a king, the people will not be sustained. He asked, "Who will succeed our king?" And the people replied, "O Minister! What to do? Having sought a [natural] successor for this king, we feel that there is no one to offer the kingship to besides Siṃhalasārthabāhu. There is no one else. For what reasons? He has the knowledge of different hand weapons, projectile weapons, different scripts; he is generous, compassionate, and devoted to the four gods. If we make him king, he would be the sort of king who would always serve the *Triratna* and [show] great virtue. And he would make all of the people happy."

All having agreed, they went to Siṃhalasārthabāhu's house. Having knelt with left knees on the ground, with joined hands they said, "O Siṃhalasārthabāhu! We have no king any more. As there is no natural successor to this king, so we must choose another. A country without a king will not remain a country. Please become king and sustain the people. You must come and look after the kingdom."

Siṃhalasārthabāhu replied, "O Ministers! I am of the trading caste. I am one who has lived by commerce. If I took up the responsibility of the kingdom, I could not do it. For me to be king is not suitable. Think again and look for another one more qualified to be the king."

The ministers replied respectfully, "O Siṃhalasārthabāhu! Except for you we do not have another fit to be king. In all our opinions, we see that you have the necessary traits. Please mount the (royal) lion's throne!" Then he went to the throne and received the royal initiation; during the coronation, he became known as Siṃhalarājā.

Thereafter in Siṃhakalpa town, the [new] King looked after his subjects like sons and caused them to serve the Buddha, Dharma, and Saṃgha and to observe the *Shrī Aṣṭamī Vrata* so that most enjoyed happiness and peace.

One day, the king called upon his minister and said, "O Minister, organize a strong army in four divisions. We will go to defeat the *rākṣasīs* of Tāmradvīpa and rule Ratnapura." After skillfuly assembling the fourfold army, he informed the king. Then Siṃhalarājā called together the strong four-division army—elephant chariots, horse chariots, horsemen, and infantry—and assembled the hand weapons, projectile weapons, bows, arrows, maces, lassos, hammers, axes, nooses, elephant discuses, *mantra* weapons, and fire weapons. He also raised many umbrellas, flags, and banners, and after having the martial musical instruments played, bid an auspicious farewell. In this way, Siṃhalarājā departed to do battle facing Tāmradvīpa.

He passed through many countries, villages, mountains, and rivers, then crossed the Brahmaputra and had his army camp near Tāmradvīpa. As they reached there, all the flags that the *rākṣasīs* of Ratnapura had raised fluttered ominously. Seeing this happen, all felt amazed and terrified. The senior *rākṣasī* then spoke, "O Younger Sisters! From ancient times, the flags have never fluttered like this. This fluttering we have not heard or seen before. On this day, an evil omen has occurred. What was that? Siṃhalarājā, King of Siṃhakalpa town, has come to destroy us. Make ready the hand and projectile weapons!" The leader called upon all the *rākṣasīs*, "Let us go; let us go! We all must go and fight! Come let us defeat them!" Having armed themselves with weapons, they assumed their dreadful forms, projected out their fangs, displayed their red eyes, and raised up their hair. They made noises indicating extreme agitation and yelled loudly in such a way that the frost there turned to hail.

After they made noises like those made by a dark cloud, Siṃhalarājā noticed them, united his four division army, and sent them into battle.

Then, having gone forth as their king commanded, all in the four-division army fought fiercely against the *rākṣasī*s. Once the *rākṣasī*s saw this army ready for battle, they became enraged and descended onto the battlefield; some showed their fighting skill with fire arrows, *mantra* weapons, and arrows; others, suspended in the air, wielded discuses, tridents, maces, and swords. They all did battle, crying out. Seeing the *rākṣasī*s using various weapons, the soldiers of Siṃhalarājā yelled out in many ways, made their weapons empowered with *mantra*s, and fought on. Some got into the elephant chariots and some [stood] on the ground. All showed their own skills in battle as they fought.

What happened on that afternoon? It became dark just as on the night of a dark fortnight when a cloud covers the earth and when lightning roars and the rain falls. Only the flashing of many weapons was visible and arrows fell like a rain deluge. Shouting was heard amidst the darkness. At last, due to the influence of the *Aṣṭamī Vrata*, the power of the king's boldness, and the four-division army's bravery, Siṃhalarājā finally turned back the *rākṣasī*s.

Though the *rākṣasī*s revealed their own skills in fighting, they finally could not fight on. Several ran away; staying at a distance and feeling afraid, they only looked on. The others threw down their weapons, joined their hands, and bowed at the feet of Siṃhalarājā. Feeling afraid, they spoke in a manner betraying their terror, "O Master Siṃhalarājā, after we saw that you had come to wage war, we also came to fight. But due to your bravery, we have lost our ability to wage war and so have come to your feet for refuge. You must pardon the crimes committed by us as we are helpless. This is because we are not equal to one with your fighting skill. To kill women like this is not ethical. It would be a great sin, O Mahārājā!" they said respectfully, touching their heads to his feet and joining their hands. They praised him saying, "Thinking we are not your worthy rivals, to us you have become a great compassionate one, virtuous, one who has the highest knowledge of merit who is also a great benefactor and learned; devoted to the gods, you have become popular among the people as 'The One Who is an Endless Store of Favors.' And so, O Master, these unkillable women cannot be virtuous or avoid committing crimes. Having forgiven all our mistakes, after manifesting compassion and grace, you must protect us!" Weeping they pleaded with him in many ways.

After hearing the *rākṣasīs*' humble requests, [the king] felt great compassion and replied, "O *Rākṣasīs*! After seeing all of your crimes, you deserve to be killed immediately. But what to do? If having understood what I say and you obey me, then I will heed your plea." The *rākṣasīs* joined their hands, touched his feet, arranged their shawls humbly, and said with respect, "O Gracious Mahārājā, Leader of Siṃhalakalpa! We certainly shall do as you say. To wherever you say 'Go,' we certainly will stay there. Please protect us."

Siṃhalarājā then replied to their plea, "O *Rākṣasīs*, up until now you have lived in Tāmradvīpa in Ratnapura. I have just completely conquered this kingdom. And in this land I have conquered, you should not live. You must never come back here so go and live in a dense forest in a far-off land. If you ever return to this town, I will certainly kill you all." Having given this ultimatum and bid them farewell, he left. According to Siṃhalarājā's command, each *rākṣasī* took an oath never to come there again and to leave for a distant forest. Then they ran off.

Then, O Shākyamuni Tathāgata, the *rākṣasīs* from this very city called Ratnapura did go to a different land. King Siṃhalarājā, after making victory banners and calling many people of different countries, gave shelter to the people in Ratnapura. Promoting the religious life among them, he caused the people to serve the Buddha, the Dharma, and the Saṃgha and conveyed the highest importance of observing the *Aṣṭamī Vrata* of Amoghapāsha Lokeshvara, and sponsored its performance. He also set up the professions, law and order, and trade and then showed them the jewel, silver, and gold mines. He also established a statue of himself. Having shown the path of happiness to the people, he addressed them, "O People! Formerly this place was called Tāmradvīpa, but now I have conquered it and so it will be called Siṃhaladvīpa in the future. And this name will become famous. You who live in this country called Siṃhaladvīpa must remember the *Triratna* and observe the *Aṣṭamī Vrata* and so live in peace and happiness. I am returning to the kingdom of Siṃhalakalpa in Jambudvīpa; I will show the Dharma to the people and live happily there." Having given these assurances to the people of the Siṃhaladvīpa kingdom, Siṃhalarājā departed for Jambudvīpa.

At that time, having reached the shore of the Brahmaputra River, in order to have the army cross, he made a boat and called it "Syāmkarṇa", placed an image of [the horse] Ashvarājā on it, and so made Syāmkarṇa famous. After crossing over with his four-division army, he returned to Siṃhakalpa and taught the *dharma* to people living in various places and countries.

Once he reached there, he called together the ministers, officials, and others, saying, "O People! From the grace of the Shrī Shrī Shrī *Triratna* and the influence of the *Aṣṭamī Vrata*, I conquered the *rākṣasī*s of Tāmradvīpa and made the name of Siṃhaladvīpa famous. From today on, all of the people will recall the Shrī Shrī Shrī *Triratna* and observe the bright fortnight *Aṣṭamī Vrata* of Lokeshvara." Following the king's command, the ministers and others all remembered the *Triratna* and prepared the holy *Aṣṭamī Vrata*; making their minds compassionate, they lived happily. From the merit of remembering the *Triratna* and the influence of the *Aṣṭamī Vrata*, in Siṃhakalpa town there was always and everywhere abundant food, virtuous conduct, and timely rainfall; and diseases, dangers, unhappiness, troubles, thieves, thugs, and evil ones were all eliminated; and only virtuous, artistic, learned, and auspicious people lived there. The king, ministers, officials, and all the people cultivated virtuous minds, served the *Triratna*, and found [both] pleasure and happiness.

The Domestication of the Text

Newar-Tibetan Trade and the Siṃhala Text

Trade with Tibet was an important undertaking throughout the last millennium for Buddhist Newars of Kathmandu and Lalitpur as leading families could profitably trade goods by caravan across the Indo-Tibetan frontier. To trade effectively in Tibet, Newar families sent family members to the major cities—Lhasa, Shigatse, and Gyantse—to live for years at a time, forming a classic "trade diaspora." These men learned to speak Tibetan, took part in the cultural life centered on Buddhism, and frequently married Tibetan women.

The trans-Himalayan journey to and from central Tibet was perilous: personal illness, the natural hazards of traveling high mountain trails, as well as banditry, could end in death or destroy years of profit, especially when returning with gold coins and with other treasures. Newars in the great cities of Tibet (Shigatse, Gyantse, and Lhasa) were generally tolerated and treated well, with some having commercial ties with high Tibetan officials. But even in these places there were scattered incidents of uprising against them, including murder.[29]

In the face of the contingencies and dangers involved in this trade, it should not be surprising that the *Siṃhalasārthabāhu Avadāna* would be incorporated into Newar culture and into Tibet. For example, several ferries across the Brahmaputra were constructed to resemble the horse Vārāhaka. There was also a *stūpa* in Lhasa known as the Siṃhalasārthabāhu *chorten* and in the Jokhang, Tibet's central shrine, Newar merchants state that there was an image of his "wife" that Newar traders venerated.

The domestication of the textual tradition was even more elaborate in Kathmandu. The hero of the story is regarded as a *bodhisattva* and a large gilded image of him is enshrined in one of the Kathmandu's oldest Buddhist temples (Vikramashīla Mahāvihāra of Thamel) dating back to the eleventh century.[30] A visit to this shrine was felt propitious before commencing the one-month overland journey to Tibet.

This bodhisattva is also worshiped in the yearly monastery festival. For this, an image of Dīpaṃkara Buddha associated with the hero (who bows in front of the fixed Siṃhala shrine before the proceedings set out) is carried in procession around the city, accompanied by a gold-inscribed *Prajñāpāramitā* text housed in a palanquin. This entourage, accompanied by musicians and *goṣṭhi* members, visits many neighborhoods, especially those where Tibetan traders predominate.

Case Study: The Multiple Levels of Meaning in Buddhist Narratives

A popular song composed in the early nineteenth century about this tale expresses the Newar identification with the hero:

> I fell under the sway of the bodily charms of the beautiful *rākṣasī*. But I, Siṃhala, want to escape, looking for a way out. Wherever I went, I went with my mind impassioned. Then you manifested yourself before us.
>
> There was the horse Balaha, and all the people were put on his back and were carried across the ocean. Moved by love, my companions looked back and fell from the horse's back. Claiming them to be theirs, the *rākṣasī*s carried them back.
>
> By invoking your name and bowing down to your feet, Siṃhala alone reached his home. . . . (Lienhard 1984b: 25, with minor emendations)

We now can examine the ways of reading this text in context.

Literal Buddhist Teachings. The text is an exemplary tale depicting many facets of Mahāyāna Buddhism in practice: the main hero is identified as an earlier incarnation of Shākyamuni; the savior-deity taking the form of the white horse is Avalokiteshvara; the ritual lauded is the *Aṣṭamī Vrata*,[31] still a popular form of devotion to Avalokiteshvara. The closing lines of the Newari text highlight all the benefits of observing this rite: prosperity, virtue, elimination of disease and evil, and rule by a moral and compassionate king.

In its most straightforward doctrinal message, the text is a morality or *karman*-retribution tale that underlines the dire consequences of damaging *stūpa*s and of failing to recall and honor the *triratna*. In the previous chapter, we pointed out that this concern with *stūpa* veneration and the great penalties for desecration were common themes in all Buddhist schools. More Mahāyāna in tone is the utter need to rely on the saving graces of the bodhisattva, whose help is necessary in order to avoid a disastrous death. This *avadāna*

Fig. 3.7. The Yearly Festival Associated with Siṃhalasārthabāhu

also holds forth with some general teachings about the ideal Buddhist king and society.

Symbolic Renderings of the Feminine. Newar Buddhist savants in Kathmandu also have pointed to a deeper, metaphoric reading to the story: for instance, that the *rākṣasī*s should be decoded as symbols of the uncontrolled sense faculties by which people are deluded, making this a tale upholding detachment. Among the earliest textual formulations of this symbolic association are those accounts of Shākyamuni's temptation by Māra's daughters who personify lust (*rāga*), aversion (*arati*), and craving (*tṛṣṇā*).

The theme of women's wayward effects on male spiritual attainment is encountered in many *avadāna*s and *jātaka*s, as we have seen in the previous chapter. The Siṃhala text graphically depicts the "feminine temptation" situation: the drama of men grasping a savior, trying to focus on Buddha-Dharma-Saṃgha as their former paramours entice them, is a powerful existential image. This theme is reiterated in the Newar text twice again by the hero's parent and by the king through their blunt assertion, "All women are, in fact, demonesses (*rākṣasī*s)"[32].

Text as Allegory: The Newar Redaction. The allegorical reading of the story builds upon the "woman as danger" sentiment. While the first two messages constitute the general program of Buddhist renunciatory teachings, connecting the text to the Himalayan context takes us into the specific Newar domestication of the *avadāna*. It is now necessary to examine several additional points regarding the ethnohistoric setting.[33]

It was the custom of many Newar merchants in Tibet to marry Tibetan women. These wives were usually younger than their merchant husbands and often quite beautiful. Their children were called *khacarā* (New.) or *khaccar* (Nep.). (Both terms derive from the latter meaning "mongrel" or "offspring of forbidden intercaste union" [Turner 1931: 111]). These children normally resided in Tibet supported by their fathers. Most Lhasa traders kept their dual families separated by the Himalayas. How was this practice viewed from Kathmandu? First, polygamy was (and is) legal in Nepal, although it was usually only the rich who could afford to support two households. The Tibetan wife, however, has an attribute that a second Newar wife, even if from a lower caste, would not: the Tibetan wife is called a *seṃ*, a derogatory Newari term expressing high caste disdain for Tibetans as dirty and low in status. For the original Newar wife, then, a husband's marriage in Tibet was often a source of heartache, jealousy, and competition. Affection and ultimately inheritance resources were at stake.

The first part of the *avadāna* provides a graphic cautionary tale: to wed non-Newar women who are alluring and sensually adept is an illusion, as it entails forgetting one's primal loyalty to Newar wife and kin while introducing the danger of enslavement, drowning, and being cruelly eaten alive by the foreign mistresses.[34] Older popular songs from Kathmandu articulate the "nightmare fears" that Newar wives of Lhasa traders confronted (Lienhard 1984b).

Further contextual analysis points to yet other related factors underlying the story's broad appeal. Occasionally *khaccar* children did return to Kathmandu; and conforming to the logic of the *avadāna* in which they are "half-demonic," they brought the potential for chaos and destruction with them. There are cases of *khaccar* girls marrying into merchant families, since in community reckoning the children would retain their father's status (although this was a minor blemish on the patrilineage). But *khaccar* sons, like Siṃhala's own "son," were another case entirely. They were of course not welcome in their father's Kathmandu homes or in the Valley, either, since they could under customary Nepalese law claim a share equal to that of the "pure" Newar sons from their father's estate. They were also not of acceptable status for marriage to proper Urāy girls, either, and the *khaccar* men in the Kathmandu Valley have mainly married other *khaccar*s or Tibetans. Since the boys were excluded from Newar *guthi* membership and from caste-sensitive family dining and ritual participation, they could not be integrated into their father's caste community.[35]

The Newar redaction of the Siṃhala tale presents a dramatic allegory of this problem. In part A, the hero's ethno-specific sentiments are implicit in his curious failure to extend his salvific leadership to the imprisoned, soon-to-be cannibalized merchants who arrived before Siṃhala's caravan from another land. (This is apparently part of the literary editing involved in redacting the local Newar text: earlier versions of the story [up through the *Guṇakāraṇḍavyūha*] contain an account of the magical fortress that defies mundane escape, in explanation of this omission.)[36]

In part B, the ethnic Himalayan resonances continue: unlike the hero, who refuses to admit the former wife-*rākṣasī*—and son—into his house, the lustful king does and his entire family is devoured[37] because he admitted the outsider. Like a Tibetan woman taken in marriage, the *rākṣasī* arrives without property and with the burden of a son, a *khaccar*; she, too, expresses pious Buddhist affirmations. The text's unmistakable message for a Newar merchant of the Kathmandu Valley is to impart the danger of breaking the circle of Newar ethnicity and kinship: one invites demons into the home and all can be lost. Even the apparent common devotion to Buddhism should not cloud recognition of impending disaster.

A final note must be made on the destiny of this domesticated tradition. Newar trade with Tibet effectively ended in 1959 after the Dalai Lama's government fled Lhasa into exile. The traditions just described have in several respects declined over the past thirty years. Most striking is the fate of the *cakañ dyaḥ jātrā*: always held on the same lunar day overlapping Holi's week-long celebration, for at least twenty years this festival procession into the bazaar has seen greatly diminished numbers of participants and patrons. For many, it has also lost its meaning and dignity due to the fact that the gilded image and palanquin are now a prominent target for water balloons and the festival attendants are treated rudely as just another raucous Holi procession of young men. This is a striking simulacrum for the modern city's shifting religious allegiances and the general drift toward Nepal's state Hinduism (Rose 1970).[38]

Observations on the History of Practical Buddhism

The analysis of the Siṃhalasārthabāhu *avadāna* and of the Newar Buddhist traditions that developed around it looks beyond the explicit didactic messages of the text, although they surely matter, to the contextual factors to explain why this *avadāna*, among the hundreds of stories, came to enjoy unique literary articulation and domestication in the Kathmandu Valley. We can also observe how a pan-Buddhist story of caravan merchants crossing the ocean was translated—linguistically and culturally—into a trans-Himalayan adventure in Kathmandu-Lhasa trade that crosses the Brahmaputra River.

The pan-Asian popularity of this *avadāna* can also be explained by the universal presence of diaspora merchant groups as Buddhist *upāsaka*s. In several ways, the *avadāna* is a strong cautionary tale for all diaspora merchants, aligning the central ideas of Buddhism with *both* practical and sacred counsel to remain chaste while abroad and loyal to one's own ethnic group and kin.

The literary evidence shows how the last Nepalese redaction went beyond mere geographic transposition to achieve a finely tuned and nuanced narrative with strong local resonance within the Newar mercantile community. The heartache and fears of Newar wives who stayed at home while their husbands lived for years in Tibet is aroused, while devotions to the Bodhisattva Avalokiteshvara (at the yearly festival and especially through the *Aṣṭamī Vrata*) simultaneously highlighted and alleviated the anxiety. These themes would also resonate with all male traders who stayed home to run the trade enterprise and whose interests (profits and inheritance) were threatened by brothers/fathers who traded abroad.

The Siṃhala tale alludes to the problem of upholding primordial boundaries, an allegory reaching deeply into kin and ethnic awareness. It was precisely because of the possibility of admitting "foreign" wives and their children into the nexus of kin and inheritance that this text received elaborate attention across the Buddhist world. As redacted, it upheld the integrity of "home and family" boundaries even to the point of overruling countervailing sentiments of Buddhist universalism. The details of the case study suggest as well the pliability of Buddhist *avadāna*s, as here the Newar adaptation leaves the domesticated story out of exact alignment with Mahāyāna doctrinal teachings. The Newar Siṃhala traditions indicate how certain voices of Buddhist interpretation are domesticated by entering the life and logic of the local context on multiple

Fig. 3.8. Simhalasārthabāhu Leads Battle Against *Rākshasīs*

levels. Although the Newar redaction on one level upholds Mahāyāna traditions, on others—in its historical, social setting—it cautions about the dangers of embracing outsiders, even those who may also claim to follow the Dharma.

The universal process of the domestication of narrative traditions again suggests how problematic it is to rely upon the literal narratives in the formal literary canon or upon the general philosophical texts to "center" representations of Buddhism. In imagining the tradition's history, there was never a general or generic Buddhism stemming from the classics, but only local Buddhist traditions. Further, with a small minority of any Buddhist community ever being literate, written documents were always being translated into local vernaculars and recurringly transposed into story-telling situations and rituals that inevitably intersected with the unfolding of local events. To reconstruct such contextual contingencies in the past is, of course, quite difficult. But the Newar case study does suggest that texts cannot stand on their own terms in order to construct Buddhist belief and practice in history.[39] The data from modern Nepal, then, converges with Gregory Schopen's work on inscriptions and on neglected *Vinayas* to suggest that Buddhism in practice was

Fig. 3.9. Scene of *Stūpa* Dedication Associated with the *Avadāna*

far more complicated by calculations of wealth and kinship than scholars have imagined and that the tradition "on the ground" was much less tidy and more diverse than indicated by the documents generated by the monastic elite and stored in their libraries.

CHAPTER 4

Devotions to a Celestial Bodhisattva: The Tārā Vrata

> In short, religious propositions cannot be believed apart from practice and even if they were so believed could not really found practice.
>
> Martin Southwold, *Buddhism in Life: The Anthropological Study of Religion and the Sinhalese Practice of Buddhism*

> The most important task for the student of Buddhism is the study of the Buddhist mentality. That is why contact with present-day Buddhism is so important, for this will guard against seeing texts as purely philological material and forgetting that for Buddhists they are sacred texts which proclaim a message of salvation. . . .
>
> J. W. de Jong, "The Study of Buddhism, Problems and Perspectives"—(J. W. de Jong 1981: 28)

This chapter and the next are concerned with an Indic ritual called the *vrata*, a form of devotion Mahāyāna Buddhists adopted to venerate the celestial bodhisattvas, Buddhas, *stūpa*s, and powerful divinities. Although the following chapters shift the genre from narrative texts to ritual guidebooks, the overlap between these designations will be immediately obvious: just as the stories just referred to (and arguably were built around) rituals, the three ritual texts that follow include stories. Indeed, one important point that is very clear in the Newar Buddhist context is that "belief and practice" are not separate phenomena in anthropological analysis. The *vrata* rituals entail doctrinal assertions and usually a long segment in which the assembled hear stories (*vratakathā*) related to the origins, practices, and boons associated with the ritual itself; the *vratas* also involve modest fasting, assembling offerings, chanting holy words declaring faith and taking refuge, and participating in choreographed rituals that are common in the local Buddhist tradition.

To examine Buddhism through rituals is one long-neglected area of historical investigation. The problem goes far beyond the biases that the field inherits from scholars who are trained primarily in translating philosophical texts.[1] There is also the deeper (and less self-consciously addressed) scholarly cultural influence, a paradigmatic imprint from Euro-American modernity strongly shaped by Protestant Christianity, which skews the definition of religion toward valuing belief over ritual (e.g., Eckel 1994; Prothero 1995) and texts over other forms of historical data (Schopen 1991d).[2] As Southwold has pointed out, this bias of distancing rituals from the center of religious tradition is coded in English language usage:

> The bias that belief is basic to religion is built into our culture, into our language itself, so that the very idiom in which we most easily talk about these matters itself sustains the bias. We commonly term an adherent of religion "a believer", and an opponent an "unbeliever." It is common for a person to explain his rejection of religion by saying, "I cannot believe that" . . . as if believing and disbelieving were causes, and not consequences, of attitudes toward religion. . . . We call a religion a "creed" or a "faith", and regularly identify faith with belief. It is not easy to abandon so deeply rooted and axiomatic a pattern of thought. (Southwold 1983: 135)

These observations, stimulated by the ethnographic study of Sri Lankan village Buddhists, are based upon the recognition that it is the near-universal norm in traditional societies that individuals starting from infancy are socialized into their religious identity by their participation in rituals. This perspective resonated well with my own studies of religious belief in the Newar context: in taking life histories of both Buddhist householders and priests, their own spiritual autobiographies were recounted in terms of the rituals, initiations, and pilgrimages they had undertaken (Lewis 1996c).

Southwold develops the view that ritual and belief ultimately impact humans through separate sensory-neural pathways; building from Robertson Smith and Rodney Needham, he argues that "belief" cannot stand autonomously in meaningful anthropological analysis: "Belief-statements are neither the precursors nor the successors of ritual practice, but part of it; that the ritual unit comprises not only the more obvious acts of presentational symbolism . . . but also verbal behavior, whether it takes the form of myth or the proclamation of belief or doctrine" (Southwold 1983: 136). My interest here is not to enter into this theoretical area of ritual studies, but simply to underline the methodological value of studying ritual texts to understand Buddhism. In chapter 7, I will return to this issue as I speculate on how our imagination of Buddhist history would be different if we wrote Buddhist history as a history of practice, not belief.

*Vrata*s are priest-led and lay-sponsored worship programs lasting one or more days. In this chapter, its Indic origins and history will be traced and the most popular contemporary Newar *vrata* observances summarized. Following the presentation of the Tārā Vrata text and its domestication here and after a similar treatment of the Mahākāla *vrata* in the subsequent chapter, the discussion of both observances in Buddhist history will follow.

Background

Historical

The term *vrata* dates back to Vedic times, where it means "will" and "law" (Monier-Williams 1956:1042; Kane 1974:5). In ancient India, the *vrata* was originally an obligatory ritual prescribed for high-caste individuals to atone for different misdeeds. By the time the *purāṇa*s were composed, it also referred to a religious vow or a voluntary ritual practice designed to please a particular deity. In these texts, and in the popular tracts produced by medieval Hindu commentators, *vrata*s dedicated to a divinity were highly elaborated, occupying substantial portions of the popular religious literature (Wadley 1983:148). Brāhmaṇ-led *vrata*s are still an important part of modern Hinduism (Babb 1975) and are performed throughout the Indian subcontinent, including modern Nepal.

*Vrata*s are one example of the many Indian religious practices that have been adapted into later Mahāyāna Buddhism. That *vrata*s date back many centuries in the Newar tradition is attested to by the antiquity of manuscripts describing the proper forms of observance (Malla 1981). To date, textual scholars have not explored the early Indic precedents of these popular Nepalese observances. (In Chap. 5 I do speculate on the origins of these Mahāyāna observances.) Texts outlining observances and recounting the tales associated with them (*vratakathā*) remain one of the most common genres of printed Buddhist literature in modern Kathmandu.

Newar Vratas: Overview

Every modern *vrata* involves special programs of priest-led rituals that immerse householders in the essentials of the faith and focus intensively on one particular divinity. Groups of individuals devote one or more days to making offerings, while maintaining a high state of ritual purity and while abstaining from certain foods. Tradition specifies a series of boons for each type of *vrata* and all are supposed to add appreciably to one's stock of *puṇya*. By so doing, the *vrata*s here, as in India (Wadley 1983), are performed to improve the devotee's destiny.

In the modern Newar *vrata*s, there is a standard structural order: led by a *vajrācārya* priest (with his *vajrācārya* assistants), layfolk worship a *guru-maṇḍala* that includes all major deities of the Mahāyāna Buddhist cosmos. In the *guru maṇḍala pūjā* they take refuge, repeat the *bodhisattva* vow, and recite the *pāramitā*s and eightfold path. After performing the *vrata* in unison they make a series of offerings, first to three *maṇḍala*s dedicated to each refuge in the *triratna*, then on another *maṇḍala* on which the divine being of the *vrata* is depicted. For those conversant in the practice, a visualization meditation is part of this last offering.

The central rituals in almost every *vrata* are the priest's *kalasha pūjā*[3] to the *vrata* deity, taking refuge in the *triratna-maṇḍala*s (Buddha, Dharma, and Saṃgha), and sets of offerings to the *vrata* deity, again on a *maṇḍala*. Most texts specify that the *vajrācārya* should explain the *maṇḍala* symbolism(s) and tell the story (*kathā*) (or stories) associated with the particular *vrata*. As the latter is done, all participants must hold a special thread (New.: *bartakā*; Skt.: *vratasūtra*) unwound from the *kalasha*. This symbolic act links the deity to each individual and binds the circle of devotees in worship. Broken up and tied around the neck, this thread is a special amulet that Newar layfolk take away from all *vrata* ceremonies.

According to a recent *pūjā* manual, there are texts specifying *vrata*s for every deity in the Indic pantheon and for every special religious occasion (R. K. Vajracarya 1981: 135). A group may be organized to perform the *vrata* once, or monthly for one or more years; it can also travel to different temples in the Kathmandu Valley or choose other sacred landmarks in the religious geography where the ritual can be performed. In whatever context, each person usually performs the *vrata* individually, although a woman may sometimes perform it for an absent husband, making two sets of offerings. *Vrata*s are open to all; nowadays women are by far in the majority. We now survey the most important *vrata*s still observed by Mahāyāna Buddhists in modern Nepal.

Dhalaṃ Danegu or Aṣṭamī Vrata. By far the most popular of the Buddhist *vrata*s, *dhalaṃdanegu*, has ancient roots in Nepal (Gellner 1988: 347ff). According to a Tibetan source, an early version of this rite can be found in a twelfth-century manuscript (Roerich 1953: 1008) and notes its transmission from Nepal to Tibet (Lewis 1989c). John K. Locke (1987) has provided a useful description of this observance, noting that variant traditions exist across the Kathmandu Valley. This *vrata* should be enacted on one of the two *aṣṭamī*s, that is, the eighth days of either lunar fortnight. The deity is one of the forms of Avalokiteshvara, popularly called Amoghapāsha Lokeshvara or Karuṇāmaya.

Basundharā Vrata. Newar Buddhists regard Basundharā *(Skt.: Vasudharā)* as a goddess of fertility and prosperity. In a recent printed text, Kumārī, Lakṣmī, and Basundharā are all said to be forms (*rūpa*) of Pṛthivī, the Earth goddess (Vajracarya 1981: 81). If pleased, Basundharā can multiply the family's wealth and sustain the vitality of the lineage. Given these benefits, it is understandable that most Newar Buddhist merchants have performed the Basundharā *vrata* at least once in their lifetimes and that there are *guthi*s responsible for insuring that it is performed annually (Lewis 1984: 242). All of the *pūjā* accessories, including the ritual thread and the women's shawls, are made with gold fabric, the goddess's favorite color.

Pūrṇimā Vrata (or Dharmadhātu Vrata). This *vrata* is performed to worship Svayambhū, the great *stūpa* of the Kathmandu Valley. According to local histories, this was the *vrata* first articulated by the *stūpa*'s mythological founder, Shāntikar Ācārya (Shakya 1977). The proper moment for this observance is the day when there is a conjunction of a full moon (*pūrṇimā*) and the day marking the start of a new solar month (*saṃkrānti*). Performing the *Pūrṇimā Vrata* is intended to awaken the desire for reaching complete enlightenment (R. K. Vajracarya 1981: 84).

Satya Nārāyaṇa Vrata[4]. This *vrata* to the Indic deity Viṣṇu is performed on *ekādashī*, the eleventh day of either lunar fortnight. The ritual specialist is usually a Newar Brāhmaṇ. Though the requirement of fasting and purification is the same in the Buddhist *vrata*, the ritual is simpler, a straightforward exoteric series of offerings to a Viṣṇu image placed in a small vehicle (*ratha*) located in the midst of the devotees. As it is done across the Nepalese hills, the Brāhmaṇ also tells stories about Viṣṇu. The *Satya Nārāyaṇa Vrata* is common in modern Parbatiya and Newar Hindu practice. Most Newar Buddhist layfolk do not express embarrassment at their participation in a ritual guided by a Brāhmaṇ priest.

Swasthānī Vrata[5]. This is a *vrata* originating in Nepal, possibly Buddhist Newar in inspiration, as the goddess Swasthānī has since early Malla times elicited strong devotional traditions, including dramas and musical compositions. Although the goddess is Hindu and the ritualist is usually a Brāhmaṇ, as with the *Satya Nārāyaṇa Vrata* Buddhists commonly participate at least once in a lifetime. (Many scribes associated with the text have also been *vajrācārya*s and doctrinally Buddhist redactions of it do exist.) The *Swasthānī Vrata* involves taking vows involving one month's abstention from sex, certain foods, and sources of impurity, as well as attending nightly recitations of the stories associated with the goddess. This *vrata* may be performed at home, but is also observed yearly in the town of Sankhu, where not only Newars but individuals from other ethnic groups come to reside each year in order to perform an especially strict version of the *vrata*. It is primarily women who perform the *Swasthānī*. I will return to the subject of Hindu-Buddhist relations in chapter 5.

Tārā, the Feminine Bodhisattva

Tārā is the most popular goddess in northern Buddhism's bodhisattva tradition (Beyer 1973; Sircar 1967): she is regarded as the embodiment of Avalokiteshvara's compassion and has twenty-one incarnations. In Tibet, the veneration of Tārā became an important religious activity for all strata in the socioreligious hierarchy, inspiring the composition of special hymns and a special tantra (Willson

1996). According to Tibetan historical accounts some of these traditions were transmitted through Nepal.

Tārā is most often worshiped in her white and green incarnations; *Saptalocanā Tārā*, the "Seven-eyed Tārā," is also often seen in Newar home shrine paintings. The classical relationship with Avalokiteshvara is expressed spatially in the Kathmandu temple found in Jana Bāhā dedicated to Avalokiteshvara, where two images of Tārā placed on tall pillars are located: they face devotees who enter the courtyard just outside the sanctum's entrance.

Translation

Notes on Author and Text

The two modern *vrata* texts translated in this volume were redacted by the Kathmandu pandit Badri Bajracarya, the same scholar whose text was quoted in Chapter 2. These volumes arise both from a patron's needs to have new ritual manuals for the family's own *vrata* observances and from Bajrācārya's own effort to revive the performances of Newar Buddhism.

> Badri Bajracarya. *Shrī Āryya Tārā Devyaiḥ Vrata Vidhi Kathā*. Kathmandu, Nepal: Popular Art Printing Press, 1980.

Stories and Guide to the Shrī Ārya Tārā *Vrata*

Rites for the Worship of Ārya Tārā

> Construct a Tārā *maṇḍala*. Place in the center of the *maṇḍala* an iron tripod. Place on the tripod a big *kalasha*. Arrange the following items in their proper place around it: medicine powder (*kalashavāsa*), five different kinds of grain (*pañcabihi*), jasmine flowers grains of unpolished rice (*ākhe*), parched rice (*tāye*), buds from a kind of long lasting grass (*pañcapallava kosbuṃ*), a jasmine branch, a tuft of broom grass, a ceremonial umbrella (*chatra*), a feather from a peacock, and a tiny earthen bowl filled with polished rice with a whole betel nut and a coin set on it (*kisalī*). Place grain powder symbolic of the *aṣṭamaṇgala* on a traditional dish called a *thāybhū*.

Fig. 4.1. Making the *Vrata Maṇḍala*

Place on the *mandala*'s four corners: ceremonial metal mirrors (*jolānhyākam* and vermilion powder stands [*sinhahudmū*]. Pass the string of five strands five times round the *kalasha* space. Place the *aṣṭamañgala* and wind bells (*phaygam*) in their proper places. Also put up a canopy [over it]. Arrange around the *maṇḍala* of Ārya Tārā items: Buddhist begging bowls (*gulupā*), water bowls (*tiñcā*) and barley flour images (*tormā*). Place oblation pots (*baupā*), curd bowls (*pati*), a small *kalasha*, and tiny earthen vessels with serpents painted on them (*nāgabhoñcā*), and put a lamp (*mata*) in front of the *maṇḍala*. Consecrate the *pañcagavya* in a small earthen bowl and in an oval-shaped bowl of rice beer (*patra*), and perform the *gurumaṇḍala pūjā* on a *maṇḍala* with a lotus pattern with an image of a deity at the center.

Do a ritual cleansing with water from a holy river. Perform *argha pūjā* (an offering of water to the Sun god). Consecrate the votive offerings. Perform the *gurumaṇḍala pūjā*. Purify it with the five cow products (*pañcagavya*). Sanctify the clay to be used for fashioning *caitya* shrines. Have the shrines fashioned from the sanctified clay that has been pressed into molds. Sprinkle red power and holy water over them. Perform *samādhi* meditation. Offer *pūjā* to all of the items

set out. Worship the image of the deity installed there. Offer *pūjā* to the *gulupā*, *devā*, *tiñcā*, and the *tormā*s. Sanctify the big *maṇḍala* and place flower petals on it. Also sanctify the ball of string by sprinkling water on it. Perform *pūjā* using *mūdrā* sequences accompanied by *mantra* recitations. Make a *bali* offering [for spirits] and perform *cākupūjā* [in honor of the guardians of the four quarters].

After this, all those who are performing the *Ārya Tārā Vrata* may be asked to sit in an orderly row and to construct *maṇḍalas* before them. Have them receive the *pañcagavya* purification and make votive offerings. Have them perform a *gurumaṇḍala pūjā*. Make them worship the *mata* lamp and clay *caitya*s made with their own hands. Have them duly perform *maṇḍala pūjā* of the Buddha, Dharma, and Saṃgha. Have them take refuge in the *triratna* by repeating in chorus "*Ratna triyaṃ me* <Buddha/Dharma/Saṃgha> *shāraṇaṃ*" three times.

Method of Worshiping the Large Ārya Tārā Maṇḍala

Sprinkle on the *maṇḍala* drops of water from a conch shell while reciting these *mantra*s:[6]

OṂ TRUṂ KHAṂ HUṂ
OṂ MEDANĪ VAJRĪ BHAVA VAJRA BANDHAVAṂ
OṂ VAJRA RAKṢE HUṂ.

Keep touching the *maṇḍala* with your ring finger covered with yellow powder while reciting the following devotional couplet:

SARVATATHĀGATA SHĀNTAṆ SARVA TATHĀGATA LAYAṂ
SARVADHARMĀ GANAIRĀTMĀ DESHA MAṆḌALA MUKTAṂ

Place a flower on the small wheat cake image (*gojā*) while reciting: "OṂ TĀRĀ MAṆḌALE SARVA BIGHNĀNUTSĀRE HUṂ." Then sprinkle a drop of water on the *gojā* while reciting: "OṂ SHRĪ ĀRYA TĀRĀ BHATTARASYĀGRE PĀDYĀRGHA ĀCAMANAṂ PRACCHAMANAṂ PRATĪCCHA SVĀHĀ."

Placing Flowers on the *Maṇḍala*

Recite: "OṂ SHRADHARĀ TĀRĀYA VAJRA PUṢPAṂ PRATĪCCHA SVĀHĀ" [and place a flower] on the head [of the *maṇḍala*].

Recite: "OṂ TĀRE TUTĀRE TURE SVĀHĀ" [and place a flower] on the heart [of the *maṇḍala*].

Recite: "OṂ HRIṂ TRIṂ HUṂ PHAṬ SVĀHĀ" [and place a flower] on the navel [of the *maṇḍala*].

Placing Eight Lotus Flower Petals on the *Maṇḍala*

Recite: "OṂ PUṢPATĀRĀYA VAJRAPUṢPAṂ PRATĪCCHA SVĀHĀ" and place a lotus petal in front of the *maṇḍala*.

Recite: "OṂ DHUPATĀRĀYA VAJRAPUṢPAṂ PRATĪCCHA SVĀ HĀ" and place a lotus petal on the right corner of the *maṇḍala*.

Recite: "OṂ DĪPĀ TĀRĀYA VAJRAPUṢPAṂ PRATĪCCHA SVĀHĀ" and place a lotus petal behind the

Recite: "OṂ GANDHATĀRĀYA VAJRAPUṢPAṂ PRATĪCCHA SVĀHĀ" and place a lotus petal on the left corner of the *maṇḍala*.

Recite: "OṂ BRĀṂ VĪNĀYA VAJRAPUṢPAṂ PRATĪCCHA SVĀHĀ" and place a lotus petal on the right downside corner of the *maṇḍala*.

Recite: "BAṂ VAṂSHĀYA VAJRAPUṢPAṂ PRATĪCCHA SVĀHĀ" and place a lotus petal on the right upside corner of the *maṇḍala*.

Recite: "MṚṂ MṚDAṂGĀYA VAJRAPUṢPAṂ PRATĪCCHA SVĀHĀ" and place a lotus petal on the left upside corner of the *maṇḍala*.

Recite: "MŪṂ MŪRUJĀYA VAJRAPUṢPAṂ PRATĪCCHA SVĀHĀ" and place a lotus petal on the left downside corner of the *maṇḍala*.

Placing Twenty-one Lotus Flower Petals on the *Maṇḍala*

[Recite:]

1. OṂ TĀṂ SIDDHIPHALA PUṢṬIṂKURU TĀRE VAJRAPUṢPAṂ PRATĪCCHA SVĀHĀ
2. OṂ HRĪṂ SARVAKARMA SIDDHIPHALA PUṢṬIṂKURU TĀRE VAJRAPUṢPAṂ PRATĪCCHA SVĀHĀ.
3. OṂ TUṂTĀḤ MAMA ĀYU PUṢṬIṂKURU TĀRE VAJRAPUṢPAṂ PRATĪCCHA SVĀHĀ.
4. OṂ TĀḤ SARVA BHAYAPĀDA SIDDHIKURU TĀRE VAJRAPUṢPAṂ PRATĪCCHA SVĀHĀ.
5. OṂ HRIṂ BHAVALOKA HĀSYAKURU TĀRE VAJRAPUṢPAṂ PRATĪCCHA SVĀHĀ.
6. OṂ TUḤ SARVASYĀTUSU MAHĀNAYE TĀRE VAJRAPUṢPAṂ PRATĪCCHA SVĀHĀ.
7. OṂ HRIḤ SARVALOKASIDDHI HĀSYĀKURU TĀRE VAJRAPUṢPAṂ PRATĪCCHA SVĀHĀ.
8. OṂ SVAḤ SARVA SIDDHICITTĀRE VAJRAPUṢPAṂ PRATĪCCHA SVĀHĀ.
9. OṂ STĀḤ SARVA DUḤKHA SHANTI KURU TĀRE VAJRAPUṢPAṂ PRATĪCCHA SVĀHĀ.
10. OṂ HĀḤ SARVA LOKAHĀSYA KURU TĀRE VAJRAPUṢPAṂ PRATĪCCHA SVĀHĀ.
11. OṂ ĀḤ SARVAMAÑGALA SIDDHI PHALAHE JYO TĀRE VAJRAPUṢPAṂ PRATĪCCHA SVĀHĀ.
12. OṂ DUḤ MAMA ĀYUPUṢṬIṂ KURU TĀRE VAJRAPUṢPAṂ PRATĪCCHA SVĀHĀ.
13. OṂ ĀḤ SARVA ITITĀMU SIDDHI KURU TĀRE VAJRAPUṢPAṂ PRATĪCCHA SVĀHĀ.
14. OṂ NIḤ SARVASIDDHI PUṢṬIṂKURU TĀRE VAJRAPUṢPAṂ PRATĪCCHA SVĀHĀ.
15. OṂ AḤ SARVASHĀNTI KURU TĀRE VAJRAPUṢPAṂ PRATĪCCHA SVĀHĀ.
16. OṂ SVĀḤ SARVAJNĀNA PUṆYAḤ PUṢṬIṂKURU TĀRE VAJRAPUṢPAṂ PRATĪCCHA SVĀHĀ.
17. OṂ KIḤ MAMA ĀYUPUṆYAJNĀNA PUṢṬIṂKURU TĀRE VAJRAPUṢPAṂ PRATĪCCHA SVĀHĀ.
18. OṂ JĀḤ SARVALOKA DUḤKHASHĀNTI KURU TĀRE VAJRAPUṢPAṂ PRATĪCCHA SVĀHĀ.

19. OṂ CĪḤ DHANASIDDHA TĀRE VAJRAPUṢPAṂ PRATĪCCHA SVĀHĀ.
20. OṂ HĀḤ SARVA KARMASIDDHI PUṢṬIṂKURU TĀRE VAJRAPUṢPAṂ PRATĪCCHA SVĀHĀ.
21. OṂ TĀḤ TĀRE TUTĀRE TURE SVĀHĀ TĀRE VAJRAPUṢPAṂ PRATĪCCHA SVĀHĀ.

Placing Flower Petals at the Four Corners of the *Maṇḍala*

Recite: OṂ VAJRA LĀSYE HUṂ and place flower petals on the right up side corner.

Recite: OṂ VAJRA MĀLETRĀṂ and place flower petals on the right downside corner.

Recite: OṂ VAJRA GĪTYE HRĪṂ and place flower petals on the left upside corner.

Recite: OṂ VAJRA NṚTYE AḤ and place flower petals on the left down side corner.

Placing Ten Flowers on the Square-shaped *Dashakrodha Patra*

Recite the following *mantra*s and place flower petals in the east, in the south, in the west, in the north, in the southeast, in the southwest, in the northwest, in the northeast and, for the last two, on the either sides.

OṂ HUṂ JAMĀNTAKĀYE VAJRAPUṢPAṂ PRATĪCCHA SVĀHĀ.

OṂ HUṂ PRAJÑĀNTAKĀYE VAJRAPUṢPAṂ PRATĪCCHA SVĀHĀ.

OṂ HUṂ PADMĀNTAKĀYE VAJRAPUṢPAṂ PRATĪCCHA SVĀHĀ.

OM HUM VIGHNANTAKAYE VAJRAPUSPAṂ PRATĪCCHA SVĀHĀ.

OṂ HUṂ TAKKIRĀJĀYA VAJRAPUṢPAṂ PRATĪCCHA SVĀHĀ.

OṂ HUṂ NĪLA DAṆḌĀYA VAJRAPUṢPAṂ PRATĪCCHA SVĀHĀ.

OṂ HUṂ MAHĀBALĀYA VAJRAPUṢPAṂ PRATĪCCHA SVĀHĀ.

OṂ HUṂ ACALĀYA VAJRAPUṢPAṂ PRATĪCCHA SVĀHĀ.

OṂ HUṂ UṢṆIṢA VĪJAYĀYA VAJRAPUṢPAṂ PRATĪC-CHA SVĀHĀ.

OṂ HUṂ SUMBHARĀJĀYA VAJRAPUṢPAṂ PRATĪC-CHA SVĀHĀ.

Placing Flowers on Four Entrances of the *Maṇḍala*

[Recite:] OṂ VAJRĀM KUSHĀYA VAJRAPUṢPAṂ PRATĪ CCHA SVĀHĀ [and place flower petals] on the eastern entrance.

[Recite:] OṂ VAJRA PĀSĀYA VAJRAPUṢPAṂ PRATĪC-CHA SVĀHĀ [and place flower petals] on the southern entrance.

[Recite:] OṂ VAJRASPHOTĀYA VAJRAPUṢPAṂ PRATĪC-CHA SVĀHĀ [and place flower petals] on the western entrance.

[Recite:] OṂ VAJRĀṂBESĀYA VAJRAPUṢPAṂ PRATĪC-CHA SVĀHĀ [and place flower petals] on the northern entrance.

Placing Flowers for the *Lokapāla* of the Ten Directions

Do *pūjā* with [offerings consisting of] wheat, maize, peas, rice, sweetmeats, fruits, betal leaf, betal nuts etc.

Sprinkle holy water from the conch shell on the string. Apply a yellow *tika* mark to its knot. Have the worshipers bow twenty-one times to the sacred string with their palms, the right for males, the left for females. When bowing, the *mantra* for recitation is: "OṂ NĀMO ĀRYA TĀRĀ DEVĪ DHARMA SŪTRAṂ PRECCHĀMI VAJRADHARMA TĀṂ TĀṂ TĀṂ SVĀHĀ".

After this, the string is placed round the *maṇḍala*. [The *mantra* recited is:] "OṂ SHRĪ SHRAGDHARĀRYYATĀRĀ MAṆḌALE BODHYĀṂGA DṚḌHA KAVACA VAJRAVASTRA VĀSASYE SVĀHĀ." Now do *pañcopacāra pūjā*.

Then twenty-one jasmine flowers are placed in the center of the sacred thread with the recitation of the *mantra*: "OṂ NĀ MAḤ SHRĪ SHRAGDHARĀRYYA TĀRĀYAI SARVABHAYADHARANĪ SARVABIGHNA SHĀNTĪ KARI PRAKṚTI PRABHĀSVARE SARVA DUḤKHA NĀ SANĪ MAMA SARVASATVĀNĀÑCA SHĀNTĪ SVASTIṂ PUṢṬIṂ KURU RAKṢAMĀṂ HUṂ HUṂ PHAṬ PHAṬ SVĀHĀ."

Perform another *pañcopacāra pūjā*.

Offer *argha* water. Recite the *dashā kushala*[7] and offer the [whole] *maṇḍala*.

OṂ SAMAṂNVĀ HARAṂTUMĀṂ BUDDHĀ DASADIGA LOKADHĀTU SANNI PATITĀ BUDDHĀ BHAGAVATO BODHISATVA MAÑJUSHRĪ UPĀ DHYĀYASHCĀRYYA TĀRĀ, AHAṂ MEVANĀMĀ YATKIṂCITA KĀYAVĀKA MANOBHI SARVABUDDHĀ BODHISATVEBHYO MĀTĀ PITARAU TADAṂNYĀNI SAGAMYA YAHA JANMANI BHABĀNTAREṢU MAYĀ PĀPA KARMA KṚTA KĀ RITA BHABET TATAḤ SARVAM EKAṂ PIṆḌAYITVĀ TARAYITVĀ SARVABUDDHA BODHISATVĀ NĀMĀCĀRYA SHĀNTĪKE AGRAYĀ VARAVĀ PRAVALAYĀ STHĀNEMAHAṂ PRATIDESHYĀMI MANASMṚTA PRATĪCCHĀ DAYĀMI SHRĪ DHARMADHĀTU BĀGĪSHVARA SHRAGDHARĀRYYA TĀRĀ SAGAṆA MAṆḌALE IDAṂ PUṢPAṂAṆḌALAṂ NIRYYĀTAYĀMI.

Take rice and flowers dipped in water and let the liquid flow down to the *gojā*. [The *mantra* recited is:]

OṂ SHRAGDHARĀTĀRĪṆA SARVADUḤKHA BHAYAHĀRAṆĪ CATURMĀRAṆĪ VARAṆĪ SARVADEVĀSURA GARUḌA GANDHARVA KINNARA MAHORAGĀDI UPADRAVA PRASHAMAṆĪ SARVA BHŪTA PRETA PISĀCA YAKṢA RĀKṢASA ḌĀKA ḌĀKINYĀDI BHAYABIDHVAṂSANĪṂ PARAKṚTA JANTRA MANTRA PRAYOGĀDI BINĀSANĪ BHAGAVATĪ DURGĀTĀRAṆĪ

ĀGACCHA IDAṂ BALI GṚHNAGṚHNA MAMA SARVASATRŪ HANAHANA KHAKHA KHĀHIKHĀHI SARVABANDHANA BYĀDHI BIPRAHĀDI NĀ SANĪ HUṂHUṂ PHAṬPHAṬ SVĀHĀ.

[Chant:]

//STROTRA//

TĀRĀMĀRA BHAYAṆKARĪ SURAVARAIḤ
SAṂPŪJITĀ SARVADĀ
LOKĀNĀṂ HITAKĀRIṆĪ JAYATISĀ
MĀTEVAYĀRAKṢATI
KĀRUṆYENA SAMĀHITĀ BAHUVIDHĀNSASĀRA
BHĪRUÑJANĀN
MĀTĀ BHAKTIMATĀṂ VIBHĀTĪ JAGATĀṂ
NITYAṂBHAYA DHVAṂSINĪ.

Offer the *ratnamaṇḍala* and bow to it. Put the sacred string round the worshipers' neck. Read from the holy manuscripts the teaching of the *dharma* [i.e., the *vratakathā*]. Offer a special fruit-scented bath (*phalābhiṣeka*). Construct [a small] *maṇḍala* and worship it with offerings of rice and

Fig. 4.2. Sand *Stūpa* and Final Offerings by the Riverside

sanctified food (*sagaṃ*). Dispense the *tika* benediction. Then the *pūjā* is over. Gently rub the sacred string with sacred water from the *kalasha*. Give out the *aṣṭamaṇgala* stuff from the special ritual plate (*thāybhū*). Holy water from the *kalasha* may not be distributed at this time: it is distributed only on the riverbank.

Hand over the mirror and *sinhaḥmū* [ready for carrying]. Let the chief worshiper carry the *kalasha* and other worshipers carry the [main] *maṇḍala* to immerse them in the river.

Place the *kalasha* on the river bank. Fashion a *caitya* and *nāga* from sanctified sand, then worship and circumambulate them. Take water in the cupped palm and splash it gently on the *kalasha*. Take consecrated water collected from the *kalasha* as a blessing. Return home and have a feast.

The *Vratakathā*: The Sanctity of Tārā *Tīrtha* at Bāgduvāl

A Brāhmaṇ named Guṇākar dwelled in a village called Himavati Nagar near the Himalaya. He had only one son named Dhanākar. He was married to a lovely woman of high status. Dhanākar was addicted to the habits of eating forbidden food, drinking alcohol, and visiting prostitutes. Guṇākar, his father, insisted that he give up these addictions, but was unable to deter him.

Ultimately his father died. After the death of his father, Dhanākar became much more addicted to the habit of drinking alcohol and visiting prostitutes. His wife, on the other hand, was very kind and faithful to her husband. Although he had such a good wife, he did not abstain from visiting prostitutes, eating unclean food and drinking alcohol. His wife, who finally grew impatient with his bad habits, [one day] implored him, "My lord, why have you taken up to the harmful habit of drinking? Your father did all he could to prevent you from becoming an addict. He is no more and now there is no one to tell you not to be given over to such bad and harmful habits. Since you have not [yet] given up your bad habits, I pray that you not be an addict."

Dhanākar grew very angry with his wife for all that she had said to him. He beat her and sent her away. She did not know where to go and so went to the forest with her heart broken. Finally she sat down to rest under a tree and sobbed to herself, "I might have acted sinfully in my previous life as a result of which I am now punished and married to such a cruel husband. I must be the most ill-fated woman in the world. Where am I to go? Who shall I stay with? I am distraught with my life. I wish I were taken away by death but death is not imminent. So I should kill myself."

She thought about this while roaming the forest until one day she saw a sage living in a cave. She approached him and asked, "Why, saint, are you living alone in the forest?" The sage said that he would tell her something helpful and said, "All those who are born must die. Everyone in this present life must face the consequences of the actions performed in previous lives. Similarly in our next lives we reap the results of the deeds that we do in our present life. If we do good deeds, we live a happy life. If we do evil deeds, we live an unhappy life. To be born, to be old, and to die are great sufferings. The cause of my living in such a lonely place near the Himalayas is to get rid of all this suffering." He further went on to ask, "Oh gentle lady! Whose wife are you? What is your name? Why have you come to this forest? Who is here escorting you? Who have you come here with? Tell me the truth."

Upon his asking these questions, the female Brāhmaṇ could not hold back her tears and sobbed out her story to the sage: "Close to this village lived a Brāhmaṇ named Guṇākar who had a bad-natured son called Dhanākar. He was addicted to drinking and prostitution. His father died without being able to correct his character, despite great exertions. After the death of his father he went from bad to worse and even stopped returning home. Once when he came home I begged him to give up his bad habits. But he beat me and sent me away. I am this wretched man's wife. I feel I am very unfortunate and roam this forest now with the intention of committing suicide."

After hearing the tearful female Brāhmaṇ's words, the sage

said, "O gentle lady! I am going to tell you something good. Listen! Human life, you know, is very precious. Only very fortunate beings can [ever] attain a human life. You need to remember with reverence Ārya Tārā and pray to her for deliverance from your suffering. Remember, O gentle Lady! Those committing suicide become scarred with an evil destiny, as illustrated in the following story:

> "Once there lived in a city a devout and pious merchant whose wife was arrogant, unfaithful, and ill-natured. No matter how well fed and nicely clad she was by her husband, she never acknowledged him gratefully. She always found fault with him and picked a quarrel. Dissatisfied with this wife, the merchant married a second wife. Upon doing this, his first wife committed suicide by throwing herself into a pond. Because of this suicide, she was doomed to hell and subjected to untold sufferings."

For this reason, O Gentle Lady, do not commit suicide! If you want to be liberated from your sufferings, pray to the Goddess Ārya Tārā. To the east of this Sankhod Mountain is the bathing spot of the Ārya Tārā who, as instructed by Amitābha [Buddha], visited the holy spot to liberate suffering people from their miseries. Go bathe at this holy *tīrtha* and offer sincere prayers to the goddess Ārya Tārā. Then you will be delivered from your sufferings." Hearing this from the sage, the female Brāhmaṇ asked him how the Tārā *tīrtha* came into being. The sage replied, "O Gentle Lady, Listen, I'll tell you how it originated."

> "Once when the demons ousted Lord Brahmā, Viṣṇu, Maheshvara and Indra from their thrones, these gods went to take refuge in Ugra Tārā, a goddess who in turn asked them to pray and to recite the *mantra* of Ārya Tārā.
>
> Straight away the gods went to the present site of the *Tārā tīrtha* and recited the *mantra* of Ārya Tārā as directed. After the recitation of the *mantra* by the gods, the Ārya Tārā made her appearance right at the *tīrtha* and liberated Brahmā, Viṣṇu, Maheshvara, and Indra from their miseries. O Gentle Lady! You also may perform *pūjā* to Ugra Tārā Bajrajoginī; then go to bathe at [this] *Tārā tīrtha* where you should also meditate and offer prayers."

Hearing this [second story] from the sage, the female Brāhmaṇ climbed up the hill with enthusiasm to have a sacred vision (*darshan*) of Ugra Tārā Bajrajoginī [of Sāṇkhu] and thereafter went to the *Tārā Tīrtha*. On reaching the *tīrtha*, she bathed and offered *pūjā*, and said heartfelt prayers.

In answer to her prayers, the Ārya Tārā took pity on the female Brāhmaṇ and appeared before her in green complexion and in *abhaya mudrā* while holding a flower in her other hand. The female Brāhmaṇ fell prostrate on the ground before the goddess and offered her *pūjā* while chanting devotional songs. The goddess blessed her and then vanished. The female Brāhmaṇ spent the rest of her life at this *Tārā tīrtha* living upon fruit and water while meditating and observing the Ārya Tārā *vrata* and offering prayers to the *triratna*. When she finally died whe was transported to *Sukhāvatī* [Amitābha Buddha's paradise].

The Domestication of the Text

In the Kathmandu Valley, there are two especially popular places for performing this *vrata* nowadays: the Tārā temple in Itum Bāhā in Kathmandu city and the Tārā *tīrtha* at Bāgduvā, the headwaters of the Bāgmati River up on Shivapuri, the mountain that defines the northern boundary of the Kathmandu Valley. The rituals described are directed to the Green Tārā and the narratives of the *vratakathā* describe an incident from the sacred history of the latter place.

We also should note that the old Newar Buddhist greeting, Tāremāṃ (popularly thought to be derived from "Tārā Shāraṇam": "I take refuge in Tārā" [Gellner 1992: 352, fn #33]), indicates the community's sense of invoking the celestial *bodhisattva*'s name in everyday social exchanges.

According to the popular Newar understanding, the *Tārā vrata* should be performed at least once early in one's lifetime, since this can avert a premature death. For this reason it is also observed in the name of a person who is seriously ill.

This very detailed text alludes to several practices that merit special comment. The requirement of *tormā* offerings suggests connections with Tibetan Buddhist ritual traditions and is doubtless a marker of trans-Himalayan cultural history (Lewis 1989c; Templeman 1981:38). The guide also prescribes that the participants make clay *caitya*s, performing a ritual called *dyaḥ thāyegu* in Newari, a practice described in chapter 2. It is during *Guṃlā*, the monsoon month holy to Newar Buddhists, when groups are usually organized to perform this *vrata* (Lewis 1993c).

Observations on the History of Practical Buddhism

See the next chapter.

CHAPTER 5

Invoking the Powers of the Buddhist "Dark Lord": The *Caturdashī Vrata* of Mahākāla

> Hail to you with the stamp of Akṣobhya Buddha on your crown and clothed in tiger skin!
>
> Mahākāla *Vratakathā*

> Yet this Lord, the deity Mahākāla, is the servant of the gods, the demons, and the men of the three worlds
>
> *Sādhana* of Mahākāla
> (Ratna Kaji Vajracarya, *Buddhist Ritual Dance*)

Background

Our second study of a Newar Mahāyāna *vrata* concerns Mahākāla (New.: Mahāṃkāl Dya:), another popular deity among Hindus and Buddhists in Nepal. This deity most probably evolved from the Indic Shiva-Bhairava, as later Buddhists incorporated this fierce deity into their pantheon. By the time of the compilation of the *Sādhanamālā*, at least seven specific *sādhana*s had been composed for this fierce deity (B. Bhattacaryya 1968a: 583–92). The deity's Buddhist identity is also shown iconographically: in Nepal he is depicted with the eastern celestial Buddha, Akṣobhya, on his crown. There are also numerous *tantra*s dedicated to Mahākāla known in Sanskrit and Tibetan recensions found in the Kathmandu Valley (Stablein 1976a, 1976b).

In textual sources, Mahākāla is referred to as King of Yakshas (demons), the subduer of Māra (demonic tempter of Buddhas and aspirants), and a powerful deity who comes to protect the Dharma as well as individual Buddhists. A personification of the syllable

"Hum", Mahākāla in another source is called "servant of gods, the demons and humans of the three worlds" who spreads the rule of the Buddha in all directions (Kalamandapa 1986, 35). In the *Mahākālatantra* translated by William Stablein (1976a), Mahākāla is variously called a *bodhisattva* and Vajrasattva (cosmic or Adi-Buddha, embodiment of the Dharmakāya) (Stablein: 211); his tutelary deity is said to be the *yoginī* Vajravārāhī (216); in more esoteric-symbolic discourse (meant for advanced devotees), Mahākāla conveys other associations:

> He whose body possesses great time. (183)
>
> The dreadful one for whom the enumeration of time constitutes the absorption of each being. (ibid.)
>
> *Saṃsāra* is the form/body of Mahākāla. (1976: 192)

Another passage from the tantra, using language close to that in our *vratakathā*, promises the following to adept practitioners,

> Those sentient beings who are devoted to the Dharma and who have completed the mantras will easily obtain the powers: 1) sword, 2) ointment, 3) pill, 4) slipper, 5) medicine powders, 6) "the power of certainty," 7) mercury, and 8) long life. (182)

Translation

Notes on the Text

The introduction to the printed version cites the textual source of the *vratakathā* as "the *Kanitāvadāna*"[1] in which Shākyamuni Buddha explains the rite to his famous disciple Sāriputra. This text differs in its depth of coverage: the *Tārā vrata* manual in the previous chapter was intended more for *vajrācārya* priests, as it contains a detailed outline of each ritual, complete with *mantras*. Our *Caturdashī vrata* text is more for layfolk: it is much shorter, giving only the most minimal ritual outline, and focuses mostly on describing the supernormal powers (*siddhi*) that can be attained by performing the *vrata*.

Badri Bajracarya. *Mahāṃkāl*. Kathmandu, Nepal, 1978.

Mahākāla

Bathe in a holy river. With the purity of mind and body, clad in clean clothes, display a scroll painting of Mahākāla in a pleasant place. Decorate the site with flags, festoons, and a canopy. Get all of the materials required for the *vrata* ready and then begin the *pūjā*.

The *pūjā* may begin by invoking the great teacher for blessings. Seek refuge in the triple gems. Construct a *maṇḍala* of Mahākāla, the guardian deity of the Buddhist Dharma, and worship it by making offerings of flowers, incense, a lighted wick, and then make a *bali* offering.[2] Look at Mahākāla and pledge to observe the eight precepts.[3] He who on this fourteenth day of the dark lunar fortnight performs this fast, pledging to observe the eight precepts wholeheartedly, will have full control over his enemies and can ascend to the status of head of state. The emancipation that can result from this *caturdashī vrata* is well illustrated in the following story:

"In the remote past there dwelled in the city of Vārānasi a king named Brahmadatta. Every month on the fourteenth day of the dark lunar fortnight he visited the Shiva temple located to the south of the city, bathed, worshiped Mahākāla, fasted, and then pledged to observe the eight precepts. As a result of this meritorious act, his country never suffered from natural disasters and his reign was blessed.

One day, a foreign king came to attack Vārānasi with an army that was well-armed with weapons. At the sight of the enemy, the people of Vārānasi were panic-stricken. They approached the king, led by their leaders. One of them said, "Your Majesty Brahmadatta! Our country is about to be attacked by a foreign enemy. The country is in a panic. Oh Your Majesty! Command us as to what we should do!"

The king responded: "Citizens! Pleasures are short-lived. They are as precarious and transitory as silvery water drops on lotus leaves. Do not panic because of this king's army. Be assured that they will be driven away through my meritorious action."

Upon hearing this, the spokesperson replied, "Your Majesty! We have no knowledge of what powers you have by virtue of your meritorious actions. We want you to demonstrate this power by resisting and destroying the present enemy. It will be pointless to repent after our country has fallen into the hands of its enemies."

After hearing the request of his people, King Brahmadatta immediately went to the holy river and bathed. Then he went to the Shiva temple that night, fasted, and worshiped Mahākāla. He also meditated upon Mahākāla constantly without diverting his attention from other things. As a result, the deity Mahākāla in his terrifying form appeared before the king and asked in a kind manner: "O King! Why are you invoking me in meditation?" Once the king saw Mahākāla, he bowed down to him and chanted a hymn of praise that is written here:

[1] Hail to you Mahākāla, destroyer of evildoers and bestower of boons!
[2] Hail to you of the round red eyes, bright like a flaming light!
[3] Hail to you with curly brown hair and rough skin!
[4] Hail to you with a big and terrifying dark body that is surrounded by a halo!
[5] Hail to you with shapely body and shapely limbs!
[6] Hail to you with a fierce-fanged face that loves flesh and blood!
[7] Hail to you with the stamp of Akṣobhya Buddha on your crown and clothed in tiger skin!
[8] Hail to you, the world in miniature, you with the thousand arms!

After chanting this hymn, the king then said, "O Lord Mahākāla, the mightiest of the mighty, I am going to the battlefield. I pray to receive your boon of the *aṣṭasiddhi*, the eight powers that will enable me to vanquish my enemies."

Upon hearing this supplication, Mahākāla granted him the *aṣṭasiddhi* powers and then vanished. These *siddhi*s are as follows:

1. *añjanasiddhi*: power of being invisible to enemies;
2. *kuṭhikasiddhi*: power of being invulnerable to enemies;
3. *padukasiddhi*: power of being able to fly in the sky;
4. *sidhausadhisiddhi*: power of being immune to diseases and for living a long life;

5. *manisiddhi*: power of being able to have inexhaustible wealth;
6. *mantrasiddhi*: power of being able to materialize what one desires;
7. *basyasiddhi*: power of being able to vanquish enemies;
8. *rajyasiddhi*: power of being able to rule over the country peacefully.

Armed with such precious powers, when King Brahmadatta went like a lion to the battlefield with his hand raised high, his enemies were panic-stricken and ran to him for refuge.

Mahākāla, who has been regarded as an effective ally in vanquishing enemies and who has acted as a guardian for the protection of the Buddha, Dharma, and Saṃgha, deserves our veneration and invocation."

Buddha, the Enlightened One, narrated this story to Sāriputra on how the *Mahākāla Vrata* helped King Brahmadatta single-handedly vanquish the enemy-king and his army and peacefully rule over his country for many years. Therefore he who observes the *Caturdashī Vrata* invoking Mahākāla will succeed in his work and be free from all dangers posed by enemies.

The Domestication of the Text

The introduction to the *vrata* text states that the *Caturdashī Vrata* is also called the *Mahākāla Vrata* and that it has been popular in Nepal "from ancient times." This *vrata*, although less popular than the *Tārā* or *Aṣṭamī Vrata*s, is observed only on the fourteenth day of the dark lunar fortnight, that is, the day right before the new moon, a time typically associated with dangerous, blood sacrifice-taking deities. It may be observed at the large Kathmandu temple, at a riverside *tīrtha*s, or at home. I know of only a few modern devotees who have actually performed it.

Mahākāla is found in many different settings. Opposite Gaṇesh or Hanumān, his images guard the entranceways of most Newar *vihāra*s (Locke 1985:8). As part of the restorations of the great Svayambhū *stūpa* directed around 1500 by the Tibetan lama gTsan-smyon Heruka, Mahākāla was established as the shrine's main protector (Lewis and Jamspal 1988). This great Tibetan teacher also initiated local devotees into the tantric practice featuring the white Mahākāla. The *Kriyāsaṃgraha*, a Sanskrit ritual manual used in the valley to guide the construction of religious buildings (Lewis 1994a: 8), specifies establishing Mahākāla on the door's right side during the consecration of a Buddhist monastery. Mahākāla is also commonly found alone as a protector inside the exterior niches of private homes.

The fierce deity is also domesticated inside the Newar home. In the *Sthirobhavavākya*, a Buddhist chant used in house consecration rituals, a host of deities are identified with household objects that are associated with "establishing Gṛhalakshmī ['Lakshmī of the House']" in the new building. Among the seventeen mentioned, "Mahākāla is the rice cooking pot" (Slusser 1982: 421).[4]

There is also a free-standing two-roof Mahākāla temple located just outside the former eastern town boundaries of Kathmandu, a site associated with the Newar myth of "first contact" with this deity by a local *vajrācārya* adept:

> There once dwelt in Mantrasiddhi Mahāvihāra, the present Saval Bāhā, a Vajrācārya named Sasvat Vajra. One day he was sitting in the sun after an oil massage. At that time a large cloud mass came floating by in the sky, cutting off his sunlight. When Sasvat Vajra looked up he saw that the clouds had remained stationary. He then left the *bāhā* and went to Tundikhel, the large open field, for the purpose of bringing down the cloud. By means of a secret *pūjā* and utilizing his *mantrasiddhi*, he succeeded in bringing the cloud to the field and there saw Mahākāla inside of it. Sasvat Vajra then worshipped Mahākāla with a hymn of his own composition. He soon discovered that the deity always

> moves between Tibet and Kashi [Varanasi] and made Mahākāla promise to stop at this site during his travels in the future. Once the *pūja* was complete, Mahākāla blessed Sasvat Vajra, went up into the sky, and then disappeared. (Translation in Lewis 1984: 75)

Mary Slusser dates this temple and icon to the later Malla period (Slusser 1982: 292). The main image itself has received countless ornaments and votive additions; it is kept oiled and twice yearly is garlanded with special human bone ornaments.

This temple receives great attention from both Hindu and Buddhist devotees daily, especially from passing motorists! There are elaborate family offerings on full moon, no moon, and eighth lunar days and especially on Saturdays, the day on which the myth guarantees his presence. The regular priests of this temple are *vajrācārya*s from Suval Bāhā, whose members claim Sasvat Vajra as their ancestor. On Saturdays, the *vajrācārya pūjāri* may also offer *puṣṭa pūjā* (Book Ritual): holding an old copy of the *Mahākālatantra*, he touches the heads of devotees in exchange for a donation. The preferred offerings presented here by devotees are black in color, be they foodstuffs (e.g., black sesame seeds), cloth, dough offerings, or powders.

For some Buddhist and Hindu families this Mahākāla site remains a locale where they can visit their family lineage deity (*digu dyaḥ*) for *pūjā*.

Observations on the History of Practical Buddhism

Buddhism as a Communal Tradition

*Vrata*s create one of the main religious constituencies within the Newar Buddhist community, uniting families and friends who regularly perform rites to a chosen deity. Once again, it can be observed that Buddhist practices are highly communal: most Newar *vrata* groups are not caste-exclusive, have shifting memberships, and are relatively ephemeral.

Further, the *vrata*s in their Nepalese setting also emphasize the interdependence between the *saṃgha* and the lay community. Newar Buddhist tradition is centered in the *vajrācārya saṃgha* who preserve the *vrata* texts and who serve as "masters of ritual ceremony." The traditional observance is outlined in these texts, but it must be "extracted" recurringly by those taking on the roles handed down through *guru-guru* lineages within their householder *saṃgha*. Here, as elsewhere, the vitality of Buddhism is as dependent on the ritualists as on the lay patrons who support the *saṃgha*'s specialist livelihood. The Newar *vrata* observances suggest that this interrelatedness was fundamental in societies adhering to Mahāyāna-Vajrayāna traditions.

*Vrata*s underline the typical Buddhist layperson's focal religious orientation as a Mahāyāna devotee. The most popular *vrata* rituals, not surprisingly, are to deities with the most important temples in Kathmandu: Avalokiteshvara, Mahākāla, Svayambhū, and Tārā. Relying on priests from the *saṃgha*, layfolk make offerings (*dāna*) to these deities who, in return, are thought to grant specific boons, good fortune, heaven, or even supernormal powers and the possibility of enlightenment itself. The stories appended to the *vrata*s convey the laity's overall religious motivation in performing them: to make large quantities of *puṇya* that can unambiguously improve their destiny in *saṃsāra* and to derive a wealth of side benefits associated with the particular divinity.

It is also important to highlight the *vratakathā*, stories inserted in the proceedings. Recounted by the ritualist for the patron, these tales provide a doctrinal element in the performance of the *vrata*. Both translations provide examples of the literary style common in "popular" Buddhist texts: to illustrate a doctrinal point or to explain a practice, the Buddha tells a story and often, as we see in the Tārā text, stories are embedded inside of stories. The plots are simple and the lessons clear. All the *kathā* also assert linkages between their accounts and the Buddhas, making explicit claims for their authority.

Uposaḍha, Vratas, and the Context of Later Buddhist Ritualism

Each fortnight on the new and full moon days, Indic *saṃgha* members were required to recite and to affirm the *Pratimokṣa*, a summary of the community's *Vinaya* regulations. This recitation came after any transgressions were confessed (*ālocanā*) in private to the monk's superior. *Uposaḍha* became the regular occasions to review, correct, and certify the proper standards of monastery discipline (Prebish 1975a; Wijayaratna 1990).[5]

Emphasizing the fundamental interdependence between *saṃgha* and the lay community, householders were encouraged to visit their *vihāra*s on the *uposaḍha* days to make offerings (*dāna*). On these days, devout layfolk could take the opportunity to observe eight of the ten monastic rules while residing continuously on the *vihāra* grounds. (The frequent lay observance of fasting after midday (until the next morning) led to their being commonly referred to as "fasting days" (e.g., Beal 1970: lxxiv). In many places across India, *upāsaka*s donned white robes while living under their extended vows (Dutt 1945a: 176). Another common *uposaḍha* custom was for layfolk to remain in the *vihāra* to hear monks preach the *dharma*.

Thus, it was the lunar fortnight rhythm that clearly dominates the Buddhist festival year: each year's passing had the regular succession of *uposaḍha*s. Given the Sanskrit title of the Newari "Uposaḍha Vrata" and of the early ritual precedents for lay-*saṃgha* devotionalism, it seems likely that the *vrata*s were orchestrated by Mahāyāna communities wishing to utilize the day for their own distinctive *bodhisattva* venerations, keeping the earlier custom of having the laity take extra precepts (eight) and take up short-term asceticism.[6]

Vratas and Hindu-Buddhist Relations

The dual identities of Tārā and Mahākāla, whose names are also used by Hindus for Devī and Shiva as well as for Newar Buddhists performing the *brāhmaṇ*-led *Satya Nārāyaṇa Vrata* raises the complex issue of Hindu-Buddhist relations. The Newar *vrata* text for Ārya Tārā illustrates the great influence that Brahmanic ritual orthopraxy exerted on Vajrayāna ritual practice: the priests use *pañcagavya* (the five cow products: milk, curd, ghee, dung, and urine) for purification; they pour oblations (*argha*) from conch shells, chant *mantra*s essential for the success of the ritual, and bestow *prasād* and *tika* marks to patrons' foreheads. In short, Newar *vajrācārya*s conform to most of the ritual procedures derived from ancient Brahmanic traditions. In this sense, *vajrācārya*s can be seen as "Buddhist Brahmins" serving their society by orchestrating rituals that are highly orthoprax in terms of classical Indic purity and procedural norms (Greenwold 1974).

But this is only a partial truth: most Buddhist ritual implements differ from Hindu analogs, the *mantra*s chanted are distinctly Mahāyāna-Vajrayāna, and later Buddhist doctrine is interwoven in a thoroughgoing manner. One must emphasize the transformations as well as continuities between the *vajrācārya*s and *brāhmaṇ*s in order to understand later Indic religious history. The proper assessment of later Buddhist ritualism in relationship to Hinduism must proceed from a historical perspective recognizing Hindu-Buddhist interdependence: modern Newar Buddhist and Brahmanic ritualism represent two evolving lineages originating from ancient Indian religious traditions; both draw upon a common core of symbolism, ritual procedure norms, and basic cosmological assumptions to develop their distinctive spiritual systems. Hindu and Buddhist traditions have, at times, profoundly affected each other, as Hindu-Buddhist relations until 1200 C.E. defined the chief dialectical poles in Indian religious history. Both should be seen as totalizing cultural phenomena, with philosophical doctrines and myths that proclaim their spiritual domination in any religious environment, including over each other. (See Lewis 1984: 468–81 for a more in-depth treatment of this complex issue.)

Beyond the fact that their outward form is congruent with Brahmanic ritual norms, both *vratas* clearly exemplify the Buddhist textual tradition's classical statements of spiritual superiority over Hinduism. First, the rites are always anchored in worshiping the *triratna*—Buddha, Dharma, and Saṃgha—and the *guru maṇḍala pūjā* that connects with and honors the Mahāyāna-Vajrayāna pantheon. Second, the great gods of the Indian tradition are specifically proclaimed as converts to Buddhism. We have two cases of that here: it is Shiva-Mahānkāl who "wears Akṣobhya Buddha on the crown," and it is the grace of Ārya Tārā that saved "Brahmā, Viṣṇu, Maheshvara, and Indra" from demons.

But what of Buddhists performing a Hindu *vrata*? The willingness of Newars to perform the Hindu *vrata* exemplifies the extent to which urban Newar Buddhists feel free to utilize the extraordinarily broad spectrum of religious options in their midst. It is not surprising that business families would take to this *vrata* for winning the worldly goal of prosperity, just as they, like Hindus, readily worship Lakṣmī during the annual Tihār (Hindi.: Divali) festival. For Mahāyāna Buddhists to worship Viṣṇu for worldly boons is not a "syncretic action," as some observers have claimed: it is consistent with the textually specified norm that allows the laity the choice of worshiping all gods for their worldly betterment (Robinson 1966). (See, e.g., the *Anguttara Nikāya* passage in chap. 7.) To perform a Mahāyāna *vrata* is to be reminded explicitly of this subordination of all "Hindu" deities, as the classical norms of Buddhist hierarchy are translated into popular devotional practice.

CHAPTER 6

The Refuge of Mantra Recitation: The *Pañcarakṣā*

> The pattern of disease with which we are familiar differs radically from the disease experience of our ancestors. Among them the sporadic outbreak of pestilence, in any of its dread forms, was a terrifying and ever-present possibility.
>
> William H. McNeill, *Plagues and Peoples*

> Having realized the powers, heightened awareness, analytical knowledges, mystical spells and the doors of liberation:
> May I simultaneously be of benefit to sentient beings throughout the immeasurable expanse of the universe.
>
> Āryashūra, *Praṇidhānāsaptatināmagāthā*
> (Brian C. Beresford, *Āryashūra's Aspiration and a Meditation on Compassion*)

The modern dismissal of ritual as a primary religious activity and a collective amnesia about epidemic disease in premodern societies have made contemporary students of Asian history prone to ignore the cultural resources that Mahāyāna Buddhism provided its faithful community. Focusing on the *Pañcarakṣā*, one of the most copied and used among all Buddhist texts, the last case study allows for a reconsideration of this important problem.

Buddhism amid Disease in the Premodern World

The realities of disease, mortality, and medical remediation in the ancient world must be imaginatively evoked to comprehend the human context in which Buddhism flourished as a successful and pragmatic missionary religion. McNeill's work on the role of epidemic disease in world history has demonstrated why this restoration of memory must be attempted. His *Plaques and Peoples* has articulated the major contours and starker dimensions of mortality and the limitations of medical treatment. First, the typical infant mortality rate for children under five years old in the premodern era was likely that still found in the most underdeveloped regions of the world today: about 50 percent. This means that the typical mother and father experienced the death of about half of their children, a heavy existential toll for every parent and surviving family member. (Some Buddhist story texts seem to refer to this experience as an expected burden that comes with marriage. As the *Mahākashyapa Avadāna* puts it, those who get married must "hear the loud bewailings of their wives uttered at the time of their children passing away from this world" (Vidyabhusan 1895: 19).

A second factor ever-present in premodern social life was the existence of epidemics. As the world's first urban culture hearth zones concentrated people and animals as never before, they also drew toward their settlements highly contagious diseases. Selection favored those who could survive the sickness induced by microbe or parasite after one (usually childhood) exposure. These urban populations, however, did not eliminate the sources of regional infection through such selective pressures, but over generations only reached a general equilibrium (in which both infected humans and parasites coexisted). As larger-scale civilizations emerged and as trade developed, the pattern of human-parasite "containment" changed and these local "disease pools" could pass over to distant peoples lacking resistance. As reconstructed by McNeill,

> . . . at about the beginning of the Christian era, at least four divergent civilized disease pools had come into existence, each sustaining infections that could be lethal if let loose among populations lacking any prior exposure or accumulated immunity. All that was needed to provoke spillover from one pool to another was some accident of communication permitting a chain of infection to extend to new ground where populations were also sufficiently dense to sustain the infection. . . .
>
> When, however, travel across the breadth of the Old World from China to India to the Mediteranian became so organized on a routine basis . . . both on shipboard and by cara-

> van, then conditions for the diffusion of infections . . . altered profoundly. The possibility of homogenization of those infections . . . opened up. (McNeil 1977: 102ff)

McNeill's historical research also suggests that although Gangetic South Asia harbored high levels of multiple-parasitic infestation, there is still little evidence for the disastrous epidemics known in later centuries in the Mediterranean, China, and Indianized Southeast Asia. In the latter cases, however, the expansion of Buddhism outward on the trade routes placed the tradition, and the need for its resources, up against the outbreak of infectious diseases and the anomie of death (Diamond 1997).

The continuing migration of traders and conquerors, particularly the Mongols, sustained the pattern of periodic epidemic outbreaks in urban areas. One famous Tibetan lama's diary recounting his visit to Nepal in 1723 indicates the continuing danger of contagious diseases there:

> At this time in Nepal, there was an epidemic which was occurring in the summertime but not in the winter. Once striken by this disease, most people died within thirty hours. The king reported that on a single night during the rainy season over one hundred dead bodies had to be removed [from town]. He also said to us: "Such a thing has gone on for three years and two-thirds of the population has perished." (Lewis and Jamspal 1988: 199)

A demoralized king then asks the lama to do something to help end the epidemic. (The disease was probably cholera.)

Thus, this public health existential baseline of the premodern world must inform the modern imagination of such basic Buddhist notions as suffering, the emphasis on the rarity of human life, and the resonances of the Buddha, *dharma*, and *saṃgha* as precious gems and refuges for vulnerable humanity. If, as the *Aṣṭsahashrika Prajñāpāramitā* assures, "A bodhisattva will not be afraid in a district infected by epidemics. . . ." (Conze 1962: 140), then we must now understand how rituals made this fearlessness possible.

Background

The Refuge of Buddhist Mantra Recitations

In common with the pragmatic religious practices shared by all South Asian religions, formula verses (*mantra*, *dhāraṇī*, and *vidyā*) composed by enlightened Buddhist saints were regarded as concentrated expressions of truth which, if spoken correctly and by qualified individuals, could affect both the world and the mind of the reciter in highly beneficial and desired ways (Gupta 1987). Verses to elicit the support of deities, to heal the sick, to understand the language of animals (e.g., *Pali Jātaka* #410), for repetition at sunrise and sunset (e.g., #498), to control and charm *nāga*s (e.g., #506), or to cure snakebites are found in the Pali literature and they are, like salvation expositions, considered part of the Buddha's *dharma* (Thomas 1933: 186ff; de Silva 1993: 30). The mastery is seen as another means to worldly prosperity and compassionate action; as the *bodhisattva* states in one story: "Sire, I do know magic. . . . For wise men who have learnt magic, when danger comes, deliver both themselves and others" (*Jātaka* #546, in Cowell 1957, 6:235).

Dhāraṇī texts are among the earliest attested for Indic Mahāyāna tradition. As Gregory Schopen has pointed out, "It is of some significance that inscriptional evidence suggests that *dhāraṇī* texts were publically known much earlier and more widely than texts we think of as 'classically' Mahāyāna" (Schopen 1989b: 157). The *Pañcarakṣā* developed in communities for whom meditation and ritual practice extensively utilized these precisely defined Sanskrit utterances. The *Bodhisattvabhūmi*, for example, explains that *dhāraṇī*s can be used to aid in the development of insight (*prajñā*) and memory, in understanding the meaning of entire texts, and for cultivating eloquence in public discourse (Braarvig 1985). Both merit (*puṇya*) and worldly benefits could be earned as well. Such *mantra*s were used to build the later procedures of Mahāyāna meditation and of ritual performance.

Mahāyāna-Vajrayāna theory in this field evolved so that sages identified "heart *mantra*s" for the entire pantheon—that is, the *buddha*s, *bodhisattva*s, Tārā, and so forth. Command of these short verses was essential for worship and meditation: *mantra* practices enliven the divine visualization in the mind's eye, as the meditator "assumes the divine ego" (Beyer 1973). Grounded in the *shunyatā* theory,[1] communion with the *bodhisattva*s through *sādhana*s became one important avenue of meditation that was pivotal to the performance of Mahāyāna ritual. The Mahāyāna masters developed these practices on a vast scale, as hundreds of *mantra*s and *dhāraṇī*s became popular for specific sacred and mundane purposes (Snellgrove 1987: 143). There was such faith in them that *dhāraṇī* recitations constituted a separate branch of early Indic Buddhist medical practice (Zysk 1991: 56), a tradition of applied spirituality that was exceedingly influential in east Asia (e.g., A. F. Wright 1959: 56; Overmyer 1980; Veith and Minami 1966). I will note below the breadth of such situations covered by the testimonial stories of the *Pañcarakṣā*.

From ancient times, it seems that recitation rituals became so integral to the devotional lives of Buddhists that *dhāraṇī*s were collected and copied by the thousands. *Dhāraṇī*s even comprised a separate division in early Buddhist Sanskrit literature, including the Mahāsaṃghika *Vidyādharapitaka* (Bharati 1955: 104). It is also likely that monastics and lay practitioners compiled their own written collections for personal use, as they still do in Nepal. Mastery of such formulas was so important that ninth-*bhūmi bodhisattva*s are specifically expected to acquire and to develop *dhāraṇī*s (Dayal 1932).[2]

The *Pañcarakṣā* links layfolk's wishes for well-being with the *bodhisattva*'s vow for compassionate occupation, containing story passages in which Shākyamuni Buddha divulges *dhāraṇī*s to the *saṃgha* and gives explicit instructions on harnessing the powers of the *buddha*s and *bodhisattva*s' words. The *Mañjushrīmūlakalpa* also connects *bodhisattva* theory with taking refuge in *mantra* practice, making the striking assertion that *bodhisattva*s even *become* the chants or their agents:

> Other bodhisattvas, those Great Beings . . . for the purpose of establishing all living beings in the irreversible path which is their aspiration, they assume the form of unaccountable spells (*vidyā*), of *mantra*s and mnemonics (*dhāraṇī*) and various kinds of medicinal herbs, or they take the form of different sorts of winged creatures, of *yakṣa*s and ogres (*rākṣasa*).[3]

The same sentiment and identification with "becoming a *mantra*" is found in the popular *Bodhicaryāvatāra* (e.g., Gomez 1995a: 190). The *Mahāvastu* states this explicitly, "All charms and medicines . . . which have been devised for the benefit and welfare of the world and for the services of men, were discovered by bodhisattvas" (Jones 1949, 1: 107).

History of the Pañcarakṣā as a Single Text

The protective *sūtra*s comprising the *Pañcarakṣā* were among the most popular across the Mahāyāna world; the *dhāraṇī*s with their associated testimonial stories have undergone many redactions through translations into Chinese, Tibetan, Mongolian, and

Japanese.[4] As Peter Skilling has pointed out (Skilling 1992: 138–39), there are, despite similar titles, at least two different early *Pañcarakṣā* collections attested, one extant in Sanskrit (datable to only 1100 C.E.), and one in Tibetan (datable to 800 C.E.). These collections vary in two of the stories.

It is likely that several of the five conjoined ritual texts were originally separate traditions since individual manuscripts of the *Mahāmāyūrī dhāraṇī* alone are much older in Chinese translation than any of the collected *Pañcarakṣā* recensions. Four of the five are still known through separate Sanskrit texts in the Kathmandu Valley (Takaoka 1981; Mitra 1971; Mevissen 1989). The *Mahāmāyūrī* is by far the most famous of the five, and its Indic genesis can be dated to at least as early as 320 C.E., as six versions were translated into Chinese over ensuing centuries (DeVisser 1976: 196). The earliest known *Pañcarakṣā* compendium, however, is only attested much later, in an eleventh-century Bengali manuscript (DeVisser, 194). The five *Pañcarakṣā* deities and their *maṇḍala*s are also found in the *Sādhanamālā* and *Niṣpannayogāvalī*, texts dated to roughly this same era, and in the later *Vajrāvalī*. (Although all of these texts became important in Nepal, it has been *Sādhana* #206 in the *Sādhanamāla* that has been almost exclusively followed in the Newar *paubhā* painting tradition [Mevissen 1989: 417]).

The Newari recension of the *Pañcarakṣā*, a modern translation from a Sanskrit original, is actually a collection of five *sūtra*s, to use the term employed for each in the text itself. These are the *Mahāmāyūrī*, *Mahāpratisarā*, *Mahāshītavatī*, *Mahāmantrānusāriṇī*, and *Mahāsāhasrapramardinī*. Although the stories in the Mahāyāna *sūtras* do not bear a close resemblance to any of the stories that Theravādins have in their modern *paritta* collections, there are a few place-names and descriptions that they do share.[5]

The Five Rakṣā Deities

Modern scholarship has found no evidence that the *Pañcarakṣā* deities were ever important apart from their apotropaic texts. Their origins, like others in the Mahāyāna-Vajrayāna traditions, stem from their being embodiments of the Dharma: "In the same way that the book comes to stand for the source of Buddhahood, the *dhāranī*, as the epitome of the wisdom and power of the Dharma, can be conceived as a protective deity" (Gomez 1987: 448). Scholars have noted attempts to correlate the five with the five senses (Foucher 1900) and with the Pañca Buddhas (DeVisser 1976: 196; Mallman 1975:

290), as well as with a theory of emanations from Tārā (D. C. Bhattacharya 1972: 87). An assembly of five is also the number needed for a proper arrangement of a *maṇḍala* (Malleman 1975: 287ff).[6] Other *Pañcarakṣā* manuscripts describe deities having both peaceful and wrathful incarnations (DeVisser, 1976 195); in China, Mahāmāyūrī was represented as male, as opposed to the depiction in the Sanskrit and Newari versions.

Judging by the manuscript collections, it is likely that the goddess Mahāmāyūrī and her snakebite treatment is the oldest part of the tradition (Levi 1915). The *Kriyāsaṃgraha*, however, also applies the recitation of the Mahāmāyūrī *mantra* specifically to the protection of trees (Skorupski 1996: 10). Besides the healing *mantra*, the *Sādhanamālā* (#97) also records a *Mahāmāyūrī maṇḍala* as does the Vajrāvalī-Nāma-Maṇḍalopāyikā of Abhayākaragupta, dated to 1130 C.E. (Bhattacharyya 1981). The deity is also represented in the archaeological finds at Nalanda and at Ellora (D. C. Bhattacarya 1972: 90). Texts from China indicate the great popularity of the Mahāmāyūrī tradition there as well. Two of the six extant Chinese texts summarized by M. W. DeVisser are quite similar to the Newari narrative; others recount aspects not cited: one version links the Mahāmāyūrī with the revelation and protection of the *Prajñāpāramitā*, a connection between texts that is also evident in an illustrated Newar manuscript published by Pal (Pal 1975: 60–61); another is more tantric in orientation, and is especially associated with rain making, having been used in a famous incident in Chinese Buddhism by the Indian monk Amoghavajra (DeVisser, 1976: 207); yet another Chinese recension contains the first known description of a Buddhist *homa* ritual (Matsunaga 1977).

Mantra Theory in the Pañcarakṣā

In the stories translated here are explanations of the powers underlying the *mantra*s, as well as dramatic testimonials to their effectiveness. These texts contribute several theories to explain the authority and efficacy of Buddhist *mantra* practice through Shākyamuṇi's explanations of each chant's history (cf. Skilling 1992). In the *Mahāpratisarā*, the Buddha states that the *mantra*s are "enshrined in the hearts of Buddhas." In the *Mahāsāhasrapramardinī* story, he connects their effectiveness with a long list of fundamental doctrinal ideas and meditation practices known from the earliest eras of the tradition (though without specifying any theme or theory explaining their interrelationship):

Shamatha and *vipashyanā*
the three *samādhi*s
the four *ṛddhipāda*s
the four *pradhāna*s
the four *smṛtyupasthāna*s
the four *dhyāna*s
the four Noble Truths
the five *indriya*s
the five physical powers (*bala*s)
the six *anusmṛti*
the seven factors of enlightenment (*bodhyaṇga*s)
the eightfold Path
the nine *anupūrvika vihāra samāpatti*s
the ten Tathāgata powers (*tathāgata bala*s)
the eleven *vimukta āyatana*s
the twelvefold *pratītya samutpada*
the twelve *dharmacakra*s
the sixteen *ānāpānānusmṛti*s
the eighteen *āveṇika Buddha dharma*s
the forty-two letters.

One passage in the *Mahāmāyūrī*'s testimonial narrative agrees with the *Dīgha Nikāya* as to how *mantra*s work: the Buddha asserts that *dhāraṇī* chanting bears results because it rouses throughout the cosmos the powerful beings who can take remedial actions (as fully given): *yakṣasī*s (esp.: Lambā, Vilambā, and Kūṇākṣī),[7] *nāgarāja*s and *tathāgata*s (esp.: Vipashvi), *bodhisattva*s (esp. Maitreya), the holy Gangā, mountain kings, heavenly bodies and planets, and herbs and plants.

Chanting the Pañcarakṣā: The Field of Blessings

All the texts in the *rakṣā* literature promise both merit and worldly blessings as a result of the proper recitation of the specified passages. In places, the effects of recitation operate mechanically; in other passages, the reciter's morality, or an act of relic worship (in the *Sāhasrapramardinī*), or stance at the town's Indra Pillar (in the *Mahāmantrānusāriṇī*) is said to affect the chant's efficacy, potentially multiplying the blessings and *puṇya*. The specific boons can overcome most human misfortune; in table 6.1, I summarize all the boons promised as a result of reciting the respective *dhāraṇī*s. This list can be taken as one typical sample of the human fears and "life insurances" that Buddhism offered its adherents.

Table 6.1
Boons in the Pañcarakṣā

1. *Mahāpratisarā*
Welfare and happiness
Destruction of all obstacles to success
Freedom from dangers posed by poison, weapons, fire, water, wind, and contagious diseases
Birth of a son (2X)
Easy childbirth
Life blessings with plenty and honor
No evil omens or bad dreams
Acquisition of a *vajrakāya* (indestructible body)
Cure of snakebite
Defense of city against enemies
Pain relief from serious illness
Defense from torments of hell
Escape from misfortune at sea
Wish fulfillment
Subduing demons
Safety from execution by sword, monster, or drowning

2. *Mahāsāhasrapramardinī*
Prevention or relief from natural disasters
Immunity from diseases
Protection of cattle and help for sick trees
Insuring the effectiveness of medicines

3. *Mahāmāyūrī*
Cure of snakebite
Freedom from snares
Deities and demons grant assistance
Buddhas and *bodhisattva*s grant assistance

4. *Mahāshītavatī*
Removal of fear
Tranquillity

5. *Mahāmantrānusāriṇī*
Relief from pestilence

The Refuge of Buddhist Amulets

To observe the practice of Buddhism in the modern world is to find that amulet use is everywhere a part of the tradition. Buddhist culture has always included this economic and pragmatic dimension, one area in which artisans (producers), merchants (sellers), monks (sources of empowerment), and pilgrims (purchasers) interacted (Tambiah 1984; Lewis 1993c; Reader and Tanabe 1998).

The *Pañcarakṣā* provides information about the use of amulets by devout Buddhists, an area that Buddhist studies has hardly explored for ancient South Asia, although there has been some recent research on modern practices (Tambiah 1984). The *Pañcarakṣā* refers to wearing an amulet as "a righteous deed." It mentions the efficacy of a *Mahāpratisarā dhāraṇī*-inscribed amulet for assuring the birth of a son and easy childbirth, and as a defense against all attempts at harm, both individually and for those on a ship at sea. The use of the *Mahāsāhasrapramardinī dhāraṇī* inscribed on cloth will even revive a dying tree. An amulet of the *Mahāshītavatī dhāraṇī* will free the wearer from "fear of ghosts, demons, tigers, bears, etc." The texts enjoin writing out the *mantra*s on a paper or cloth that is tied to the body (on the wrist or neck, or tree trunk), appended to clothing, or affixed to a king's crown and armor. Having the *dhāraṇī* printed on flags to flap in the breeze is also recommended.

In places, the use of amulets as described in these stories creates a seeming contradiction between the tradition's theory of *mantra* power and *karman* doctrine that asserts moral retribution to be the supreme, inescapable law operating in the universe. Perhaps the most striking scenes of moral paradox are found in the stories of the *Mahāpratisarā*. In its last tale, a person who committed an unspecified capital crime is sentenced to death but escapes three forms of execution due to the use of an amulet: an executioner's sword smashes, monsters retreat, and a river dries up because the criminal is wearing this amulet. (The king even grants clemency and decorates him as an "honored citizen" after observing the amulet's effects!) Another paradoxical scene is found in an earlier narrative from the same text where a bodhisattva who lands in hell[8] can evade karmic retribution because of the amulet; his presence there even suspends all punishments suffered by the other tortured bystanders! Here, again, we find a transindividual, collective dimension to Buddhism in practice.[9]

Pañcarakṣā Texts in Nepal

The earliest Sanskrit edition of the *Pañcarakṣā* found in Nepal dates from 1105 C.E. (D. C. Bhattacharya 1972: 91). The *vihāra* libraries of Nepal also preserve numerous versions of the composite five-part work under a host of titles. Over fifty different manuscripts with the name *Pañcarakṣā* are extant in the libraries of the Kathmandu Valley. There is one often used today by Kathmandu *vajrācārya* ritualists called the *Pañcarakṣā Samādhi* that provides practical instructions in the use of the *dhāraṇī* and *maṇḍalas*: access to this work is restricted to those who obtain an initiation (*dīkṣā*). Other manuscripts listed in the Japanese microfilm collection (Takaoka 1981) include fifty-six with the name *Pañcarakṣā* or using one of the separate *sūtra*s. It is also noteworthy that there are bilingual Sanskrit-Newari versions of the most commonly copied texts.[10]

Notes on the Newar Text

The five *sūtra*s in our published text share a common format. Similar to the process of evolution within other Mahāyāna texts (e.g., the *Prajñāpāramitā*), each *dhāraṇī* tradition evolved to have a deity embody the respective protective power. All five in this Newari recension begin with a line drawing of the deity, followed by an exact iconographic description in Newari[11] and then the Sanskrit *dhāraṇī*. Each closes with the testimonial narrative(s) in Newari.

In the Newari prose text for each of the *sūtra*s, there is a frame narrative. Two of the five add testimonial stories that are given in traditional Buddhist *avadāna* format. Each claims to be *buddhavācana* (the Buddha's words), as an incident brought to the attention of Shākyamuni becomes the occasion for his narrating one or more tales in support of the specific *dhāraṇī* recitation practice. Since remarks on the specific content of these stories follow in the next section, I merely note here the story outlines. The outer frame narrative and stories are summarized in table 6.2.

Table 6.2
Stories in the Pañcarakṣā

1. ***Mahāpratisarā***
   - A. Frame Narrative: As part of a sermon atop Mt. Meru
   - B. Testimonial Narratives
     - a. Gopa and the Fetus
     - b. The Merchant Son's Snakebite
     - c. King Brahmadatta's Defense
     - d. An Evil Monk Saved from Hell
     - e. Bimal Shaṇkha, Saved Seagoing Merchant
     - f. King Prasāritapāṇi
       - f.1. Previous Birth of King as Servant
     - g. Previous Buddha and Demons
     - h. The Failed Execution of King Brahmadatta
2. ***Mahāsāhasrapramardinī***
   - A. Frame Narrative: Buddha Confronts Natural Disasters of Vaishālī, invoking the Guardian Kings
   - B. Question of Monastic Discipline When Chanting *Mantra*s: Meat Eating[12]
3. ***Mahāmāyūrī***
   - A. Frame Narrative: Monk Bitten by Snake
   - B. Testimonial Narrative: The Ensnared Peacock
4. ***Mahāshītavatī***
   - A. Frame Narrative: Rahula Afraid in Cemetery
5. ***Mahāmantrānusāriṇī.***
   - A. Frame Narrative: Disease in Vaishālī

Translation

The Newar Translator and the English Translation

The text translated here is that published in Newari by one of the great modern Sanskrit *pandita*s of Kathmandu city, Divya Vajracarya. The Sanskrit text he utilized appears to be nearly the same as the Sanskrit texts from Nepal now found in the Royal Asiatic Society Library in Calcutta as reported by Rajendralala Mitra (Mitra 1971: 159–64; 168–69). The first printed Newar edition was published in 1980 by a small private press.

Vajracarya comes from one of the few distinguished Newar Buddhist scholar families of Kathmandu and is the long-recognized Buddhist master of Sanskrit living in the capital. Since the mid-1970s through public lectures and courses for *upāsaka*s, Vajracarya has been Sanskrit *guruju* to the small number of young *vajrācārya*s still learning their canonical language. He has also written many similar works, most notably the *Dharmasaṃgraha Koṣa* (1979), a dictionary of terms drawn from the *Abhidharmakoṣa* and from other Mahāyāna *sūtra*s.

In his short introduction to this text, the scholar notes that chanting the *Pañcarakṣā* is an old Newar ritual similar to the Theravādin *Paritrāṇa* that over the past few decades has become popular as part of the latter tradition's successful mission in the Kathmandu Valley (Kloppenberg 1977; Tewari 1983; Lewis 1984: 494–517). Vajracarya's publication of this *Pañcarakṣā* can be seen as yet another of the many works designed to strengthen the older Newar Mahāyāna-Vajrayāna tradition by making texts more accessible for both the laity and the *vajrācārya saṃgha*.

Vajracarya's other pertinent comment in the introduction states that the author chose his final Sanskrit source after consulting several manuscripts from the library of the venerable teacher who is the *vajrācārya* Rājaguru, Pūrṇānanda. He notes that this teacher is the most renowned at maintaining the Newari *Pañcarakṣā* traditions: the practices of *maṇḍala* drawing; chanting the *dhāraṇīs*; making special *maṇḍala*s, *yantra*s, and the incense for ritual use that have been "handed down from antiquity" in Pūrṇānanda's lineage.

There is a common format between this published text and the five chapters in the Newari recension: each begins with a line drawing of the deity, followed by an exact iconographic description in Newari, followed by the *dhāraṇī*, and ending with the testimonial narrative(s). Though alluded to in several stories, the *maṇḍala* for each or for the entire group is not provided.[13]

The published Newari text has been translated with Sanskrit terms recorded as given in the text, and paragraph breaks designated as in the original. The line drawings were those redrawn (with minor deviations) by a modern Valley artist after those found in the original published text. The proper Sanskrit title, *Pañcarakṣā-kathāsāra* (A Compendium of *Pañcarakṣā* Stories) is the Newar compiler's own designation for his printed redaction of the Sanskrit sources that were available to him.

THE PAÑCARAKṢĀ KATHĀSĀRA

(Kathmandu, Nepal: Jana Kalyana Press, 1980)

A COMPENDIUM OF *PAÑCARAKSĀ STORIES*

Mantra

Oṃ maṇidharī vajriṇī mahāpratisare rakṣa rakṣa māṃ sarvasattvānaṃa hūṃ hūṃ hūṃ phaṭ phaṭ phaṭ svāhā

Mahāpratisarā Meditation

[The goddess] emanates from the seed syllable "pra", seated in the lotus position; four-faced: the left one black, the back one yellow, the right one green, the middle one white; eight-armed, holding (on the left) the 8-spoked wheel, *vajra*, arrow, sword; on the right side, an ax, noose, trident, bow; each head has three eyes with a shrine (*caitya*) on the crown.

Oṃ Homage to Ārya Mahāpratisarā!

The Mahāpratisarā Mahāyāna Sūtra

Once the Lord Buddha was dwelling in a monastery atop Mount Sumeru. It was a delightful place covered with fruit-laden trees, and dotted with ponds full of lotus blossoms. A splendid palace of Indra also stood there. The whole estate was surrounded by a footpath covered with raw gold dust. A large number of superhuman beings were there such as the Vajragarbha bodhisattvas, the perfect ones; Arhats, including Shārīputra; Maheshvara accompanied by a host of gods including Brahmā and Indra; and countless demons, spirits (*gaṇa*s), and *nāga* kings. All assembled there calmly turned to the Buddha, ready to listen to his sermon. At that time the Buddha in a simple and intelligible language gave a sermon on *brahmācārya*, the renunciation of sensual pleasure that applies to all epochs—past, present and future—and that is full of knowledge that can lead one to the blissful state of *nirvāṇa*.

At that time there shone forth miraculously from the Buddha's brow a radiant light known as "the vision of all Buddhas." Immediately after the radiant light shone forth, the whole world was illuminated and everything was visible including the reincarnate Buddhas giving sermons to their disciples. Then Lord Buddha paid his respect to all of the Buddhas dwelling in all the worlds and said "OṂ NAMAḤ SARVATATHĀGATEBHYO ARHADBHYA: SAMYAK SAMBUDDHEBHYAḤ." He turned to those assembled there and said, "Listen! I tell you that the *Mahāpratisarā dhāraṇī* is for the welfare and happiness of humanity. Hearing this *dhāraṇī*, one can destroy the cause of whatever distress one is suffering from. One who recites this *Mahāpratisarā dhāraṇī* will be free from harm by *yakṣas*, *rākṣasas*, *bhūtas*, *pretas*, *pisācas*, *gandharvas*, the nine planets (*navagraha*), *kuṣmāṇḍas* (*shiva*-demons), madness, epilepsy, and dangers from all beings, human and nonhuman. All one's sworn enemies will be reconciled. One will be immune from the dangers posed by poison, fire, weapons, water, wind, and so forth and will be immune from contagious diseases. If one wears around the neck or wrist an amulet containing the *Mahāpratisarā dhāraṇī*, one will succeed in all endeavors, besides being free from all dangers. This places one under the protection of the goddess Māmakī. A woman wanting to be blessed with a son will have a son if she wears such an amulet. And she will conceive and deliver the baby with ease. A person, male or female, who follows the teaching of the *Mahāpratisarā* and observes the moral precepts solemnly will live in plenty. He or she will earn honor. Misfortune from certain evil omens or bad dreams will disappear. A large store of religious merit will also be accumulated. There will be prosperity all around. I will now reveal this *Pratisarā dhāraṇī*, so listen to me."

When the Buddha was preaching the discourse, among those in his audience was the great Brahmā. Addressing Brahmā, the Lord said, "Hearing this *dhāraṇī*, one can be free from danger of all sorts. One who learns it by heart will have an invulnerable body [*vajrakāya*], strong like a thunderbolt."

[He continued:] "Once in the city of Kapilavastu, [a woman] Gopā was made to leap into a blazing furnace. At that time Rāhula Bhadra Kumāra, the unborn offspring in her womb, who remembered the *Mahāpratisarā dhāraṇī* since the time when Siddhārtha Kumāra touched his navel with his big toe, called to mind this *dhāraṇī*. As a result of his recollecting this holy *dhāraṇī*, the flame died in the furnace and Gopā was found in the embers as if she were seated in the middle of a lotus blossom.

"Not only this, O Brahmā! In the great city of Surpāraka there once dwelled the merchant's son Kaushāmbika who had skill in catching snakes. The son compelled Takṣaka, the *nāga* king, to come to him, but he locked the *nāga* by mistake in a closet. But the serpent king struck Kaushāmbika before it could be brought under his magical control. [The pain from] the snake bite become unbearable and he lost consciousness.

A number of healers then came to cure him, but they could not do anything. In the city of Surpāraka, there was a devout lay Buddhist named Bimala Bishuddhi who had committed the *Mahāpratisarā dhāraṇī* to memory. Taking pity upon him, Bimala Bishuddhi went to recite the *dhāraṇī* for him. Immediately after the recitation of the *dhāraṇī*, the merchant's son regained consciousness. After this he was also made to repeat and recite the *dhāraṇī* and was thus saved from danger."

Not only this, O Brahmā! In the remote past there ruled in the city of Vārāṇasī a king named Brahmadatta. Once his neighboring enemy kings used their military power to seize the city and came to attack him. When the ministers went to the king, they said, "Your Majesty! We have been surrounded by enemies on all sides. Command what we should do to defend ourselves and safeguard our country." The King replied, "My dear subjects! It is my duty to safeguard the country and countrymen. You need not be afraid of anything. I will do all that is needed".

After saying this, King Brahmadatta bathed and cleansed himself with many different kinds of sweet-smelling waters. Purified in body, mind, and speech, the king appended amulets of the *Pratisarā dhāraṇī* to his crown and armor, then went alone to meet the enemy. The men in the army of the enemy kings retreated and ran away in a panic, believing that the king must have a large number of soldiers coming after him, for otherwise he would not have dared to come alone onto the battlefield. O great Brahmā! The *Pratisarā dhāraṇī* should be considered fruitful in this sense. It should be treated as something enshrined in the hearts of the Buddhas. Those born to die young will have their lifespans expanded. Those born not fortunate or lacking religious merit can have their happiness ensured.

Not only this, O Brahmā! There was once a greedy monk. He was not living up to the teachings of the Buddha: he went so far as to take something not given to him by its owner; he always asked persons for one thing or another shamelessly; he coveted the *saṃgha*'s possessions and other things belonging to many monks; he even treated the offerings left on the area surrounding *stūpa*s as his own personal belongings. After a certain time, the ill-natured monk became afflicted with a very terrible disease and had to spend his time in painful lament. There lived in the same country a kind Brāhman. He could not bear the sight of the monk's misery and placed round his neck an amulet with the *Mahāpratisarā dhāraṇī* on it. Immediately after this, the monk became relieved of all the pains and regained his consciousness.

Full of remorse for all the evil deeds he had committed before, the monk engendered an enlightened mind, but passed away the same night and was consigned to the Avīci Hell. With the effect of the *Pratisarā dhāraṇī* amulet still hanging on his dead body, those suffering in the Avīci Hell were relieved of their sufferings. The blaze of fire burning bright within the radius of several miles also died out. Those suffering for their evil deeds also were relieved of their sufferings. Aware of all these things, the messengers of death greeted Yamarāja and said, "O King Yama! Although we have tried to drive the wedge into wicked transgressors, we have not been able to make any cuts on their bodies. Although they have been led to walk on the blades of swords or laid on beds of needles, they have been found as if they were treading on velvet beds. Iron maces with spikes and hot balls of fire have broken and cooled by themselves. A huge cooking pot—with a vast holding capacity—was filled with hot molten iron but cooled by itself. Further, none of the transgressors suffered any injury although they were led into the Asipatra Forest where trees have grown with swords as their leaves. What has caused these strange miracles?"

King Yama replied to them, "O messengers of death! Events such as these are not unusual when bodhisattvas are condemned to hell for their evil deeds. If you do not believe this, you may go to the city called Puṣkarāvatī and see with your own eyes the mortal body of the bodhisattva. An amulet of *Pratisarā dhāraṇī* can be found on his body and a large number of gods must be there protecting it. After hearing this, the hell guards went to the place in question and they indeed saw gods and demigods all around the dead body, preparing the *Pratisarā Yantra* and paying their last respects with sweet-smelling flowers, smoking incense and camphor. When the hell guards went back to King Yama to make a report, they noticed that the monk who was there previously was no more to be found because he had already left for the Trāyatriṃshadeva heaven where he was celebrated as "Pratisarā Devaputra."

Therefore O Great Brahmā! Let it be known that it is a righteous act to learn by heart and to recite this *dhāraṇī* or to wear an amulet of this *dhāraṇī*. Not only this, O Great Brahmā! In the great city called Hiñga Mardana there once dwelled a well-known merchant named Bimala Shaṇkha who had great wealth, gold, silver, and supplies of food. He had hundreds of assistants at work in his business firm. In the course of his overseas trade in jewelry, one day he set out for Ratnadvīpa with his assistants in a ship loaded with merchandise. In the middle of the sea, a huge long sea monster—called Timiñgala—kept in check the motion of the ship in which he was traveling. At that time the angry *nāga* kings also caused heavy rainfall interspersed with thunder and lightning. Those on board were panic-stricken for fear of being drowned. At that time the merchant Bimala Shaṇkha comforted them and hoisted a flag in which was written the *Mahāpratisarā dhāraṇī*. He also started reciting the *dhāraṇī*. Immediately after this, the *nāga* kings became pacified and went away calmly, according respect to the *Pratisarā*. The sea monster Timiñgala also ran away, mistaking the ship for a huge ball of fire. Then the ship reached Ratnadvīpa safely. O Brahmā! Know that hoisting a flag with the *Mahāpratisarā dhāraṇī* written on it helps safeguard one's country.

"And furthermore, O Great Brahmā! In Magadha there was once a famous king named Prasāritapāṇi. He was given this name of "Prasāritapāṇi" because he was born with his arms outstretched. When someone came to him begging for something, he turned to the sky with his hands outstretched and the gods put in his hands valuables like gold, silver, and jewelry that he in turn gave generously to the beggars who approached him. (For this reason, too, he earned this name.)

"The king was born in Kushinagara in his previous life. At that time the Buddha incarnate was Prabhūtaratna. The essentials of *Mahāpratisarā* [recitation] were preached even then by Prabhūtaratna Buddha. A merchant, Dharmamati by name, used to invite this Buddha and his fellow monks to give religious discourses in his house. A poor person came to know this and approached the merchant Dharmamati with the double purpose of working in his household to earn a living and also to have the privilege of listening to the religious discourses by the Buddha. Very much pleased with the service of the poor fellow, the merchant one day gave him a gold coin as a bonus, which he then spent to organize a recitation of the *Pratisarā*. As the sponsor of this discourse, he wished that from the religious merit gained therefrom that the poverty of the poor be ended. "It was because of this meritorious deed in his past life that King Prasāritapāṇi could miraculously get the things he wanted merely by raising his outstretched hands aloft toward the sky, and could generously give them in charity to the poor.

"Sometime later, King Prasāritapāṇi was still issue-less: he could not beget a son despite his meritorious deeds, and so he had no peace of mind. One night, a celestial deity appeared to him in a dream who said, "O King Prasāritapāṇi! With the meritorious deeds of upholding the *Mahāpratisarā* in your previous life, you have now been able to give generously to all beings! If you place an amulet of *Mahāpratisarā* around your wife's neck, you will beget a son." The king did as instructed in the dream, constructed a *Mahāpratisarā maṇḍala*, made an amulet, and placed it round his wife's neck. As a result of it he begat a son showing auspicious signs." Thus the Tathāgata extolled the significance of the *Mahāpratisarā*.

[The Tathāgata continued:] "Not only have I expounded the truth of this *Mahāpratisarā*: it has been expounded by previous Buddhas as well. In the remotest antiquity there was a Tathāgata called "Vipulaprahasitavadanamaṇikanakaratnojjvala Rashmiprabhāpratyudgatarāja." Ready to preach a religious discourse, he was surrounded by fierce-looking *yakṣa*s holding dangerous weapons. They caused strong winds to blow and heavy rains of fire to fall. Then the Tathāgata recited the "Great Secret Vidyā" of the *Mahāpratisarā*. Immediately after this, within the sight of all the *yakṣa*s, there came out from each of his pores fierce beings holding weapons in their hands and shouting, "Hold fast the *yakṣa*s and knock them down." Then the *yakṣa*s lost their powers and ran away helter-skelter in panic. Some of them sought refuge in the Buddha and thereafter remained calm and quiet.

"O Great Brahmā! Those upholding the *Mahāpratisarā* are immune from premature death. In the remote past, there lived in Ujjayanī City a king named Brahmadatta. In that city once a person committed a capital crime and the king sentenced him to death. The king's executioners took him to a mountain cave and unsheathed their swords to behead him. At that time the criminal was chanting the *Mahāpratisarā dhāraṇī* with his eyes fixed on an amulet of the *Mahāpratisarā* tied round his right wrist. As a result of this, although the executioners wielded their swords over him, he did not suffer any injury; on the contrary, the swords smashed into pieces. This news reached the king and irritated him. Then the king wanted him to be eaten up by monsters. So his men took him to a cave where monsters dwelled and left him there. The monsters also came running in great delight to eat him up, but they could not cause him any harm because of the effect of the *Mahāpratisarā*. The monsters found his body ablaze with flames and they retreated in fear.

"When news of this result reached the king, he became even more irritated. In a fit of anger, he told his men that the criminal should be thrown into a river with his hands and feet bound. Accordingly, the criminal was thrown into the river. But as soon as he reached the river bed, the water in the river dried up by itself and the ropes by which he was bound also fell away.

"When this news reached the king, he was astonished and sent for the criminal. The king asked him the reason why he could not be put to death in these three consecutive attempts. After the king insisted on a reply, the criminal told him all about his knowledge of the *Mahāpratisarā* and showed him the amulet worn on his right wrist. Highly pleased with this man, the king then decorated him with the title of "Honored Citizen" [*nagara shreṣṭha*] and gave him a shawl as a token of respect.

"O Great Brahmā! Due to the effect of the *Mahāpratisarā*, premature death is thus avoided." The Buddha then proceeded to describe the correct procedures for constructing and worshiping the *Pañcarakṣā maṇḍala*, with *Mahāpratisarā* at the center.

Mantra

Oṃ amṛtavare vara vara pravaravishuddhe
Hūṃ hūṃ hūṃ phaṭ phaṭ phaṭ svāhā

Sāhasrapramardinī Meditation

[The goddess] emanates from the seed syllable "hūṃ"; brown-haired, black-bodied, trampling a hell guardian; having twisted eyebrows and fanged mouth; eight-armed: one of the four right hands presenting a boon-granting *mudrā*, and the other three right hands holding a hook, an arrow, and a sword; the four left hands holding a noose, a bow, a lotus blossom with a jeweled sword in the center, an axe; with four faces, the middle one black-colored, the one turned to the right white, the one behind yellow, the one turned to the left green; having three eyes in each of the four faces; posed in *lalitāsana*.

Oṃ Homage to Blessed Ārya Mahāsāhasrapramardinī!

The Pramardinī Sūtra

Once the Lord Buddha was staying on Gṛddhrakūṭa mountain. There he was accompanied by thirteen hundred monks including Shāriputra and Maudgalyāyana. King Ajātashatru of Magadha rendered his services by supplying them with food and drink and other necessities, for instance yellow robes, begging bowls, and lodging. Just then, the great city of Vaishālī was rocked by an earthquake and suffered the ravages of thunder, lightning, and rain. The people there knew not where to go and became panic-stricken. Greatly frightened, the monks and nuns invoked the *Triratna*. Those who are not the adherents of the Buddhist faith invoked Brahmā. Some of them invoked other deities including Indra. Others worshiped their patron deities (*iṣṭa-devatā*s), Mahādeva, Māṇibhadra, Hāritī, the moon, the sun, the planets, heavenly bodies, as well as mountain, tree, and river deities. The Lord Buddha through his divine knowledge came to understand the miseries of the suffering people and with the help of his supramundane power (*ṛddhi*) called all the deities from their sojourns in the three thousand realms. Brahmā and other gods came down at midnight and bowed to the Buddha who was then illuminating the whole of

Gṛddhrakuṭa mountain with the halo emitted from his body. [They then] sang a hymn of praise as follows:

Salutation to the hero among men!
Salutation to the best of men!
We pay homage to you with joined hands,
O Lord of the Dharma, Great Sage!

They also requested that the Buddha preach a discourse on the *Sāhasrapramardinī Mahāyāna Sūtra* for the purpose of controlling the ravages afflicting the country.

The Buddha observed silence for a few moments and then addressed the four guardian kings, "O Guardian Kings! What are your family members up to? Are they not giving troubles to our people, the monks and nuns, male and female novices, and the male and female *upāsaka*s? The Buddha, you know, is preaching a sermon to them. The monks are also following the Buddha's teachings. *Pratyekabuddha*s and *arhat*s have arisen in this world by the force of numerous virtuous deeds. The perfect ones and the deities now take their births in the thirty-two heavens. Similarly, great virtuous deeds can elevate beings to the status of a seven-jeweled universal monarch (*cakravartin*). I think that you all know this well. But O Guardian Kings of the four quarters! It is not proper for you to remain indifferent when the people are suffering so much. How can the Dharma be maintained when there is so much negligence on your part?

Upon hearing this from the Buddha, the guardian kings told the Buddha what diseases the people might be afflicted with, what *mantra*s they should utter, and what measures they needed to take for curing themselves of such diseases. Having heard from the guardian kings what the people had to do to get rid of the troubles instigated by the *gandharva*s, *yakṣa*s, *kuṣmāṇḍa*s, *nāga*s, the nine planets, and so forth the Buddha said to his audience, "I am endowed with energy from the ten powers (*dashabala*). I possess the Four Confidences (*Vaishāradyaṃ*). I am the one who has preached religious discourses for the welfare of humanity and who alone has given the protection needed by the people for overpowering the four Māras. Now I will tell you the *Sāhasra-*

pramardinī dhāraṇī for the good of humanity."

The Buddha then chanted the *mantra*. Immediately after this, all the cruel-natured *yakṣa*s, *gandharva*s, *kuṣmāṇḍa*s, *nāga*s, etc. left from there and ran away frightened. At that time, Dhṛtarāṣṭra was guarding the East, Virūḍhaka the south, Virūpākṣa the west, and Kubera the north. The Buddha used his supernormal power (*ṛddhi*) to go up in the sky where he remained seated in the lotus position.

Brahmā then paid homage to the Buddha and thereafter said to the guardian kings, "O Guardian Kings of the four quarters! As stated by the Buddha, *Pratyekabuddha*s, and *arhat*s: the great deities and the *ṛṣi*s well versed in the six works auxiliary to the *Veda* come to this world by the powers from their numerous meritorious deeds. It is not proper on your part to be negligent of the miseries suffered by humanity." Upon hearing this from Brahmā, the guardian kings of the four quarters brought all the cruel impure-minded demons and spirits of the four directions before the Buddha with their hands and feet bound. Then Brahmā also uttered some *mantra*s and wished all living beings health and happiness.

Then the Buddha said, "The Buddhas have arisen in this world for the welfare not of any particular person but for the welfare of all living beings. Therefore for the welfare of the people living in Vaishālī I am going there." So saying, the Buddha put on his robe and, while holding a begging bowl, came down from Vulture Peak accompanied by his thirteen hundred fellow monks. At that time the Buddha was seen flanked by Brahmā on the right and Indra on the left, who were fanning him gently with whisks; the guardian kings were seen holding an umbrella over the Buddha from behind. Following behind the Buddha were a large number of gods as well.

The Licchavis saw this scene from a distance and swept clean all the lanes and by-lanes, decorated both sides of the streets with flags and festoons, and covered the ground all over with flowers and puffed rice. The whole atmosphere was scented by smoking incense and pervaded by the gentle musical sound of bells ringing. The Buddha was lustrated, ceremonially welcomed, then escorted into the city of Vaishālī. He entered the city saying that the purpose of his visit was to bring peace and prosperity to the people living there. He also comforted them by saying that there was nothing for them to be afraid of.

In those days, long poles [*Indrakīla*] were erected in all four directions as the boundary markers of the city. The Buddha stood beside one of these poles, held aloft his hand, and addressed the citizens assembled there: "That monk or nun, male or female *upāsaka* who does the following will be immune from diseases and dangers of all sorts: respects me here and my earthly remains hereafter as relics no matter how small they are in size; memorizes or helps others to memorize the *Sāhasrapramardinī* text or teaches the essentials of it.

Upon hearing this, Brahmā begged the Buddha to recite the *Sāhasrapramardinī vidyā* to him. At his request the Buddha recited it and said that the *dhāraṇī* was based on the following:

kāye gatānusmṛti shamatha vipashyanā
the three *samādhi*s
the four *ṛddhipāda*s
the four *pradhāna*s
the four *smṛtyupasthāna*s
the four *dhyāna*s
the four Noble Truths
the five *indriya*s
the five physical powers (*bala*)
the six *anusmṛti*s
the seven factors of enlightenment (*bodhyaṇga*)
the eightfold Path
the nine *anupūrvika vihāra samāpatti*s
the ten Tathāgata powers (*tathāgata bala*)
the eleven *vimukta āyatana*s
the twelvefold *pratītyasamutpada*
the twelve *dharmacakra*s
the sixteen *ānāpānānusmṛti*s
the eighteen *āveṇika Buddha dharma*s
the forty-two letters.

"This is all in the *Sāhasrapramardinī Vidyā*, the seal of the Buddha. It constitutes the Buddha's treasure." After saying this, the Buddha uttered the following verse:

IMASKI LOKE PURIMASMI VĀ PUNA: |
SVARGEṢU YADA RATNA VARĀṆI ShANTI. ||
SAMOSTI NAIVEHA TATHĀGATENA DEVĀTIDEVENA NAROTTAMENA |
TASMĀDIDAṂ RATNAVARAṂ PRAṆĪTAṂ ETENA SATYENA IHĀSTU SVASTI ||
KṢAYAṂ VIRĀGAṂ HYAMṚTAṂ
TVASAṂSKṚTAMĀJÑĀ YA YAC SHĀKYAMUNI
PRABHĀVITAM NA TENA DHARMEṆA SAMOSTI
KASHCIDA AMṚTENA SHĀNTENA HYASAṂSKṚTENA
TASMĀDIDAṂ RATNAVARAṂ PRAṆĪTAMETENA
SATYENA IHĀSTU SVASTI ||

Upon hearing this, Brahmā, Indra, and the four guardian kings praised the Buddha, extolling his virtues. Seeing the loving-kindness of the Buddha, the impure-minded beings also felt pacified and then conformed to his teachings. Immediately after this, the whole of Vaishāli City became free from all sorts of plagues and diseases. The citizens extolled the virtues of the Buddha, Dharma, and Saṃgha. The four guardian kings then spoke reverently to the Buddha, "O Lord! Now it has been affirmed that the recitation of the *Sāhasrapramardinī* that you have preached helps not only to get rid of all dangers, diseases, and evil planetary influences, but also that it safeguards the country. You have also conveyed how its recitation leads to the protection of cattle etc. The *dhāraṇī*s of protection that one needs to utter when one takes medicine have also been taught. The symptoms of specific diseases—namely *mañjuka* and *mṛgarāja*, and so forth—and their methods of cure were also revealed at the request of Brahmā. Many other things were discussed in the assembly, including the use of an ointment made from many different herbs like *shirīṣa*, *apāmārga*, and from the burning of *añan* incense powder as medicine against innumerable diseases. After the end of the discussion, all the gods including Indra miraculously disappeared.

In the evening the Lord came out of his meditation abode and addressed the monks assembled there, "O Monks! You too learn this *Sāhasrapramardinī Mahāvidyā* and memorize it; repeat and recite it because doing so is good for protecting not only living beings but also the plants and trees. If a piece of cloth inscribed with this *mantra* is tied to the trunk of a dying tree, it will start sprouting green shoots again.

Then the companion monks said to the Buddha, "O Lord! You have told us that those who recite these five *sūtra*s—

1. *Sāhasrapramardinī sūtra*
2. *Mahāmāyūrī sūtra*
3. *Mahāshītavatī sūtra*
4. *Mahāpratisarā sūtra*
5. *Mahāmantrānusāriṇī sūtra*

—should refrain from taking the five kinds of forbidden food called *pañcāmiṣa*.[14] But when going from door to door for alms, what if we are offered one of these kinds of meat?"

Then the Buddha replied, "In that case when you are forced to accept such food, consider it to be the opposite of what you actually perceive; take it as something that does not contain any of these things; remember that everything is produced by causes and conditions that are not eternal, and that every noneternal thing is painful; since everything is painful, realize that there is no such thing as the *ātman*. The one who keeps in mind the thought of abandoning dual discernment will cease to be conscious that he is taking one of the forbidden foods. Try to take delight in the destruction of the *ātman*."

Mantra

Oṃ amṛtavilokinī garbhasarakṣaṇī ākarṣaṇī
Hūṃ hūṃ hūṃ phaṭ phaṭ phaṭ svāhā

Mahāmāyūrī Meditation

[The goddess] emanates from the seed syllable *"maṃ"*, yellow complexioned, posed in *satvaparyañkāsana*; three faced:

the middle one yellow colored, the right one blue, and the left one red; three-eyed; bedecked in jeweled ornaments; eight armed: one of four right hands presenting the *varada mudrā*, and the rest of the three right hands holding a pitcher of jewels, a *vajra*, and a sword; and the four left hands holding a begging bowl, a peafowl feather, a bell crowned with crossed *vajras*, and a flag with a jeweled pinnacle.

Homage to Blessed Mahāmāyūrī!

The Mahāmāyūri Sūtra

Once the Lord was staying at Jetavana monastery built by Anāthapiṇḍa in Shrāvastī accompanied by numerous companion monks. About the same time in the same monastery there was also dwelling a newly-ordained monk named Svāti who had little understanding of the rules of discipline. One day, Svāti was piling up logs to make a fire for heating the bodies of other companion monks who were suffering from rheumatism. From one of the logs came out a big black cobra who bit his right big toe. Immediately after the bite, the monk fell down and lay unconscious. His eyes rolled up and his mouth was full of foam. Venerable Ānanda saw him in this condition and reported it to the Buddha. Upon hearing the report from Ānanda, the Buddha said that he had his loving kindness (*maitrī*) extended to all of the serpent kings. Saying so, the Buddha preached a discourse on the knowledge of the *Mahāmāyūrī*.

The Lord said to Ānanda, "O Ānanda! Long long ago on the southern slopes of the Himālaya Mountains, there lived a famous peacock-king named Suvarṇa Vibhāsa. Every day, the peacock-king recited this *dhāraṇī* in the morning and evening and he lived happily. One day the peacock-king went out for a romantic encounter with a number of peahens and finally entered a mountain cave fully consumed with sexual desire. Inside the cave there was a snare set by a fowl hunter and the peacock-king got enmeshed in it. At that time, the peacock-king became vigilant and recited the same *dhāraṇī* and freed itself from the entanglement and lived cheerfully. O Ānanda! Keep it in mind that the peacock of that time was myself.

"In this world ["earth *maṇḍala*"] there are countless demons possessed of supernormal powers. Recite this *dhāraṇī* for their help succoring the monk Svāti. The army of demons pervading all the directions may come to his rescue. The *rākṣasī*s Lambā and Vilambā also may rescue him. The demoness *Kūṇākṣī*, also may protect him. The *nāga* kings may also protect him. The Tathāgata Vipashvī and other Tathāgatas may protect him, too. Maitreya or other Bodhisattvas also may protect him. The holy rivers like the Gangā flowing on the earth and the powerful beings living within it may protect him. The mountain kings and powerful beings living in their kingdoms can also protect him. The heavenly bodies and planets also may protect him. This earth abounds in many different herbs and plants which may protect him.

After saying this, the Buddha commanded Ānanda, "Let all the powers of the Tathāgata be with you. Go to the monk Svāti and protect him. Ānanda bowed to the Buddha and as instructed went to the monk Svāti and recited the *Mahāmāyūrī Vidyā* over him. Due to the effect of this recitation, the poison lost its effect and he recovered. When this matter was reported to the Buddha, he told the assembly of monks, nuns, and lay disciples (*upāsaka*s) that they all needed to learn the *Mahāmāyūrī Vidyā*. Since then, the practice of reciting this *dhāraṇī* came into usage among the people.

Mantra

Oṃ bhara bhara saṃbhara saṃbhara indriyavara vishodhanī
Ruru care hūṃ hūṃ hūṃ phaṭ phaṭ phaṭ svāhā

Mahāshītavatī Meditation

[The goddess] emanates from the seed syllable "shaṃ"; she is green complexioned; three faced: the middle one green colored, the right one white and the left one red; having three eyes in each of the three faces; six armed: one of the three right hands presenting the "fear not" *mudrā*, and the other right hands holding a *vajra* and an arrow; the three left hands hold a noose, a *vajra* gem, and a bow; she wears the headdress of a Tathāgata.

Homage to Mahāshitavatī!

The Mahāshītavatī Sūtra

Once the Lord was staying in Rājagṛha. In the famous Shītabana forest there was a cremation ground called "Iṇghikāyatana". The Buddha was one day imparting instructions on the methods of meditation to his companion monks and at that time the monk Rāhula was present as well. The surroundings of the place were such that it created a sense of fear in Rāhula. He then went near the Lord and bowed to him and remained seated in front of him with his eyes full of tears. Upon seeing Rāhula with a tearful face, the Buddha asked him why he was crying. Then he replied [to the Buddha], "Ever since you came to Iṇghikāyatana, the fear of ghosts, demons, tigers, bears, and snakes has been haunting my mind." Upon hearing this, the Buddha said to Rāhula, "You recite and repeat the *shītavatī mahāvidyā*. Wear an amulet with this *vidyā* written on it. Free from all fears of ghosts, demons, tigers, bears and snakes, you will be fine." Saying so, the Buddha told him the *Mahāshītavatī* recitation. Chanting this *dhāraṇī* has ever since been popular for inducing tranquility and for exorcising evil effects of various sorts.

Mantra

Oṃ vimale vipule jayavare jayavāhini amṛta
Viraje hūṃ hūṃ hūṃ phaṭ phaṭ phaṭ svāhā

Mahāmantrānusāraṇī Meditation

[The goddess] emanates from the seed syllable "trāṃ"; she is red complexioned and twelve armed: two of his hands present the *dharmacakra mudrā*; two other hands join in a *samādhi mudrā*; the other right hands present *abhaya mudrā* and hold a bow and an arrow; the remaining left hands hold a noose, a water pot with a lotus blossom in it, an umbrella with jewels and a lotus on it, and a bow; she is seated in the half-*paryañka* position.

Homage to Mahāmantrānusāriṇī!

The Mahāmantrānusāriṇī Sūtra

One day the Lord Buddha said to Ānanda, "Let us go to Vaishālī" and the Lord accompanied by Ānanda went to the Bṛji republic, and from there they reached Vaishālī. There they stayed in the grove belonging to the Āmrapālī family. At that time, a pestilence was rampant in Vaishālī. To free Vaishālī from its misfortunes, the Lord called Ānanda and said, "O Ānanda! For the purpose of quelling disasters of all sorts, you go to the Indra pillar, sit under it, and recite the *Mahāmantrānusāraṇī*. With the effect of the recitation, everything there will be happy and at peace." Saying this, the Lord revealed the knowledge of the *Mahāmantrānusāraṇī*.

As instructed, Ānanda recited the *Mahāmantrānusāraṇī* sitting under the Indra pillar. Due to the effect of this recitation, the misfortunes in the country were all eradicated. Since then the practice of reciting the *Mahāmantrā-nusāriṇī* became popular.

The Domestication of the Pañcarakṣā Texts

> In whatever house the *Pañcarakṣā* is located or whoever causes it to be read, the merit will certainly bring peace if there is trouble, anxiety, disease, or accident.
>
> Adivajra Vajracarya, *Pañcaraksā Pātha Sūtra*

The *Pañcarakṣā* is among the most traditionally utilized Mahāyāna texts in the Newar Buddhist community of Nepal (Gellner 1992: 127). It is clearly an "efficient text" (Strickmann 1990: 80) meant for ritual use. The text's very presence in Newar households is thought to be beneficial, and many families call upon members of the local *saṃgha* to read their manuscripts for a variety of reasons, especially during the Buddhist holy month of Guṃlā (Lewis 1993c). It is also read at the completion of a series of Mahāyāna *vrata*s (Locke 1987; Lewis 1989a), especially the *Lakṣacaitya Vrata* when the community creates a hundred thousand miniature *stūpa*s (Lewis 1993c; Rajapatirana 1974). Kathmandu Valley *guthi*s (Skt.: *goṣṭhi*s, "voluntary associations") have been in existence for at least several centuries and were organized by devotees wishing to sponsor regular recitations of this text.

One general reason why Newar Buddhists feel it's important to have the *Pañcarakṣā* text in their households is the widely held belief that the five deities provide thoroughgoing protection from any dangers posed by the five elements. As summarized by a recent text (A. Vajracarya 1993: jh), table 6.3 lists the correlations involved in this protection:

Table 6.3

Danger	*Deity*
Earth	Mahāsāhasrapramardinī
Space	Mahāmāyūrī
Water	Mahāpratisarā
Wind	Mahāshītavatī
Fire	Mahāmantrānusāriṇī

On the three lunar days of each month when the majority of Newar Buddhists visit major *stūpa*s and *bodhisattva* temples—the full moon and the two eighth days (*purnimā* and *aṣṭamī*, respectively)—*vajrācārya*s can be found sitting in adjacent rest houses chanting their *Pañcarakṣā* texts. It is local practice for layfolk to visit them for a short blessing ritual: in exchange for some small coins and/or rice as *dāna*, the priest will chant a *dhāraṇī* from the text, inserting the person's name, then touch the manuscript itself to the devotee's head. Periodic surveys over the last decade have shown that the *Pañcarakṣā* is by far the most used text.

It is also noteworthy to observe that the goddess Mahāpratisarā is alone invoked in the *gurumaṇḍala pūjā* performed at the start of any *vajrācārya* ritual (N. M. Vajracarya 1989: 5; Gellner 1991b).[15] Kathmandu *vajrācārya*s typically consult a text called the *Pañcarakṣāsamādhi* to construct the *Pañcarakṣā maṇḍala* needed for a householder ritual.

The *Pañcarakṣā* was once read routinely on an individual's birthday, or on the recommendation of a Buddhist astrologer if there is an inauspicious influence (*doṣa*) concerning a special occasion about which he is consulted: a wedding, the laying of a house foundation, the beginning of a journey, or a serious illness.

For birthdays, Newar Buddhists usually worship both the nine planets and the *Pañcarakṣā* deities. Each of the latter is represented by a small leaf or clay cup that contains different grains. In the simplest form, and as shown in figure 6.1, a *vajrācārya* priest leads the individual celebrating the birthday to make offerings to the deities with the correlations listed in table 6.4:

Table 6.4

Food	*Deity*
Black sesame seeds	Mahāsāhasrapramardinī
Mustard seed oil	Mahāmāyūrī
White sesame seeds	Mahāpratisarā
Green lentils	Mahāshītavatī
Red lentils	Mahāmantrānusāriṇī

For moving into a new home,[16] the family's *vajrācārya* priest usually performs a ritual called *bau biyegu*. Essential to this is when the *vajrācārya* empowers and directs the household head in nailing a *Pañcarakṣā yantra* to the main house lintel along with other items (Lewis 1984: 121). Hemraj Shakya has also noted that for completing the restoration of the great Svayambhū *stūpa*, the *Pañcarakṣā* and four other texts (*Prajñāpāramitā*, *Dashabhūmīshvara*, *Ṣaḍdharmapuṇḍarīka*, and *Svayambhū Purāṇa*) must be chanted (Shakya 1978: 286).

For elaborate *dhāraṇī* protection, especially in the face of a period of major inauspiciousness, Newar astrologers may prescribe *dāna* to each of the five deities. (See the appropriate offering list in table 6.3.) Others who attune their lives to astrological influences may chant the text at any other inauspicious times, for instance, during eclipses or intercalary months.

Another such occasion is for the *ghaḥsu* rituals performed on the twelfth day of Buddhist mourning; when the house and those

Fig. 6.1. Vajrācārya Giving *Pañcarakṣā* Blessings

living within are repurified (Lewis 1984: 322–23), a *vajrācārya* may also be called to recite *Pañcarakṣā dhāraṇīs*, an observance especially recommended by Kathmandu *vajrācāryas* when *ghaḥsu* falls on a Monday or, most dangerously, on Wednesday. This ritual is felt to be so effective that some Hindu Newars who normally utilize Brahman *pūjāris* for other life-cycle events may call a *vajrācārya* for this ritual. Thus, the *Pañcarakṣā* even has a role in Newar Hindu families.[17]

The Newar *vajrācāryas* may serve their patrons by reciting the text at any important moments in the householder's life cycle. Special resort to the *Pañcarakṣā* tradition has been incorporated into three important life-cycle rites. The first is for the baby rite called *Macā Jaṃko*,[18] when an amulet in the form of a necklace includes five items symbolizing the *Pañcarakṣā*. Second, the *Pañcarakṣā* has a role at the end of the life span in a ritual called *Buḍa / Buḍi Jaṃko*. This two-day observance is performed when an elder reaches seventy-seven years and seven months (Lewis 1984: 299-307; Pal 1977): as part of the many rituals done to achieve merit and to assure longevity, chanting and *dāna* are offered to the five deities arrayed on a *maṇḍala*. At the center of this *maṇḍala* is *Mahāpratisarā*, with the other four deities directionally situated as in the *Sādhanamālā* (#206). (In the usual Newar rendering, only the symbols of each are drawn; see fig. 6.2.) In the concentric rings around the *Pañcarakṣā* are found the eight *bodhisattvas*, the nine planets, and the ten *lokapālas* (R. Vajracarya 1981: 49–50). Note that this practice is consistent with the promise made in the *Mahāpratisarā Sūtra* story in which control over the planets and other deities is achieved with this *dhāraṇī* recitation. The offerings made to each over the two-day ritual are specified precisely in a modern manual:

Mahāpratisarā

flowers, white flowers, diamonds, pearls, sandalwood, white sesame seed oil, yogurt, sweet puffed rice, brown sugar, white sesame seeds, gold leaf with flame inscribed on it, *taṣī* fruit;

Sāhashrapramardinī

scent, blue sapphire, flowers, musk, dark sesame oil, gold leaf with *vajra* and a flame inscribed, yogurt, ghee, rice pancake, wild *jhamsī* fruit, black sesame seeds;

Fig. 6.2. Lintel *Pañcarakṣā Yantra*

Fig. 6.3. Making the Navagraha *Maṇḍala*, Featuring the *Pañcarakṣā* in the Center

Mahāmāyūrī

scent, *Aju* flower, gold flowers, sandalwood, mustard oil, gold leaf with jewel inscribed, ghee-honey mixture, turmeric-flavored rice, *khaisī* fruit, bread, yellow mustard seed;

Mahāshītavatī

musk, *kule* flower, ruby, lotus, red vermilion, black mustard, gold leaf with lotus inscribed, sweet bread, milk-soaked brown rice, red lentils;

Mahāmantrānusāraṇī

camphor, *shāla* incense, blue sapphire, mustard oil, gold leaf with peacock inscribed, puffed rice, boiled rice, wild fruit, green lentils.

These *pūjā* offerings are in fact appropriate for all other ceremonies involving the *Pañcarakṣā*.

Another use of the *Buḍa/Buḍi Jaṃko* rites, a function consistent with their apotropaic function generally, finds the five *Pañcarakṣā* deities on the Uṣṇīṣavijayā painting or sculpture that families must also make as part of the ceremonies designed to strengthen the elderly and to prepare them for death (Chakravarti 1969: 128–29; Pal 1977: figs. 1–6; Lewis 1996a: 15–16).

The third use of the *Pañcarakṣā* text in life-cycle rites is at the time of death. The *Pañcarakṣā* deities form a circle of guardians around the *Durgatiparishodhana tantra maṇḍala* drawn by the family *vajrācārya* immediately after death (R. K. Vajracarya 1981: 104; Lewis 1984: 316–20). Having the text read is especially important in cases when an individual dies inauspiciously: it should be read as part of the last rites and in the year of mourning. Newar Buddhists feel that doing this is essential when a person dies in a violent accident, especially when the corpse cannot be recovered for proper cremation (and only the horoscope is burned at the *ghat*).

There is one final Newar astrological death belief of note: according to informants conversant in Vajrayāna astrological systems, of the twenty-seven stars (*nakṣatra*), five are "evil stars." In the event that someone dies while the moon is in the rising phase and located in the first of these five, Newar belief is that four more people will die and so the *Pañcarakṣā* must be read out of compassion to save those in danger.

Amulets derived from the *Pañcarakṣā* and the system of medicine described in the text have also been popular in Nepalese healing traditions. Special incense and *yantra*s are made based upon the text to ward off troublesome *bhūta*s and *preta*s. There is even a common piece of jewelry made by local artisans to be worn by layfolk: a bracelet fashioned of the five metals (iron, copper, brass, silver, and gold) that represent the five deities of the *Pañcarakṣā* text.[19]

Prominent practices associated with royalty and government likewise illustrate the text's domestication in the local polity, Each year during the Kathmandu Indra Jātra festival,[20] there is a chariot procession led by the royal *kumārī* throughout the city that includes five *vajrācārya*s representing the Pañca Buddhas. Before this procession begins with the king's appearance outside the royal palace, the *Pañcarakṣā dhāraṇī*s must be read. Another use of the text was in pre-1950 legal proceedings: the *Pañcarakṣā* was the book used when Buddhists had to swear an oath (Hodgson 1972: 18). The kings of late medieval Nepal also had the text read whenever inauspicious omens were noted or when misfortunes occurred (Shakya 1977: 163, 223). For example, King Bhaskar Malla of Kathmandu (ruled 1700–22) had it read twenty-one times at several points in his reign (Shakya 1977: 223).

Ritual Sites, Architecture, and Painting

The *Pañcarakṣā* text is located in most monasteries and in many homes. Sometimes these works are illustrated with fine miniature paintings or line drawings of the goddesses (e.g., Pal 1975); and there are also extant examples of hanging paintings showing the *maṇḍala*-like arrangement of Buddhas and allied *Pañcarakṣā* deities (e.g., Kreijger 1999, #28 and 32).

Several sites in the Kathmandu Valley's sacred geography have special associations with the *Pañcarakṣā* tradition. A ritual guidebook from Kathmandu lists the *Pramoda Tīrtha* that is located on the Bagmati River among the twelve main Buddhist pilgrimage sites and it is especially here where the *Pañcarakṣā* should be read (R. K. Vajracarya 1981: 122).[21] Another temple is the Maitidevī temple northeast of old Kathmandu. Mary Slusser has suggested that "Maitidevī" is derived from "Māyūrī Tīrtha" and was once a center for worshiping the *Pañcarakṣā* goddesses, but later this identity was superseded by an *aṣṭamātṛka* shrine and by the later identification of the Hindu goddesses there as the "Pañca Kaumārī" (Slusser 1982: 335). Such blurring of Hindu-Buddhist boundaries in the pragmatic traditions of the Kathmandu Valley was especially pronounced in the late medieval period.

Another association of the *Pañcarakṣā* goddesses has been with Hārītī, the *rakṣasī* converted by the Buddha who came to safeguard children. The major Hārītī temple in the valley located at Svayambhū has images of the *Pañcarakṣā* deities adorning its main *toraṇa*. But there may be more ancient precedents here as well: a Newar ritual text describing the method of Buddhist offerings to Hārītī, the *Hārītī Pūjāviddha*, also lists short invocation *mantras* for each of the five deities (B. Bajracarya 1988: 5).

Other Newar Buddhist monuments bear the *Pañcarakṣā* in sculpture. The most common location is on the roof struts of the *vihāras*. The most well-known set is in Kathmandu's Guṇākara Vihāra (New.: Chusya Bāhā, constructed in the seventeenth century), where all five deities are depicted in an unusual two-handed form (Van Kooji 1977) according to the *Nispannayogāvalī* (Mevissen 1989: 422). Along with other protective deities associated with the days of the week and with the lunar mansions, the *Pañcarakṣā* deities at this site are arranged in the order of one old and often-used ritual chanting book, the *Dhāraṇīsaṃgraha*; the strut positioning in the Chusya Bāhā courtyard enables devotees to recite their respective spells in textual order as they circumambulate the monastic courtyard. Here, again, we find texts and artworks established to serve the purpose of ritual practice.

Observations on the History of Practical Buddhism

The Pañcarakṣā and Spiritual Conquest

Wherever Buddhist missionaries established the faith, they proclaimed the spiritual superiority of the Three Jewels. In service of spiritual and cultural conquest, famous Buddhist saints of the Buddhist *saṃgha* converted the *nāgas* or *yakṣas* of the new territory (e.g., Falk 1973: 13), defeated competing ritualists in duels of magic (e.g., Samuel 1993: 265–69), and incorporated local practices into their hierarchy of spiritual disciplines (Nakamura 1973; Lehman 1971). Likewise, the texts of popular Buddhism are replete with stories showing that all deities are limited, semideluded beings who are always inferior to the Buddha and *bodhisattvas*, and that rituals stemming from the Buddha and his utterances (*dharma*) are preeminently effective.

The *Pañcarakṣā* stories, like others in this ritual protection genre (e.g., the "Consecration Sūtra" [Strickmann 1990] or the "Prajñāpāramitā Sūtra for Humane Kings Who Wish to Protect their

States" [Orzech 1989]), provide examples of Buddhism's style of dominating the religious landscape, with Buddhist supremacy achieved through compassionate, bloodless conquest.[22] Chanting the *Mahāpratisarā Sūtra*, for example, should be seen as a potent missionary tool in non-Buddhist cultural environments: it can repel the fiercest *yakṣa*s, causing their fear and leading to their taking refuge in the *triratna*.

The *Mahāsāhasrapramardinī Sūtra* contains a more extended discussion of how Buddhism reorders and dominates the entire pantheon, with the Four Guardian Kings charged with controlling the lesser deities, demons, and spirits.[23] Granted the Buddha's recognition of their mundane powers, the great deities are then respected for the healing and controlling *mantra*s they reveal, although the Buddha-revealed *mantra*s are clearly deemed superior. This text is congruent with the modern Sri Lankan Buddhist concept of the Buddha's *varan* (warrant) that legitimizes and controls all divinities (e.g., Obeyesekere 1964).

Buddhist Boundary Maintenance, Social Philosophy, and Statecraft

It was Buddhist missionary practice to accept local deity traditions after subordinating and rearranging them according to the norms of dominance. This made it easy for myriad ethnic groups in Asia to adopt the faith and not to abandon their ancestral identities. But given this great tolerance, Buddhism in practice seems to have emphasized certain texts—and their related ritual practices—that *emphatically* reasserted Buddhist dominance. This has been noted in relation to the Tibetan yearly festival of masked dances depicting the original conquest of Tibetan deities and their ritualists by Buddhist saints (e.g., Samuel 1993). The *Pañcarakṣā* stories express this same theme: all local spirits submit to the power of the Buddha and to those who chant his words.

The *Pañcarakṣā* also orders the pantheon in a manner that renders all deities subservient to Buddhist divinities and ritualists. The implicit social ramifications of this doctrinal assertion are significant: they establish the fact that monks and devotees have higher standing than ritualists of competing "local" deities.

In several narratives in the text (esp. I,6), like many *jātaka*s, kings are the main actors and the stories seemed to be directed to them. For them, the text includes instructions on how a king can defeat foes in battle without bloodshed by resorting to *Pañcarakṣā* amulets. It also promises prosperity if monks chant the text or make the empowered amulets as prescribed. The history of medieval Nepal, which has already been noted, offers examples of the *Pañcarakṣā* text being used just as intended. The text likewise found royal audiences in both China and Japan where it was used to impress emperors by demonstrating Buddhism's beneficent utility. Buddhist traditions in both countries emphasized the chanting of the *dhāraṇī*s, especially those of the Mahāmāyūrī cult (DeVisser 1976: 207).[24] In this use of *Pañcarakṣā* rituals, it is evident how some Buddhist monks, far from being aloof or apolitical, were doubtless major actors who sought to affect their polities.

The Tradition of Ritual Power

There have been claims of *dhāraṇī* efficacy in the *Pañcarakṣā* that are hard to reconcile with theories of individualistic Buddhist moral retribution as expressed in more philosophical tracts. The sense of Buddhist orthopraxy outlined in the text also seems to express the evolutionary pattern of later South Asian Buddhism, emphasizing an individual's contact with the power of Buddhist *mantra*s and hierophants as a priority over the goal of personal transformation through moral observance or meditation.[25] The ultimate case of this paradoxical situation has been the time of death; compassionate counsel is offered to the dying so that they pass on to the best possible rebirth . . . regardless of the person's prior *karman*. This practical approach to death, most known by modern students of Buddhism from *The Tibetan Book of the Dead*, is actually found in the early Indic canons, including the Pali *sutta*s (de Silva 1993: 36). It was the masters in the Mahāyāna-Vajrayāna traditions who developed the pan-Buddhist sense of ritual intervention to their greatest level of elaboration.

The study of Newar Buddhist practice opens up one final digression regarding a transregional pattern of cultural evolution: did the emphasis and elaborate ritualistic development promoted by Mahāyāna adepts contribute to the tradition's institutional history by legitimating householder *saṃgha*s that claimed legitimacy through ritualistic expertise rather than strict moralism or spiritual charisma? What were the sociohistorical effects of later Mahāyāna traditions' "it works" attitude that evolved concerning prosperity, power, and *karman* diversion at death, a view supported by the myriad miracle claims in the *Pañcarakṣā* and in similar Mahāyāna texts? One causal line seems to have culminated in the viewpoint expressed in tantric texts like the *Tattvasaṃgraha*, a *tantra* source that often is cited in modern Nepalese ritual guidebooks:

> Even those beings who cling to wealth and food and drink and detestable things, who take no pleasure in the vow and are not proficient in the preliminaries and so on, even they, by acting in accordance with their understanding and entering the *maṇḍala*, will bring to perfection what they have in mind. (Translated in Snellgrove 1959: 211.)

What were the consequences of Mahāyāna Buddhism's extravagant claims for rituals, especially when it de-emphasized moral retribution in favor of the power of *mantra*s and rituals?

CHAPTER 7

Summary and Conclusions: The Domestication of Indic Buddhism and Its Construction in Modern Scholarship

We of the higher classes (so called) . . . are trained to seek the choice, the rare, the exquisite, exclusively, and to overlook the common. We are stuffed with abstract conceptions, and glib with verbalities and verbosities; and in the culture of these higher functions . . . we grow stone-blind and insensible to life's more elementary and general goods and joys.

William James
(Quoted in Lawrence W. Levine, *The Opening of the American Mind: Canons, Culture, and History*)

The authentic tradition of orthodoxy was not a matter to be decided by an intellectually formulated "rule of faith" set forth by scholars and theologians, but by the "rule of prayer" of "the thousand of silent believers, who worshipped in spirit and truth."

Jaroslav Pelikan, *The Vindication of Tradition*

The claim of supernatural power of recitation may be disputable among scholars as well as sectarians, yet one point has clearly emerged. . . . From an insider's viewpoint, the power of recitation is extremely powerful, and in certain cases, it is claimed to be even more powerful and preferable than either a philosophical understanding or the excellence in moral disciplines.

Jan Yun-hua, "Buddhist Self-Imolation in Medieval China"

Having examined the "practical Buddhist traditions" derived from five texts domesticated in the Kathmandu Valley, what do these case studies suggest about the dynamics of community belief and practice that shaped Buddhism elsewhere? Is the vibrant center of Buddhism that inspired the laity's patronage that of meditation and philosophical analysis? In this concluding chapter, I would like to consider the ways in which scholars have selectively conceptualized the Buddhist tradition and pose an alternative formulation that places as central figures the monastic masters who wielded ritual power and who conveyed the essentials of faith through stories.

The Intellectual Construction of Buddhism

In the study of Buddhism, as in many other fields of cross-cultural inquiry, there has been a natural propensity for intellectuals to be drawn to the study of other intellectuals. Scholars have indeed been very successful in showing how Buddhist philosophers have met high standards of logical-intellectual rigor and that Buddhist meditation masters have explored entirely unique arenas of human spiritual experience. In both areas, textual scholars have contributed a very important body of translated sources and intellectual understanding to the history of world religions. This work has won recognition for Buddhist philosophies, philosophers, and forms of meditation.

For the cultural historian, however, the narrow focus on literate elites and on their texts has left many fundamental issues skewed or unresolved, stuck in nineteenth-century categories. Historical presentations privileging philosophical texts have also constructed the Buddhist tradition without utilizing other domains of cultural evidence, remaining woefully untouched by the dissonant findings of archaeological and epigraphic sources (Schopen 1991d) and disconnected from the cultural media of art history. Added to this, modern anthropological demonstrations of the scarcity of monk-scholars in the transmission of tradition have likewise made little impact on the predisposition of Western intellectuals to assume the normative centrality of literati in portraying Buddhism.[1] Thus, textually based renderings of Buddhist tradition in history remain skewed toward the intellectuals and in modern imagination Buddhism is reduced to philosophy. In the process, too, Buddhist history contracts to be the outcome of contending ideas and the humanity of Buddhist devotees is reduced to intellect. The growing publications directed to interested Westerners or to modern Euro-American converts have also been quite friendly to this idealizing and reductive discourse.

This selective and appropriative elitism is a continuation of the early investigators and exponents of Buddhism who were hoping to find in the tradition an antidote to (in their view) the blind ritualism and irrational monotheisms of Europe[2], often importing Protestant assumptions and categories about "true religion" in the process (Eckel 1994; Obeyesekere 1991; Gombrich and Obeyesekere 1988: 202–40). It was also convenient for scholars to dismiss modern practices as "distortions" or as "degenerations" of a "true Buddhism" that Europeans alone were equipped to "rediscover" in antiquity.[3] Modern scholars in Buddhist studies have only quite recently begun to confront this legacy of colonial orientalism in their discipline. Converging with several points just made on the need for more sociocultural models, Donald S. Lopez Jr. writes of the field's "curatorship" as follows:

> But the Buddhism that largely concerned European scholars was an historical projection derived exclusively from manuscripts and blockprints, texts devoted largely to a "philosophy," which has been produced and had circulated among a small circle of monastic elites. With rare exception, there was little interest in the ways in which such texts were put to use in the service of various ritual functions. Buddhist studies has thus been to a great degree the history of master texts, dominated by scholastic categories it seeks to elucidate, what Said has called a "paradigmatic fossilization" based upon "the finality and closure of antiquarian or curatorial knowledge." (Lopez 1995b: 7)

The cost of this selectivity remains great, however, as the older paradigms endure and as "academic fossilizations" reproduce the earlier biases. As a result, there has been very slow progress in understanding how and why Buddhist institutions and cultures evolved across Asia. Textbooks still purvey a propensity to ill-founded discussions about who "true Buddhists" are (or were), on such issues as Buddhism's "atheistic" or "anticaste" ideology; they privilege belief over practice in defining Buddhist identity, fail to make intelligible the 95 percent of Buddhists who were householders, and ignore the idealistic and inclusive utopian vision that Buddhism held for entire societies. I suspect, as I will indicate, that even the Western construction of the small sector of Buddhist virtuosos as resolutely isolated from the popular traditions is, as well, a distortion. As a result, the wider public audience who reads this scholarship—students, scholars in other fields, journalists, and so forth—still encounter Buddhism and Buddhists with naive, elitist biases.

Buddhist scholarship has yet to bring the tradition into comparative religion discussions in a coherent manner: if one of the first principles of comparative religion methodology is "to compare like with like" and to carefully match level to level, modern representations of Buddhism through textual evidence still hardly attempt to convey socioculturally informed renderings of the tradition. These distortions in representing the tradition also give no foundation on which to build an understanding of the vicissitudes faced by contemporary rank and file Buddhists and Buddhist institutions in modernizing Asia.

Toward a Buddhist Sociological Imagination

A *sociological imagination of Buddhism*, to adapt C. Wright Mills's terms, must recognize the fact that economic resources and political alliances have been as crucial to the tradition's successful global domestications as ideas were. It is essential that the historical imagination of Buddhist societies be built upon the textually defined norm of religious pluralism within Buddhist cultures, imagining societies composed of a broad spectrum of individuals pursuing different spiritual regimens. Monks, layfolk, and even followers of other religious schools were all seen as converging "on the path" heading through rebirth levels toward eventual *nirvāṇa*-realization. Buddhism in any social context cannot be understood as based upon unified philosophical schools in isolation; nor was the *saṃgha* centered on a singular doctrinal orthodoxy but on conformity to discipline; monasteries of course varied but their leaders were most commonly concerned with the practical perpetuation of the faith's material and spiritual culture in a manner that could dominate the socioreligious life of the surrounding community. The monastic institutions that maintained Buddhism in any locality did so through interlocking economic, ritual, educational, medical, artistic, political, and meditation activities. Service to the local community was essential to institutional survival, prior to any philosophical or scholarly pursuits. An anthropologically informed history of Buddhism cannot ignore the fact that these institutions mediated the texts and shaped the history of Buddhist cultures.

It is also time to abandon a misbegotten legacy of early anthropological theory that was merged with the curatorial text/literati bias: to us a two-level model for Buddhist communities that divides the "true ordained followers" from everyone else (Cabezon 1995: 262; Dargyay 1988). This idealization is undermined decisively in the biographies of Theravāda saints, Mahāyāna philosophers, and Vajrayāna masters. Many of these esteemed philosophers and scholars did not denounce "folk religion" or "popular devotional practices" for everyone, but only for those few in the advanced stages of practice. Yet, this "reductive orthodox" model has been quite influential among those studying the elite's Buddhist traditions; with them has followed a concomitant dismissive interpretation of the story narratives as conveying compromised and incomplete views of the teachings, being mere "vulgarizations" of proper Buddhist thought as a concession to the masses (Hallisey and Hansen 1996: 309).

Further, while the two-tier imagination of Buddhism finds little support from epigraphic or anthropological accounts pertaining to monastic roles or institutions, it also defies the tradition's own early and textually located notion of *anupūrvikathā*, "the gradual path" (Bond 1988; Pezzali 1993).[4] This model notion entailed a fundamental definition of society as a multipoint hierarchy of beings who are different according to their *karman* and spiritual capacities. In the "gradual path," too, we find the central ideal of individuals dutifully supporting ongoing exchanges in every society that shape and sustain Buddhism, linking through ritual and patronage the advanced practitioners with the beginners. As George D. Bond has pointed out:[5]

> The notion of the path links all diverse persons, stages, and goals. Although these manuals define some *sutta*s as mundane and others as supramundane, and though they identify some *sutta*s as applying to ordinary persons and others applying to adepts, the manuals do not regard these as distinct religious paths; they do not separate the kammic from the nibbanic path. Though the path has many levels and applications, the dhamma is one and the path one. This . . . is the secret to understanding the logic and meaning of the Buddha's teachings. (Bond 1988: 42)

This inclusivity applies as well to Mahāyāna contexts, with the appreciation of teaching and ritual performance as *upāya*s, expressions of a *bodhisattva*'s skillful assistance to the community.[6] In short, "normative Buddhism" exists throughout the social order.

Thus, the presentation of the elite as "the sole norm" is an ethnocentric notion, a projection doubtless agreeable to some, but it is ahistorical and not based upon textual authority. This idealizing paradigm of Buddhism dominated by aloof, meditating ascetics and controlled by intellectuals is unsuitable for portraying the typical Buddhist monk or nun; and it certainly cannot stand scrutiny as a model for the history of Buddhism's doctrinal or institutional evolution (Tambiah 1973). As Gregory Schopen has pointed out:

> The actual monk, unlike the textual monk, appears to have been deeply involved in religious giving and cult practice of every kind from the beginning. He is preoccupied not with *nirvāṇa* but above all else with what appears to have been a strongly felt obligation to his parents, whether living or dead. He is concerned as well, for example, with the health of his companions and teachers. (Schopen 1988–89: 167)

Privileging textual sources in Buddhist studies has distorted the field's historical development by directing students to high philosophy and ascetic esoterica, by inflating (even if unintendedly) the importance of the intellectual traditions, and by skewing assessments of the faith's history.[7] The hegemony of master text scholarship has caused scholars in Buddhist studies not only to neglect the articulation of Buddhist institutions, cultures, and societies; it has also impoverished the treatment of the doctrine itself. As Jose Ignacio Cabezon has pointed out:

> The claim is not simply that the investigation of other semiotic forms should exist alongside the study of doctrine as it is found in written texts, but that doctrine itself cannot be fully understood independent of culture in the broad sense of the term. (Cabezon 1995: 263)

Although this complaint is an academic one in origin, it does have implications far beyond academia. Taking texts alone as representative of Buddhism has led many Westerners—including students—to view "typical Buddhists" who do not conform to the modern construction of the elite ideal with derision or condescension.[8]

Further, this misconstruction has been one reason why Western converts and immigrant Buddhists have remained isolated from one another in North America and in Europe (Nattier 1995). The overidealizing and disembodied philosophy-centered imagination of the faith has also led to neglecting the most widespread texts and practices in every Buddhist society: story narratives and rituals.

Story Narratives as the Central Texts in Buddhist Societies

Evidence for the centrality of narratives in Indic Buddhism comes from their early compilation and the vast accumulation of story collections, indicating popular interest in these parables and the universal need for scholars to redact them; it also comes in a quite straightforward way from another often-disconnected sample of information: the record of sculpture and painting. Attention to the content analysis of Buddhist art at *stūpa*s and at monasteries from the earliest days onward likewise demonstrates that it was the story narratives that shaped the minds, spiritual imaginations, and moral landmarks of most Buddhists, including monks and nuns.

To understand the sources of doctrinal definition, moral guidance, or popular rituals in the history of Buddhism in any locality, then, one must look to the popular narratives, not to the "classics" of the intellectual elite. A tough-minded cultural historian's approach might even decide: better to assume that the latter literature was marginal in Buddhist societies unless proven otherwise. These narratives include the collections of *jātaka* and *avadāna*, as well as the stories integrated with ritual manuals.

The centrality of this genre of vernacular literature in guiding Newar tradition is not a modern innovation or peculiar to the Himalayas, but continues a long-standing dialectic of domestication from ancient sources. A large number of narratives appear to come from the *Vinaya* compilations themselves, indicating again that it was monks and nuns who were concerned with orthopraxy, ritual performances, patronage, and storytelling.[9] That these "popular" stories were taken seriously and read carefully by the literati is confirmed by their use in the early legal systems of Southeast Asia (Lingat 1937, Huxley 1997).

One strategy for reimagining Buddhism might be to construct an inductive model of doctrine from such story collections and compare it with the more systematic formulations of the philosophers. (I suspect the former will converge more closely with the inscriptional data.) The potential results from focusing on texts that we know

Fig. 7.1. Painting Showing The Siṃhalasārthabāhu Avadāna in a Nepalese *Vihāra*

were connected with the householders should prove to be salutary: "Attention to the worklike aspects of the texts may help us to educate our imaginations, such that we do feel that we have a reasonable idea about what subsequent Buddhists might have learned from a story" (Hallisey and Hansen 1996: 311).

In the Newar case studies surveyed involving narratives that have been told and retold in public storytelling, there is evidence that Buddhism in practice was much less individualistic, antiwoman, and antifamily than expected;[10] that Buddhism was quite at home with the norms of Brahmanic society in respecting caste privilege, acquiescing to the logic of widow immolation, accepting the deities of the pantheon (albeit demoting their superior status); and that rituals aimed at fostering prosperity, health, and wealth were regarded as powerful and pivotal to the "true Buddhist's" religious identity and life-style.

From ancient times narratives have performed very important roles within Buddhist polities. These include envisioning the society's moral imagination, tracing the realm of karmic retribution, and providing a venue for entertaining Buddhist utopian scenarios.[11] The Newar stories in this book illustrate these functions abundantly: husbands and wives are reunited, demonesses are removed from the scene by a merchant-king, rulers find rituals and fierce protectors to pacify their realms, monks alleviate their fear and gain support in their practice, and Buddhas bestow *dhāraṇī* recitations linked to ritual practices that can redress all forms of suffering. The *dharma* may lead elites to realize nirvāṇa; but the narratives convey that there was a more widespread and pragmatic notion of the *dharma* in Buddhist communities: *the dharma also protects those who take refuge in it*. The *dharma* as the distilled words of the Buddha can repel evil and create good; and since it articulates and upholds the law of moral causation—the central theme of most popular narratives—the *dharma* also opens up the most efficient path to winning future prosperity through teachings on merit-making. As the *Mahāvastu* states, "For verily *dharma* protects him who lives by *dharma*, as a large umbrella protects us in time of rain" (Jones 1952, 2: 77).

Thus, to make the most reliable connection with the center of Buddhist belief and practice—with *dharma* as most Buddhists regarded it—I suggest that we cease privileging the philosophers and their canons, and turn to the neglected sources: ritual texts, narratives, and inscriptions.[12] While scholarship in these areas has been scant but increasing, these voices composed by, and most often heard by, typical Buddhists offer one solution to understanding Buddhism in history free from the burden of intellectualist idealization.

The Preeminent Buddhist Ideology: Merit-Making

The dominant ideology operant in Buddhist communities throughout history, including that of the great majority of monastics, has been that of merit accumulation. The logic of Buddhist institutional history in every locality has been shaped by those householders and monastics (Schopen 1985a, 1991a, 1993a) seeking to make merit for current happiness and better rebirth either as a human or god (Lopez 1995a: 15). This point, made in a key article by Gananath Obeyesekere (1968) for Theravāda contexts, has been noted for other culture areas where Buddhism was domesticated (e.g., for Tibet [Gombo 1985; Samuel 1993]; for China [Gernet 1995]).

Yet it is striking how early canonical texts dealing with merit and with the practical ethos of proper human striving have been downplayed or ignored in Western accounts of Buddhist doctrinal tradition. Once sought, however, there are many passages that cover this territory with sublety and insight. One notable Pali text is worth careful consideration, as it connects with themes and concerns found in the modern Mahāyāna culture of Nepal. This passage from the *Anguttara Nikāya* (IV, VII, 61) treats the issue of merit and the householder life directly, as Shākyamuni instructs the ideal Buddhist to seek "The Four Conditions":

> Housefather, there are these four conditions which are desirable, dear, delightful, hard to win in the world. Which four? . . .
>
> [1] Wealth being gotten by lawful means. . . .
> [2] Good report gotten by me along with my kinsmen and teachers. . . .
> [3] Long life and attain a great age. . . .
> [4] When the body breaks up, on the other side of death may I attain happy birth, the heaven world! . . .
>
> (Woodward 1992, 2: 74, with numbering added)

The text then proceeds to specify how the moral and wealthy Buddhist householder should attain these goals by doing the "The Four Good Deeds":

> Now, housefather, that same Aryan disciple, with the wealth acquired by energetic striving, amassed by strength of arm, won by sweat, lawful and lawfully gotten, is the doer of four deeds. What are the four?
>
> [1] [He] makes himself happy and cheerful, he is a contriver of perfect happiness; he makes his mother and father, his children and wife, his servants and workmen, his friends and comrades cheerful and happy. This . . . is the first opportunity seized by him, turned to merit and fittingly made use of.
> [2] Then again, the . . . disciple . . . with that wealth makes himself secure against all misfortunes whatsoever, such as may happen by way of fire, water, the king, a robber, an ill-disposed person. . . . He takes steps for his defense and makes himself secure. . . .
> [3] Then again . . . the disciple . . . is a maker of the five-fold

> offering (*bali*), namely: to relatives, to guests, to departed hungry ghosts, to the king, and to the gods (*devatā*). . . .
>
> [4] Then again, the . . . disciple . . . offers a gift to all such recluses and brahmins as abstain from sloth and negligence, who are bent on kindness and forbearance, who tame the one self, calm the one self . . . to such he offers a gift which has the highest results, a gift heavenly, resulting in happiness and leading to heaven.
>
> (75–76)

This teaching passage starts with the praise of one whose wealth has been used fittingly, who has seized the opportunity, and who has "turned [it] to merit."

The provisions and actions articulated here are congruent with the Newar texts examined in this book, echoing their concern with family, wealth, rituals, and protection, and its themes and ideals should be taken seriously as "normative Buddhism" for householders. In the realm of the laity's spiritual imagination shaped by popular narratives and ritual, we have seen that Buddhist merit-making "cheats death" by reuniting couples after death and by reuniting the rich with their wealth. Merit-making is also *not* strictly individualistic, as actions by husbands and wives, patrons and shipmates, and monks and kings may affect the destinies of others. Finally, heavenly rebirth was recognized as an exalted religious goal to strive for as well. In short, householder practice across the Buddhist world is centered on merit-making (often collective in practice and effect), showing respect for local deities, and heaven seeking.

Yet like the archaeological findings indicating monk donors and local Arhat relic cults, texts like this and prosperity rituals concerned with less than *nirvāṇa*-seeking have been consistently discounted as sources for understanding the "true Buddhist" in the Western historical imagination. So many false assumptions and ridiculous sociocultural assertions about this religious tradition ancient and modern, could have been avoided by comprehending the worldview and ethos, to use Clifford Geertz's terms (1966), implicit in the householder tradition. In the *Anguttara* summary and in the Nepalese texts, we see that Buddhism fosters family ties, encourages an "energetic striving" after economic success, promotes the worship of hungry ghosts and local gods, justifies the rightful seeking after worldly happiness and security, applauds the religious virtues of faith and heaven-seeking, and underlines the necessity of being a donor and patron. This is the pragmatic side of the *dharma* which, however nuanced in every local community, shaped the domestication of Buddhism from Sri Lanka to the Himalayas, from Central Asia to Japan. I suggest that by shifting focus from elites to householders, committing to memory (and analysis) "The Four Good Deeds" alongside "The Four Noble Truths" as distillations of "normative Buddhism," we can recognize that pragmatic well-being, moral cultivation, and *nirvāṇa*-seeking were the interlocking triple tracks of legitimate Buddhist striving throughout history. This coexistence is evident in the narrative realm, seen in the juxtaposed images of *mithuna* couples and pragmatic deities (e.g., Hārītī and *nāga*s) at *stūpa*s, and made clear from the content and development of Buddhist ritualism.

Mahāyāna: A Religion of Philosophical Analysis or Ritual Power?

The domestication of narrative traditions in Nepal points to the ritual process evident in the later history of Mahāyāna Buddhism. We can see in these traditions how the faith in practice evolved to emphasize *puṇya*-making, health maintenance, protection from supernaturals, and powerful death rites; the *saṃgha* addressed these needs in adopting practices that ensured ongoing lay-*saṃgha* exchanges that supported the community of householders, ritualists, folklorists, and renunciants.[13] Whatever else we might surmise about the faith's variegated history, texts such as the widely traveled *Pañcarakṣā* point to the Buddhist propensity to ritualize spiritual ideals and to incorporate pragmatic traditions into monastic iconography and ritualism, textual chanting, *stūpa* devotions, the festival year, and the life-cycle rites of specific communities. By charting a text's domestication in a particular context, we can see, as David Seyfort Ruegg has noted, that "Buddhism is indeed not only philosophy and/or religion but also a way of living and being, a cultural and value system permitting Buddhists in vast areas of the world to construct so much of their mundane as well as spiritual lives" (Ruegg 1995: 104).

The neglect of ritual in the understanding of Buddhism (and Buddhists) has also obscured the application of Buddhist doctrinal constructs into the events of "real life," especially childhood, marriage, old age, and after-death contingency. Far from being a "vulgarization" or a "concession" to the masses, ritual in all Buddhist societies has been the fundamental means of applying *dharma*

Fig. 7.2. A Vajrācārya with *Dhāraṇī* Text and Ritual Object (*vajrakila*) Waits to Serve the Laity

analysis to acculturating the young or, to use Buddhist terms, to shape consciously and beneficently (*kushala*) the *skandhas*—body, sensations, perceptions, habit energies, and consciousness—of individuals, ultimately pointing them toward spiritual maturity and awakening. To use anthropological terms, ritual practice generates and shapes belief developmentally. Children question the meaning of rituals, come to understand the teachings through practical examples during storytelling, and listen very intently to the doctrinal testimony that swirls around them when death rituals are being conducted in the family circle. Mahāyāna rituals are carefully constructed to work on multiple levels, too: many act and impart meanings differentially for those all along the "gradual path," from beginners to advanced tantric practitioners, from little children to elder adepts. Recognizing this (in Nepal) means to discern the *upāya* of the collective Mahāyāna tradition.

Intellectuals are prone to forget that in premodern times when literacy was rare, only a very few could read texts to learn the *dharma*; most had to learn through oral accounts and through the experience of rituals. Buddhist rituals, thus, were developed and sustained by those wishing to shape human experience consciously. As Martin Southwold has noted, "Buddhists themselves are very aware of this effect, and they stress that just as it is true that having a right or good state of mind leads to right or good conduct, so too does good conduct tend to produce good states of mind" (Southwold 1983: 199).

In the Kathmandu Valley's Buddhist libraries, among the thousands of volumes still extant, the texts concerned with *dhāraṇī* practice (e.g., the *Pañcarakṣā*), prosperity rituals (e.g., the *vrata* manuals), and *puṇya/pāp* narratives outnumber philosophical treatises by over 100 to 1. Perhaps Nepal was unique in this regard. But I suspect that this was a standard distribution of texts and a reasonable indication of the practical daily concerns that are representative of Buddhist communities elsewhere and in earlier eras. What might this material culture inventory indicate about the evolution of Buddhist practice and Buddhist history?

For the multitudes who have performed rituals associated with specific narratives or have integrated texts like the *Pañcarakṣā* into their practice of Buddhism, taking refuge in Buddha/Dharma/Saṃgha meant following a tradition that had demonstrated that its saints and masters could exert control over the powers of the universe, powers that could promote worldly prosperity. This evolutionary outcome is by no means restricted to Nepal: Jaroslav Prusek and Jan Yua-hua,[14] for example, have noted the same strong focus on spiritual power in the Chinese Buddhist storytelling traditions:

> Their purpose is to demonstrate the magnitude of their religion and the supreme power of its representatives. Apparently in the eyes of the social classes for which these narratives were intended, as well as in the minds of their authors, the essential value of the religion was tested only by the magical powers which it gave to believers. (Prusek 1938: 384)

Thus, it was ritual practice that created and defined Buddhist identity and it was faith in the pragmatic powers of the Buddhas and *bodhisattva*s accessed through ritual that held the center of Buddhist tradition.

In conclusion, I suspect that in the course of Mahāyāna Buddhism's evolution, the earliest hagiographic narratives discussing spiritual powers related to the Buddha's words (causing the quaking of the earth, rains of flowers, etc.) were elaborated upon in the ensuing centuries and were codified for practical usage by the faith's missionary exponents. Lofty moral values and blissful fruits of meditation certainly must have impressed and converted some; but the *dharma*'s control over the powers that insure health, wealth, progeny, and peace—even overcoming bad *karman*—certainly would have had the widest appeal in securing the faith's success in contexts as different as nomadic pasturelands, urban enclaves, or subsistence farming villages.

Attention to the content of locally domesticated vernacular texts and pragmatic ritualism is needed to hasten the development of the postorientalist study of Buddhism free of idealization, "protestantization," and the overestimation of the role elites played. As Charles Hallisey puts it, this means that

> We will inevitably end up having to rethink our conceptualization of Buddhism as a translocal tradition with a long and self-consciously distinct history but which is at the same time a tradition dependent on local conditions for the production of meaning. (Hallisey 1995b: 51)

To survive and to achieve the Buddha's missionary call to spread the faith with compassion, Buddhists articulated pragmatic as well as soteriological traditions. By performing *vrata*s and utilizing texts like the *Pañcarakṣā*, the great majority of Buddhists could take refuge with powers identified by the Buddha as eminently suitable for securing both temporal and spiritual benefits. This was an evolutionary development that small circles of Buddhist philosophers throughout history might have found troublesome or disconcerting. But my guess is that this was often a welcome, skillfully balanced alliance: just as one tradition identifies the five *Pañcarakṣā* deities as special protectors of the scholastic *Prajñāpāramitā* texts, and just as the intrepid Chinese *vijñānavādin* scholar and pilgrim Hsuang-Tsang chanted the *Heart Sūtra* for protection against demons in his sojourn across Central Asia,[15] so too did most Buddhist scholars likely carry amulets into their study rooms and place them down alongside their learned *sūtra* commentaries. By centering our imagination of Buddhism in ritual and in the merit-making ideology seen in the narrative traditions, and by awakening to Buddhism's contributions to "life's more elementary and general joys,"[16] we can begin the needed task of comprehending the full religious meaning of Buddhism's triple refuge.

Notes

Preface

Portions of this book have appeared, in whole or in part, in earlier publications. Chapter 2 is a revised and considerably expanded version of the article, "Contributions to the History of Buddhist Ritualism: A *Mahāyāna Avadāna* on *Stūpa* Veneration from the Kathmandu Valley," *Journal of Asian History* 28 (1), 1994, 1–38. The translation was also included in the anthology edited by Donald S. Lopez Jr., *Buddhism in Practice* (Princeton: Princeton University Press, 1995). The translation found in chapter 3 was also anthologized in this same volume; the discussion originates in the article, "Newar-Tibetan Trade and the Domestication of the *Siṃhala-sārthabāhu Avadāna*," *History of Religions* 33 (2), 1993, 135–60. Both texts in chapters 4 and 5 originally appeared in the article, "Mahāyāna *Vratas* in Newar Buddhism," *The Journal of the International Association of Buddhist Studies* 12 (1), 1989, 109–38. The first story in chapter 6 was included in the anthology edited by Lopez, *Religions of India in Practice* (Princeton: Princeton University Press, 1995).

Chapter 1

1. This is the apt translation of Etienne Lamotte (1988: 146).

2. Few anthropological studies of texts in living Buddhist contexts have been recorded, with the exception of Robert F. Spencer (1966). Margaret Cone and Richard F. Gombrich (1977) present some comments on the *Vessantara Jātaka* in *The Perfect Generosity of Prince Vessantara* as does Pierre Dupont (1954) in his study of the Mon version of the *Narada Jātaka*. Historical studies have been more numerous. John Clifford Holt (1996), has examined the relationship between kingship, art, and specific *jātaka* narratives in late medieval Sri Lanka, Ratan Parimoo (1991) examined the *Vidhurapandita Jātaka's* significance in early Indian Buddhist art. Gombrich

(1985) studied the Vessantara Jātaka in which he explored another area of research: the redaction of Buddhist texts in their Brahmanic-*dharmashastric* region of origins. D. Mackenzie Brown (1955) examined the *jātaka*s for political principles. Padmanabh S. Jaini (1966) has also explored the sources and redactions of the *Sudhana Jātaka* narrative. Apropos of the ongoing nature of the domestication-redaction process, see the recent study by Madhu Bazaz Wangu (1992) that examines the composition of a "new" Hindu text in relation to its sociopolitical context in Kashmir.

3. Ranjini Obeyesekere recounts this from her own childhood experiences in Sri Lanka:

> Many of the stories grew very familiar with time. We heard them told and retold in many different contexts; in the temples, when the elders observed the eight precepts on full moon nights, as illustrations in the sermons of monks, and in schools they were often assigned in literature classes. But the stories I remembered best, and the bits and pieces that remained stuck in my mind were those that had fired my imagination as a child. . . .
>
> I realize that we were never given religious instruction as such, either in school or at home. We participated in Buddhist rituals and ceremonies, mostly in the extended kin group, went to temple on full moon days . . . and listened to many Buddhist stories. That was how we learned to be Buddhists. (Obeyesekere 1991: x)

4. This analytical approach might be compared with another theoretical concept that long ago contributed to the anthropology of South Asia: McKim Marriot's early discussion of "parochialization" that he defines as

> . . . the downward devolution of great-traditional elements and their integration with little-traditional elements . . . a process of localization, of limitation upon the scope of eligibility, of deprivation of literary form, of reduction to less systematic and less reflective dimensions. The process of parochialization constitutes the characteristic creative work of little communities within India's indigenous civilization. (Marriot 1955: 200)

While Marriott is certainly correct in noting such transformations as universal and central to Indic history, his framework of distinct traditions is difficult to apply to the entirely urban settings of the Kathmandu Valley. Compared to other textual recensions of the same tales presented in this volume, the Newar narratives may lose some "reflective dimensions" but add others, making it difficult to assert a loss of literary qualities.

5. In Thailand, the domestication also took shape in an alliance with ritual practice. Special *jātaka*s were identified as best associated with the months of the year. In this Theravāda culture region, the observance developed that one should donate funds to the *saṃgha* to have a monk read the *jātaka* of one's birth month to make merit (Keyes 1975: 75; Ferguson 1976).

6. G. H. Luce (1956: 302) has raised this issue regarding the *jātaka* corpus as a whole for the study of early Buddhism in Burma. A still-useful early description of the Burmese art depicting *jātaka*s is found in Charles Duroiselle (1912–13). Hsio-yen Shih has similarly analyzed the early shifts in treatment and arrangement of these narrative portrayals at Dunhuang; he argues that they show a demographic broadening of the local Buddhist community in the region. "By the sixth century, appeal to the laity became an additional factor in the increasing popularity of *avadāna* . . . in less than a century, Dunhuang was transformed from the isolation of discipline within the *samgha* to interaction with a larger world where conversion and instruction required greater efforts for the faith" (Shih 1993: 88).

7. The narratives treated in this book do not form a complete set of all important local works incorporated into the religious geography and temporal lives of the Newar Buddhists. These would also have to include the *Vessantara Jātaka* (perhaps the most popular tale across the Buddhist world); the *Maṇicūḍa Avadāna* (the *bodhisattva* sacrifices his life for medicine to save a distant country from plague); and the *Mahāsattva Rāja Kumār Avadāna* (The great prince story, in which the *bodhisattva* saves a hungry tigress and cubs). The Newari *Maṇicūḍa* tale has been translated by Siegfried Lienhard (1963). The *Vira Kush Jātaka* is another popular tale. Other works in this class include the *Svayambhū Purāṇa* and the narratives connected with Padmapani Avalokiteshvara, principally those emanations found in Bungamati-Lalitpur, Kathmandu, Nala, and Chobar.

8. The levels of rebirth in the realm of desire are: heaven-dweller, hell-dweller, titan, animal, hungry ghost, and human. (Some texts conjoin the titan status with heaven dweller, making only five realms.)

9. For example, after Shākyamuni preaches his first sermon, the *Mahāvastu* describes how the effects ripple through the entire cosmos, from the earth to the heavens to the hells: "Then did the earth quake violently. In six ways, like a fallen leaf it trembled and shook. . . . Then there appeared in the world an infinite radiance . . . for at that instant all beings were lapped in entire well-being, even those who had been reborn in the great hell of Avīci. . . . (Jones 1956, 3: 327–28).

10. The practice of the Buddha blessing others is found in many of the biographical accounts. In the *Mahāvastu*, Shākyamuni gives thanks for the *dāna* bestowed by two traders soon after his Enlightenment in this way, "He bestowed a blessing on them, a blessing divine, bringing good luck and success." The text then quotes his salutation:

> Blessing be on your men and on your beasts;
> Blessing be on you when you go your ways and when you return.
> Blessing be on you by night and day; blessing be on you at noontime.

> Blessing be on you always; may no evil befall you.
> May good luck stand on your right shoulder and on your left; may good luck cling to your every limb like a garland.
> Good fortune and good luck be yours, traders; may it be well with you on whatever business you go to the regions of the east.
> May the stars that stand over that region protect you. . . .
>
> (293–94)

Andre Bareau (1959) has written on the various elaborations to this episode found in different biographical narratives. He notes that a Mahāsaṃghika *Vinaya* commentary includes an elaborate schema of protective deities that Shākyamuni revealed for the benefit of these merchants. Thus, the Budda's first utterances to followers were concerned with their pragmatic well-being.

11. The protection is against evil nonhumans: *yakṣa*s, *gandharva*s, *kumbaṇḍha*s, and *nāga*s. Another *Dīgha* passage states that when the Buddha enters a settlement, any resident evil beings cannot injure humans (Thomas 1951: 186). This idea is seen in the *Pañcarakṣā*, chapter 6.

12. It should not be assumed that the rituals described in the Pali tradition differ in intention from those in the Mahāyāna *rakṣā* literature. For example, in the *Dhammapada* commentary we find the theme of life-extension quite dramatically the focus on the Buddha's service to the laity. In one story, a Brahman mother, father, and young son go to meet the Buddha:

> The Brahman went to the Teacher, and himself straightaway saluted him. "Live long!" said the Teacher. When the boy's mother saluted him, he said the same. But when they made the boy salute him, he held his peace. When the Brahman asked the Teacher [why he did not respond to the boy, he said] "Some disaster awaits the boy, Brahman." "How long will he live, Reverend Sir?" "For seven days, Brahman."
>
> The Brahman asked the Teacher, "Reverend Sir, is there no way of averting this?" "There might be, Brahman. . . . If you erect a pavilion before the door of your house, and set a chair in the center of it, arrange eight or sixteen seats in a circle around it, and cause my disciples to sit therein; and if you then cause texts to be recited for the purpose of securing protection and averting evil consequences for the space of seven days uninterruptedly, in that case the danger that threatens him might be averted. . . .
>
> So when the Teacher came, the deities of all the world assembled. But a certain ogre named Avaruddhaka . . . who had received the boon, "Seven days hence you will receive the boy," approached and

stood waiting. But when the teacher came there, and the powerful deities gathered themselves together, and the weak deities drew back, stepping back twelve leagues to make room, then Avaruddhaka stepped back also.

The Teacher recited the Protective Texts all night long, with the result that when the seven days had elapsed, Avaruddhaka failed to get the boy. Indeed, when the dawn of the eighth day broke, they brought the boy and caused him to bow to the Teacher. Said the Teacher, "Live long!" "Sir Gotama, how long shall the boy now live?" "120 Years!" (Burlingame 1990, 2: 237–38)

13. If the extent of ritual articulation and praxis are used as defining criteria, the terms *little vehicle* and *great vehicle* do evoke the most important diachronic contrast between the two main streams of Buddhism's historical evolution.

14. An early text that defines the monks' specializations gives an indication of this broad activity within the *saṃgha*: instructors, meditators, folklorists, *sūtra* experts, *Vinaya* experts, and ritualists (Lamotte 1988: 149). Gregory Schopen (1991a, 1991b) has shown that the *saṃgha* early on also performed rituals for certain life cycle ceremonies desired by Buddhist laity.

15. Though in some early Buddhist circles it was quite possible that there was a firm basis for separating the terms *mantra*, *dhāraṇī*, and *vidyā* (Snellgrove 1987: 141, 191; Matsunaga 1977; Davidson 1981:23), the Newari texts are consistent with later Buddhist writers who use them interchangeably. *Dhāraṇī*, a term originating among Buddhists (Bharati 1965: 114), and *vidyā* are used most frequently in the *Pañcarakṣā* text and, in terms of evolved practice, elsewhere in Buddhist *sūtras*: as contractions of longer passages that impart the essence of the doctrine to the mind (as in *Pañcarakṣā* story #1) and to empower the devotee.

16. Information in the Tibetan records on Buddhist traditions extant in Nepal suggests the date for this assimilation being no later than 1200. Other studies on Newar-Tibetan connections have been published (Lewis and Jamspal 1988; Lewis 1989a). Our date conforms to the time of the precipitous decline of north Indian Buddhism, assuming a major transformation due, in part, to the closing down of the greater Buddhist network that linked the northeast hearth region to highland centers, and on which monks, pilgrims, and merchants traveled across Asia.

17. As David N. Gellner (1986: 129) has pointed out, the great majority of the Newari-language publications on religious themes dating back to 1909 have been Buddhist.

18. A recension of the *Ācāryakriyasammucaya* from Nepal states:

> The real teacher is he who apart from other qualities, does not live like a monk, does not shave his head and puts on good clothes and beautiful ornaments. Amongst other qualities of a teacher are counted his knowledge about purificatory rites, his kind disposition, pleasing humour, maintenance of all the *ācārya*s, insight into the art of architecture and in the science of *mantra*s, skill as a profound astronomer . . . and his capability to select an auspicious plot for the construction of a *stūpa* and for the installation of the idol of the Buddha. (Translation is by N. S. Shukla [1975: 127–28])

19. Accounts of Central Asia confirm this assessment that emphasizes the tendency toward elaborate ritualism in later Indian Buddhist cultural environments (Snellgrove 1987: 347). The ritualism of Tibet also conforms to this developmental pattern.

20. The resurgence of the modern Newar Buddhist literati who edit and publish new versions of their older texts over the last fifteen years contains yet another example of how problematic it is to base assessments about the state of the tradition from the activities of the textual scholars. Judging by this wave of Nepalese publications alone, one might guess that Newar Buddhism was in the midst of great intellectual resurgence; in fact, the understanding of Mahāyāna doctrine has been in steep decline throughout Newar society (Lewis 1996c).

21. It has been impractical to publish in this book all the photographs that help the reader to visualize the domestications of these Newar texts. Interested readers will find complete color documentary slide sets for each text on my website located at http://sterling.holycross.edu/departments/religiousstudies/tlewis/MasterPage.htm

Chapter 2

1. There is strong inscriptional support for asserting that monks, nuns, and laity gave *dāna* to benefit parents (Schopen 1985a: 30ff). A survey of Indic inscriptions on the subject of spouses would help clarify this orientation (e.g., Rosen 1980: 119), although the reluctance to identify a spouse might limit the ability to assess the frequency of this occurrence.

2. This is the common inscription on clay votives throughout the Buddhist world:

> Ye dharmā hetuprabhavā hetus teṣāṃ tathāgato hy avadat
> Teshāṃ ca yo nirodha evaṃ vādī mahāshramaṇaḥ

3. A recent description of the *stūpa*'s symbolic evolution reflects

concisely the developments in Vajrayāna philosophy that endure in the Nepalese context:

> Whereas the *stūpa* in the earlier tradition . . . is the sign and symbol of a Buddha's departure into final *nirvāṇa*, the *maṇḍala* by contrast represents the continual activity of Buddhahood on behalf of living beings. . . . In later Indian Buddhist tradition, the *stūpa* was adapted to this newer symbolism . . . with the great *stūpa*s of Nepal with the eyes which look forth over the dome and with cosmic Buddha manifestations enshrined at the points of the compass. . . . Thus the later *stūpa*, like the *maṇḍala* . . . at the center which a deity sits enthroned, is the sacred sphere of beneficent activity. (Snellgrove and Skorupski 1977: 13)

4. A modern Tibetan explanation of *stūpa* symbolism further expands this multiplexity by relating them to the *trikāya* theory of Buddhahood: Buddha images represent the *nirmāṇakāya*, texts the *sambhogakāya*, and *stūpa*s the *dharmakāya*. All are said to be *upāya*s for Buddhists who seek both *puṇya* and *prajñā*. Offerings to the *dharmakāya* yield the greatest *puṇya* (Rimpoche 1990).

5. A text from northwest India dramatically describes how even modest *stūpa* building is infinitely superior to making lavish material offerings of other sorts (Bentor 1988).

6. Chapter 11 in the *Lotus Sūtra* focuses on the apparition of a jeweled *stūpa* and depicts Shākyamuni instructing followers to build *stūpa*s wherever the devotees to the *Lotus* dwell: "Wherever these good men and good women sit, or stand, or walk, there one should erect a *stūpa*, and all gods and men should make offerings to it, as if it were a *stūpa* of the Buddha himself" (Hurvitz 1976: 254). These places, *bodhimaṇḍo veditavyaḥ* or "Platforms of the Path" (255), mark sites where *The Lotus* has been stored, read, recited, interpreted, copied, or practiced; they are equated with the sites where Buddhas have achieved enlightenment, taught, and passed to *parinirvāṇa*."

7. Eva K. Dargyay's study of Buddhist death practices in Zanskar (western Tibet) includes the construction of a small *stūpa* using cremation ashes and bones; this and other typical lay rituals after death (image making and text copying) have a threefold purpose: ". . . to let the previously deceased attain to the path of liberation; to purge the defilements of the living ones; and to ensure the future prosperity and power of one's dynasty" (Dargyay 1986: 87). Other Tibetan areas also preserve this cultic use of monk and layfolks' cremation remains (Schopen 1992). Gregory Schopen's speculation on the congruence between *stūpa* and *tīrtha* is supported by the living Newar Buddhist traditions: *avadāna* tales link *tīrtha*s to Buddhist saints and to the conversion of *nāga*s (Lewis 1984: 62); Newar texts specify

the necessity of Buddhist *stūpas* being established at proper *tīrthas*; and the performance of Buddhist *shraddha* rituals can involve the dispersal of ashes at such venues in the first year of mourning (326–30; 388–89).

8. Asanga's list of the ten-principle Mahāyāna rituals requires the resort to a *caitya*, one either with or without relics (Poussin 1937: 281–82). The *Bodhicaryāvatāra* also lauds worship to both kinds of shrines; an eleventh-century commentary on this text by Prajñākaramati specifically notes that *bodhisattvas* should worship "sites associated with the bodhisattvas, places [connected] with *jātakas* and *avadānas*" (Gomez 1995a: 193).

9. Alan Sponberg (1992) has suggested four views of women in Buddhist literature: soteriological inclusiveness, institutional androcentrism, ascetic misogyny, and soteriological androgyny. This is a useful schema, but as it is grounded in the monastic and ascetic field, it does not cover the subject fully from the householder *upāsaka* perspective.

10. All references to the Pali *jātakas* are indicated from the Pali Text Society's translation (1957).

11. Xinru Liu (1988: 100) has shown how the paraphernalia of Buddhist *stūpas*, shrines, *vihāras*, and temple building itself contributed significantly to overland Indo-Chinese trade by Kushan times. Of particular importance were the offerings of (Chinese) silk and the (Indian) seven jewels—gold, silver, lapis lazuli, crystal, pearl, red coral, and agate—including the building of "seven-jeweled *stūpas*." These were described as the best of offerings (97). Note that the *caitya* in the *Shṛṇgabherī* story is transformed into a "jeweled *caitya*."

12. As discussed in the next section, this is a tendency common in Buddhist rebirth narratives, affecting even Buddhist monks. The stock gloss on the recurrence of desire for former loves in *Mahāvastu* narratives often notes, "When it enters the mind and the heart becomes glad, even the intelligent man always succumbs to it, for it means that there has been acquaintance in the past" (Jones 1952, 2: 163–64).

13. The translations of the *Sigālovāda Sutta* and of the *Mahāmaṇgala Sutta* are both from Narada Thera's translation (1966: 14–15, 20). The passage is from a sermon in which the Buddha reinterprets the early Brahmanic tradition of worshiping the cardinal directions by replacing blind ritualism with ethical injunctions.

14. The great Theravādin scholar Buddhaghosha's commentary on a verse from the *Dhammapada* invokes a story of a woman reborn in heaven with her husband who then "falls down" to human rebirth into a high-caste family. She then matures, marries, and bears four sons, yet all of her tireless merit-making service and gift giving to the *saṃgha* is dedicated to achiev-

ing heavenly rebirth again with the heaven-dwelling former husband (Warren 1922: 264ff).

15. The *Mahāvastu*'s recension of the *Kusha Jātaka* strikingly expresses the power and focus of the *bodhisattva*'s desire for the future Yasodharā. As king he addresses his queen:

> I have the power, sovereign lady, to bind you and make you go wher'er I will. What can your father do?
>
> I can if I like gratify a thousand women in one night. But you are my choice. . . . (Jones 1956, 3: 18)

16. Chapters 2-9 of the *Bhadrakalpāvadāna,* another popular text in Nepal (Tatelman 1999), recount the 'trials of Yośodharā' after Siddhartha departed for the forest. I can confirm Tatelman's speculation about the text finding resonance as a model of a wife's fidelity to spouse and faith in the Newar context, both in the Kathmandu market and for wives with husbands trading in Tibet, as we'll see in Chapter 3.

17. The Newar domestication of Hindu tantra follows a similar pattern. On this and the documentation of Newar Hinduism in the town of Bhaktapur, see the monumental study by Robert I. Levy (1990).

Chapter 3

1. For example, Sylvain Levi (1929), Balkrishna Govind Gokhale (1977: 125–30), and James Heitzman (1984).

2. Recently there has been Himanshu P. Ray (1986) in his study of Satavahana patterns of trade and political alliance, and Xinru Liu (1988) in his a survey of Indo-Chinese contacts in Kushan times. Several articles from Russell F. Sizemore and Donald K. Swearer (1991) devote attention to the early merchants mentioned in the Pāli texts.

3. In the Pali Canon *jātaka* collection, for example, the *bodhisattva* takes birth as a merchant 35 times and traders figure prominently in another 24 stories. Of the 35 stories in the *Mahāvastu*, the *bodhisattva* is a merchant 7 times, 4 as a caravan leader.

4. The most famous, pan-Buddhist exemplary donors in the literature are the royal patrons: King Vessantara, the last incarnation of the future Buddha Shākyamuni, and King Ashoka. There are also two similarly renowned merchant families: Anāthapiṇḍika and Visākhā. Other prominent merchants are Ghosita of Kausambi and the merchant Purna of Shravasti (Lamotte 1988: 20–21). The most famous Mahāyāna lay sage Vimalakīrti is also described as being a businessperson who gives lavishly

to the *saṃgha* and to the poor. See Robert A. F. Thurman (1976: 21,41).

5. See Etienne Lamotte (1988: 66). The *Mahāvastu* also includes this account.

6. Lamotte (414) has noted that at Sanchi, the greatest number of lay donor inscriptions are recorded for bankers [19] and merchants [5]. Gregory Schopen (1979) has pointed out that the earliest known Mahāyāna inscription records a *sārtavāha*'s (caravan trader's) gift.

The Chinese pilgrims accounts all mention specific instances of merchants' leadership in early festivals. Consult James Legge (1886: 79); and Samuel Beal (1970 xxxii, xxxix, lvii, lxxii, lxxxvii, 81, 129, 175–77.

It is now beyond doubt that monks, too, were prominent donor patrons of Buddhist establishments. See Schopen (1991b, 1991c, 1994b). The monks' control of wealth (including laborers) must have been a factor in the economics of later Indic Buddhist history. The Kharoṣṭhī records support this hypothesis: as reported in T. Burrow (1940), monks are reported as slaveholders (65); complaining of lost goods (64); paying in goods (66); borrowing food (65); and receiving horses as compensation for land (120). Another passage even records one monk selling land to another monk (135–36). Note what one Kharoṣṭhī record states about the ethos of being wealthy:

> Just as a man traveling on a journey rests here and there when overcome with fatigue, so a man's possessions from time to time, having rested, come back again. . . .
> Alas the life of the poor; again alas the life of those rich people who have not the sense to enjoy or distribute [their] riches. (103)

7. The formula found in both Pali (*Sigalovāda Sutta*) and Sanskrit traditions (*Upāsaka Shīla Sūtra* (in Robinson 1966: 49) allot one's wealth as follows: 1/4 to family, 2/4 to business, and 1/4 held in reserve (Gombrich 1988: 78ff). Note how the Buddhist merchant *upāsaka*—sober, benevolent, honest, ascetic, and pious—would have resembled the ideal Muslim merchant.

8. *Mahāratnakūta*, as translated in Diana Y. Paul (1985: 34).

9. The text is from the *Anguttara Nikāya* (IV, vi, 61). The full passage is cited in the final chapter, where it elaborates on why "the good Buddhist" should seek wealth and how one should wisely "invest" it in multiplying happiness (for self and others) and through making merit.

10. As summarized in Radhagovinda Basak (1963: xxv).

11. The religious institutions within early Buddhist merchant communities, often called *goṣṭhi* in the epigraphic records, which did precisely this. The merit "payback" of donations generating further wealth is made explicitly in the noncanonical Theravāda text, the *Tuṇḍilovadānasutta*:

"Generosity is increased wealth, it is running streams of wealth. Generosity protects material goods, and it protects life" (Hallisey 1995a: 305).

12. In Richard H. Robinson (1954: 17).

13. In Paul (1985: 36).

14. This connection was noted by George Coedes (1971: 21). This Dīpaṃkara tradition seems to be linked to the yearly Newar festival involving the hero of the Siṃhalāvadāna festival (as discussed in the next section).

15. Lamotte (1988: 688).

16. See Jan Fontein (1990: 189–91) and Janice Leoshko (1996).

17. Pali *jātaka* 442. This deity figures prominently in the *Maṇimekalai*, a Tamil Buddhist tale translated by Paula Richman (1988).

18. See Geri H. Malandra (1993). They are also found in Tibetan texts as well. See Augustine Waddell (1893: 9).

19. See D. D. Kosambi (1964: 185), Gregory Schopen (1994a, 1994b), and Jacques Gernet (1995: 65–93).

20. As other groups did elsewhere, Buddhist merchants created diaspora trade networks, mercantile/entrepreneuring webs of import/export trade, which were often in the hands of single ethnic groups with their own core and periphery zones quite distant. This mode of livelihood, relying on business acumen, capital, family partners stationed in strategic venues, and diplomatic skills, was a pervasive global phenomenon. (On diaspora trade in comparative perspective, see Philip Curtin (1984).) Kosambi (1964: 124) suggests that there is ancient evidence for Indic and Indo-Greek diaspora traders as early as the Sātavāhana era. Another valuable source is Christopher I. Beckwith (1977: 91–92).

21. The same dynamic pattern is still reconfiguring Buddhism in contemporary Japan, with the emergence of the cult surrounding the "Senility Kannon." The development of the *boke fuji* pilgrimage involves interlocking elements: *saṃgha* ritualists garnering income and selling newly developed amulets, employment for artisan manufacturers, and marketing by merchant promoters. All are converging to attract donations, travel, and patronage by elderly Japanese and their families. See Ian Reader 1995.

22. A recent translation of the life of the Indic master Atīsha (982-1054 C.E.) has him traveling to Sumatra on a ship owned by merchants from Nepal (Decleer 1995: 532–40). This source suggests that there was a very old awareness of true overseas trade in the Newar community.

23. Important studies are found in A. W. Macdonald and Anne Vergati Stahl (1979), Dor Bista (1978), and E. Bue (1985, 1986).

24. Siegfried Lienhard (1987: 51-53).

25. Later Buddhist versions were also translated into Khotanese, Tibetan, Chinese, and Japanese Buddhist texts. Buddhist artists of different areas and eras have depicted this story: it is found on a third-century stone pillar at Mathura, in cave 17 at Ajanta, in Central Asia, as well as in Burma (Pagan), Angkor, in Borobodur, and in Nepal. The story also enjoyed popularity in East Asian art, as discussed by Julia Meech-Pekarik (1981: 111–28). Lienhard (1985) explores the early textual traditions of the Siṃhala story and presents a long scroll and a translation of its caption text.

26. The Sanskrit text version of the Siṃhala story in the *Guṇakāraṇḍavyūha* is found in Y. Iwamoto (1967: 247–94). Lienhard (1993) dates this text as late as the sixteenth century.

27. The boatman's addition is noted in the numbering here, but is not accounted for again as the set number reverts back to 499.

28. New.: *sambhoga yāye.*

29. According to Prem Uprety, there were violent incidents against Newar merchants in Lhasa in 1854, 1862, and 1871. In 1883, "all 84 shops in Lhasa were looted" (Uprety 1980: 97–98). Again in 1911–12, rioters killed 5 Nepalese and burned 38 shops (132).

30. See Purna Harsha Bajracharya (1979) and John K. Locke (1985: 405–13). Modern informants now identify a small shrine outside the Siṃhalasārthabāhu Vihāra otherwise identified as that of Hārītī Ajimā as that of his *rākṣasī* wife. Ajimā herself has been extensively incorporated into Newar Buddhist traditions: her story of child-eating and conversion is well-known (most recently, see Strong (1992: 45) and many prominent Newar *stūpa*s and *vihāra*s have nearby temples dedicated to her. The domiciling of the defeated *rākṣasī* just outside Siṃhala's monastery, although it finds no basis in the published versions of the story, is consistent with the final resolution of the conflict. Daniel Wright in a "text" compiled from local histories (*vaṃshāvali*), states the origin of this monastery and attendant temple:

> He [Siṃhala] pulled down his house and built a *vihāra*, and consecrated an image of the bodhisattva. In consideration of this *rākṣasī* . . . having been his mistress, he raised a temple for her worship, and assigned land for her support. He, having no issue, the dynasty became extinct on his death. (Wright 1990: 87)

31. See the following two chapters regarding this and other *vrata*s.

32. The designation of a seductress as a "demoness" is common in Buddhist literature, for example, in Pali Canon passages (e.g., the *Itivuttaka* (Collins 1982: 25) and in the *jātaka*s (e.g., Pali #527). Doubtless this Bud-

dhist designation is one instance of a transcultural construction of "the dangerous strange woman." A recent article on the *bori* (road siren) in modern Niger bears an uncanny resemblance to this story: "Ranging in appearance from beautiful, long-haired girls to smartly attired city women, these mysterious *femmes fatale*s often rob unsuspecting [male] travelers of their lives after having seduced them" (Masquelier 1992: 56).

33. John Clifford Holt (Holt 1991: 46–53) explores this same tale in relationship to the domestication of Avalokiteshvara in Sri Lanka, as it expresses a Mahāyāna attempt to rework the earlier "spiritual conquest" myth of Buddhism's coming to this island.

34. A psychoanalytical exegesis would take the analysis of the tale's impact into the Freudian subconscious: identifying "being eaten" as arousing castration anxiety in male listeners. I remain agnostic on this analytical belief system and unconvinced of its universal application; since I conducted no field research on this question, I can only mark the issue. See Melford E. Spiro (1992) for a broader interpretation of such gender psychodynamics in Burmese Buddhism. In his article, he cites several *jātaka*s in order to develop a "cultural complex" using Freudian paradigms without, however, demonstrating how the narratives specifically had been known or domesticated to inform the laity.

35. David N. Gellner (personal communication, 1996) writes of such a case in Lalitpur's Nāg Bāhā where the *khaccar* son did build a house and maintain a family, but had no familial connection with his half-brother, neighbors, or their families.

36. As J. W. De Jong (1981: 293–96) has pointed out, the hero in literary versions confronted an "iron fortress" that was magically charged with transformative powers to defy escape. The walls respond to any *thought* of escape by an inmate, and compensate by growing higher, lower, or thicker. The Newar version omits this situation, raising the question as to why the hero Siṃhala and, for that matter, why Avalokiteshvara did not include earlier victims in the horse-rescue operation.

37. Here, a final parallelism between linguistic use and subconscious meaning can be noted: just as the male victims of the *rākṣasī*s are "eaten," so in Newari the verb to eat (*na-ye*) can be used idiomatically to convey wasting money (as in *wa dheba na-ye* (lit. "he ate the money") or destroying a house (as in *mīṃ cheṃ nala* (lit. "the fire ate the house").

38. The influence of the *Simhalāvadāna*/Tibetan trade narrative tradition in Nepal reached beyond the circle of Newari culture and into Nepali literature. The best example of this would be Lakshmīprasād Devkoṭta's *Munā-Madan* (Rubin 1980: 29-33; Hutt 1991: 40-51). In Tibet, the story was also domesticated in art, song, and literature. The "flying horse" metaphor for *bodhisattva* striving can be found for example, in the songs of Milarepa (Evans-Wentz 1969: 216–17). The tale "The Life of Child

Padma 'od-'bar" incorporates part of this narrative and it inspired popular *mani-pa* lama storytellers and a genre of paintings used to accompany them (Blondeau 1988). Interestingly, in the Tibetan redaction it is also due to the attachment to half-*rākṣasī* children that the merchants fall to their destruction (1986: 27).

39. This methodology and conclusion have been noted by John R. Bowen in his recent review of anthropological research in Southeast Asia:

> Rather than reading events, institutions, or ways of speaking as parts of a single cultural "text," anthropologists increasingly ask how social actors interpret cultural forms, how actors change their interpretations over time, and what is most at stake for them in their interpretations. (Bowen 1995: 1050)

Chapter 4

1. In modern Buddhist communities, ritual texts are the most abundantly represented in local communities and are most commonly offered by modern practitioners as the key to understanding Buddhism. My experience in 1979–82 in Nepal (as recounted in the preface) were the same as those reported by the first Europeans who entered into more accessible Buddhist lands much earlier. As Charles Hallisey notes,

> The first texts that Europeans were given in their encounter with the Buddhist world, ritual texts for the ordination of monks, however, indicate that whoever gave those texts thought that ritual was the key for understanding the Buddha's message. The very capacity for knowledge depended on ritual preparation, and in Theravada Buddhist communities this generally presupposed ordination. (Hallisey 1995b: 46)

2. Although Buddhist scholars have awakened to these biases inherited in the academy and from our intellectual ancestors, this hasn't changed the manner of presenting Buddhism in our textbooks very much.

3. The *kalasha* is a ceremonial vessel. As stated in a modern Newar commentary, "The main aim of the *Kalasha pūjā* is to make the deity present in the *kalasha* by means of *sādhana* and then through the *abhiṣeka* of the *kalasha* bring about a participation in *nirvāṇa* itself." (Quoted in Locke 1980: 96.)

4. This *vrata* and the Swasthānī *Vrata* are included because they are commonly performed among non-*vajrācārya*s, that is, among the Mahāyāna layfolk that constitute the great majority of Newar Buddhists.

5. For an important study of a *Vrata* performed predominantly by Hindu Newar layfolk, see Linda Iltis's (1985) monumental translation and

analysis of the Swasthānī *Vrata*.

6. I have reproduced the spellings and word spacing of the *mantras* as published, with the exception of having commonly known Buddhist terms conform to standard English transliterations, especially the substitution of *v* for *b* in terms such as *vajra*.

7. This list of "ten unproductive transgressions" is very commonly chanted by a *vajrācārya* priest as part of most *vratas*. It constitutes a list of moral precepts, providing a moral element in these rites. These are to avoid harming living beings, theft, sexual misconduct, lying, slander, harsh speaking, gossip, covetousness, malevolence, and adhering to false doctrines (Gellner 1992: 118).

Chapter 5

1. The Sanskrit title for this text, the *Kanitāvadāna*, has not been mentioned in any published Nepali account. The only study of a Newari *avadāna* collection can be found in Hans Jorgensen (1931), but in this work, there is no mention of the Mahākāla story, however.

2. In colloquial Newari, the term *bali* can literally mean an animal sacrifice. While blood offerings are approved for fierce deities by some tantric Buddhist texts, in most Newar Buddhist rituals *bali* "refers to the apotropaic offerings made to ghosts or other spirits who might cause problems for the ritual. . . ." (Gellner 1992: 149). Note that even the Pali texts record passages (e.g., *Anguttara Nikāya* IV, ii, 43) in which Shākyamuni accepts ritual sacrifices made for dead relatives as long as they are free of cruelty (*nirāramba*). See Bruce Owens (1993) for a discussion of the relationship between other Newar Buddhist traditions and the issue of blood sacrifices made to them.

3. See the discussion on the history of the *vrata* in this chapter.

4. This is doubtless a schematic identification based upon a protective *maṇḍala* that priests use.

5. Based upon the Indic lunar calendar (Das 1928), *uposaḍha* includes the overnight of the full- and no-moon period; hence each can span two solar days each month (Lamotte 1988: 70).

6. Both *vratas* featured here refer to "keeping the eight precepts."

Chapter 6

1. The connection between meditation and philosophy can be traced back to the authority of Vasubandhu's *Bodhisattvabhūmi* in his discussion of *mantras* having no ultimate meaning (Dasgupta 1974: 59; Braarvig 1985: 20).

2. This view is expressed in the *Mañjushrīnāmasaṃghiti*, a text that also is quite widely used in the Kathmandu Valley. "[Chanting the text] is the quick success of those Bodhisattvas implementing their practice by means of *mantra*s, and the realization in contemplation for those intent on the Perfection of Insight. . . ." (Davidson 1981: 40). Like the *Pañcarakṣā*, this text also makes many assurances about the host of mundane blessings that the chanter of the text can garner. See also Gregory Sharkey (1994).

3. Translated in David L. Snellgrove (1987: 191–92).

4. Recensions of the Sanskrit *Pañcarakṣā* texts copied by Newar scribes were found in Tibet from at least as early as 1138 C.E. (Petech 1984: 60,96). A Sanskrit-Chinese *dhāraṇī* text for the goddess Caṇḍā in Newari script has been noted (Whitaker 1963), indicating the scope of influence of texts from early Nepal.

5. As the Newar *vajrācārya* pandit points out in his introduction, there is a vaguely discernible connection between this tradition and the Theravādin *paritta*:

> It may, however, be noted that in the *Sudatta Sutta* appearing in the tenth chapter of the book of *Saṃyukta Nikāya*, there is the description of the cremation ground called "Shītavana". Once the Buddha had his sojourn there in the cremation ground of Shītavana and it was during this time that Anāthapiṇḍa first saw the Buddha. Haunted frequently by non-human beings and demons, the cremation ground of Shītavana is described as a horrible place. This description of Shītavana and the discourse which the Buddha preached to Rāhula in the Shitavana Shmashāna bears resemblance to what has been recorded in our *Shītavatī sūtra*. (Vajracarya 1980: pg. ch)

6. The *Niṣpannayogāvalī* constructs the *Pañcarakṣā maṇḍala* as follows:

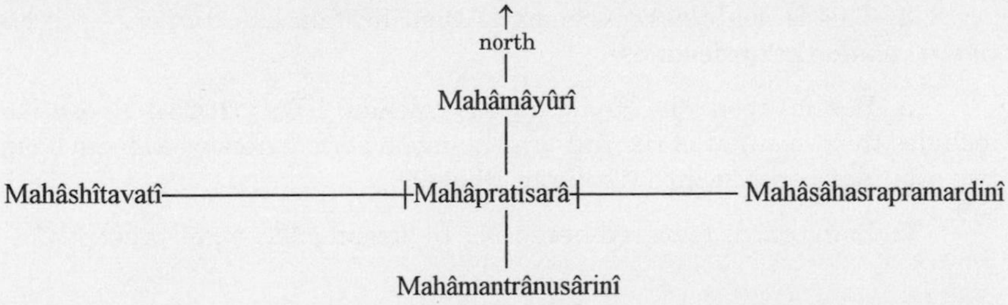

The text adds that any of the five can in fact be located in the center (B. Bhattacaryya 1968b: 302ff). The *Sādhanamālā* (#201, #206) gives alternative placements, although Mahāpratisarā is still pivotal (Mallmann 1975: 56–57). See also Gerd Mevissen (1991/2) on the variations in iconographic depictions.

7. Franklin Edgerton (1953: 461) lists Lambā and Vilambā as *yakṣasīs* occurring in the Sanskrit *Saddharmapuṇḍarīka* (chap. 21) where they, along with nine others, including Hārītī, give *mantras* to Shākyamuni and promise a host of special protections to preachers of the *dharma*, as in our text. The dictionary also notes that in one Mahāmāyūrī text, these figures are labeled *pishācī*. The goddess Kūṇākṣī is not found in any of the Sanskrit or Newari listings I consulted.

8. According to the *Mahāvastu*, it is not possible for a *bodhisattva* to be born in hell.

9. Our Newari text lacks the "escape clause" that Peter Skilling (1992: 148ff) has highlighted in other recensions: this is an editorial note in the texts that asserts that sometimes *karman* operates regardless of any ritual or amulet.

10. The following titles appear in one collection (Takaoka 1981), with the number of occurrences cited in brackets:

Pañcarakṣā	[31]
Pañcarakṣā Vidhi	[1]
Pañcarakṣā Vidhāna	[3]
Pañcarakṣā Hṛdaya Dhāraṇī	[3]
Pañca Mahārakṣā Sūtrajipari	[1]
Pañcarakṣā Nāma Dhāraṇī	[2]
Pañcarakṣā Dhāraṇī	[4]
Pañcarakṣā Mantra Dhāraṇī	[2]
Mahā Pañcarakṣā	[1]
Pañca Mahārakṣā	[1]
Ekaji Pañcarakṣā	[1]
Pañcarakṣā Mantra Kalpa	[1]
Pañcarakṣā Hṛdaya Mantra	[1]
Pañcarakṣā Mahāyāna Sūtra	[1]
Mahāmantrānusāriṇi	[0]
Mahāpratisarā	[4]
Mahāsāharapramardini	[2]
Mahāmāyūrī	[4]
Mahāshitavatī	[1]

There is obviously a wealth of *Pañcarakṣā* texts located in Kathmandu Valley libraries that need further study. Finally, the compilation of new redactions in Nepal continues: just as this manuscript was in final preparation, I received a new, larger Sanskrit-Newari edition published in early 1993 (A. Vajracarya 1993).

11. The iconographic description is for chanting in order to insure the proper visualization of arms, objects, and colors. As the text notes, by placing the image of the deity in the mind's eye, the practitioner enhances the effect of each formula.

12. Note that a practical question of monastic discipline is inserted here, implying that vegetarianism is the *Vinaya* norm. The answer draws upon *shūnyatā* doctrine to justify any monk or nun eating whatever is given as alms, arguing that ingestion of food is a conventional, not ultimate, action if comprehended rightly.

13. This constitutes the more advanced level of practice: only through oral and personal contact with a teacher can an interested disciple gain the knowledge of the *maṇḍala* ritual. In the local context of the Newar Buddhist community to which the printed text is addressed, anyone wishing for further instruction or practical assistance could easily contact the author or the *vajrācārya* mentioned in the book's introduction.

14. As David N. Gellner (1992: 31) has pointed out, this class of food in the modern understanding includes salt, onions, tomatoes, garlic, meat, and alcohol. The concern for a specific issue pertinent to monastic discipline shown here and in other stories in this collection most likely indicates that it was the *saṃgha* that recited the "popular" stories (Schopen 1996) and that many monks and nuns were interested in "popular practices."

15. The *mantra* is as follows: *Maṇidharivajriṇi Mahāpratisare rakṣa rakṣa māṃ sarvasattvānāñca huṃ huṃ phaṭ svāhā* (N. M. Vajracarya 1989: 5). In some of the *Pañcarakṣā* recensions, as in the *Niṣpannayogāvalī* (cited in the previous section), this goddess sits at the center of the *maṇḍala* and stands for the group of five.

16. The house consecration text translated in Mary Slusser (1982: 421), however, does not utilize a *Pañcarakṣā* text.

17. As Gellner (personal communication, 1996) has noted, this domination is the result of two converging trends: newly "Hindu" clients retaining their former *vajrācārya* priests for this ritual and new patronage by long-established Hindu families turning to *vajrācārya*s due to their former tantric Hindu priests, the Karmācāryas, giving up this kind of ritual service.

18. Male babies have the ritual at six or eight months; female babies at five or seven months (R. K. Vajracarya 1981: 9). See also Todd T. Lewis (1994a: 11).

19. One Chinese version of the *Pañcarakṣā* mentions a *maṇḍala* ritual using balls of five metals: gold, silver, copper, zinc, and iron. Although it is hard to know from M. W. DeVisser's terse summary (1976), apparently one chanted the *mantra* for each while the layperson held the respective ball in his mouth. Neither his text nor ours allows for correlation between the five deities and the five metals.

20. The "Indra Pillar" referred to in story #5 is still erected each year for the five-day festival in Nepal (Lewis 1984: 374–79; Toffin 1978).

21. The source for this account of local Buddhist *tīrthas* (sacred sites, especially river confluences) is the *Svayambhū Purāna*. (These are cited accompanied by a map in Gellner [1992: 194–95].) Each site has a series of resident deities, auspicious times for visitation, and special effects on the devotee. At this *Pañcarakṣā* site at the *Pramod Tīrtha*, the text states that fury (*krodha*) can be dissipated through pilgrimage due to the fact that merit (*puṇya*) will arise to infuse the mind (Kolver 1985: 149).

22. Studies in the history of diseases have noted that missionaries, like merchants, have not only been vectors of mass diseases; they have also been instrumental in the process of fostering public health adaptation through the more long-term homogenizing of virulent strains, ultimately abetting a population's widespread resistance (McNeill 1977: 97). (The former case is best documented in connection with Buddhism's introduction into Japan from Korea in 552 C.E. [124ff].) The success of the *dhāraṇī* traditions must be understood in the historical context of how survivors of these mass epidemics, especially Buddhist converts, explained their fate.

23. The Pali Commentary on the *Dhammapada* (Burlingame 1990: 237) described this same deployment of the pantheon.

24. The twelfth century in Japan was the "golden age" of this rite (DeVisser 1976: 208).

25. There was one merchant in my early fieldwork, a learned private scholar, meditator, and forceful Mahāyāna exponent, who brought this point home to me as belief and practice. For Dharma Ratna, the *dhāraṇīs* were compassionate revelations that made winning a good rebirth and even *nirvāṇa*-realization easy if one would only practice them. In 1981, when his health was clearly deteriorating, he devoted himself ever more intently to his practice of the *Aparamitā dhāraṇī* as taught to him years before by a Tibetan lama. He told me that, when the moment of death approached, if he could still stay focused on the practice, his good rebirth destiny would be assured. For a broader portrait of this remarkable individual, see Lewis (1996c: 256–57).

Chapter 7

1. I suspect that those debating the fine points of Buddhist philosophy in the past—for example, on such "huge issues" as whether the Madhyamaka or Yogācara system should be considered the "highest teaching" of the Buddha—were as marginal to the dynamics of Buddhism in history as are the technical debates raging in philosophy departments in shaping Western institutions of higher learning. Yet we still find scholars—even those trying to guide in the redefining of Buddhist studies—imagining "that the canons . . . guided the tradition" (Gomez 1995b: 205).

2. Even those who began with a highly selective Western appropriation of Buddhism have come to understand the need for a holistic approach to Buddhism. The poet Gary Snyder who has recently pointed out this persistent pattern of misconception by Euro-Americans:

> We came as westerners to Buddhism generally with an educated background. . . . So we have tended to overemphasize the intellectual and spiritual sides of it, with the model at hand of Zen, without realizing that a big part of the flavor of Buddhism, traditionally and historically, is devotional. This is not necessarily tied to doing a lot of practice, but is tied to having an altar in the house—putting flowers in front of it every day, burning incense in front of it every day, having children bow and burn incense before it. . . . You can be a perfectly good Buddhist by keeping flowers on your altar. . . .
> There's a big tendency right now in western Buddhism to psychologize it—to try and take the superstition, the magic, the irrationality out of it and to make it a kind if therapy . . . I'm grateful for the fact that I lived in Asia for so long and hung out with Asian Buddhists. I appreciate that Buddhism is a whole practice and isn't just limited to the lecture side of it; that it has stories and superstition and ritual and goofiness like that. I love that aspect of it more and more. (Quoted in Carolan 1996: 25.)

3. The best example of this might be the dismissive attitude earlier generations showed for the practice of mantra recitation. Edward J. Thomas (1933: 156) writes of mantras "infecting" the tradition; Cecil Bendall (1880: 286) even chose to omit them from his translation of a *sūtra*, calling them "mere gibberish and mysticism."

4. The early formulation called the graded teaching (*anupūrvīkathā*) established *puṇya/dāna* (merit/gift-giving) as the foundation for Buddhist practice, while also legitimating a Buddhist community's diverse cultural activities. The *anupūrvīkathā* are as follows:

1. *dāna/puṇya*
2. *shīla/svarga* ("morality"/"heaven")
3. evils of *pāpa/kāma* ("immoral acts"/"pleasure seeking")
4. value of renunciation
5. Four Noble Truths (Lamotte 1988: 77)

This hierarchy of legitimate, progressive practices defines a "syllabus" for advancing in spiritual attainment. As *puṇya* has provided the chief orientation point and goal in the Buddhist layperson's worldview and ethos, *dāna* (giving, charity, and generosity) has always been the starting practice for accumulating *puṇya*, the lifelong measure of spiritual advancement.

5. The Buddhist worldview rejects the assumption of "spiritual democracy" and a singular religious vocation for all that is so integral to Western monotheisms. In the Theravāda texts, the levels and subdivisions

of this hierarchy are specified. As George D. Bond states, "The basic classification given divides persons into three types: the ordinary person (*puthujjana*, the learner or initiate (*sekha*), and the adept (*asekha*)" (Bond 1988: 34). People can also be divided into two groups: those dominated by desire-temperament (*taṇhācarita*) and persons of view temperament (*diṭṭhicarita*). The former was also divided according to a subdivision of those dominated by lust (*rāgacarita*), hate (*dosacarita*), or delusion (*moha*) (35). Yet another division placed persons depending on their ability to receive teachings: those who need only condensed teaching, those who need expanded teaching, and those who are barely instructable. The text cited by Bond (ibid.) 35) adds that each can be subdivided by those who are bright-witted or dull-witted.

Texts, too, are designated according to human diversity: some deal with defilement, some with moral teaching, some with penetration of doctrine, and still others with the adept (ibid.). The classification scheme also divided the texts into mundane and supramundane content.

6. The seventh-century saint Shantideva's verses express this powerfully:

> May I become a wish-fulfilling jewel to all embodied beings
> A horn of plenty
> A Powerful magical formula
> The universal remedy.
> (Cited in Gomez 1995a: 190)

7. A Chinese devotee of Kwan Yin *dhāraṇī* chanting provides one example of a Buddhist practitioner overturning the logic of elitism to explicate and to apply Mahāyāna philosophy to *dhāraṇī* recitation practice:

> The conventional view of the world says that ordinary people are totally different from sages and people cannot be transformed into holy persons. Because they narrow their potentiality this way, they cannot keep the *dhāraṇī*. On the other hand, if people fall into the other extreme of nihilism and think that in emptiness there is no law in causality, they also cannot keep the *dhāraṇī* because of their recklessness. When one realizes that the common man and the sage possess the same mind and there is not the slightest difference at all, one has left the conventional view. When one realizes that this one mind can manifest as either ordinary or saintly and this is due to the clear working of causality, one has then left the nihilistic view. Leaving behind these two erroneous views and following the one mind in teaching the world, one can then chant the *dhāraṇī* [and] . . . the effect will be unfailingly efficacious. (Cited in Yu 1996: 104.)

8. I have learned to counter this usual student reaction to standard textbooks and textual readers about Buddhism by forcing an analogy: is it also the case that the only "true Christians" are those who renounce the

householder's life world and take vows as Jesuit priests or Carmelite nuns? Is it true that the rest, including all the laity who live by less strict discipleship, are "not true Christians" or, as one of my Holy Cross students once wrote, "slacker Christians?"

9. The history of the influential *Mahāvastu* and *Divyāvadāna* texts traces this connection: both are derived from the Sarvāstivādin Vinayas, indicating that the stories collected were so numerous and useful that they were eventually spun off into these narrative anthologies (Levi 1907).

10. These points on family relations have also been developed by Gregory Schopen (1984, 1985a, 1985b, 1988–89, 1991b).

11. This power of the *jātaka*s to teach disciples about the faith is not just consigned to the past. For example, John P. Ferguson and Christina B. Johannsen explain the rapid multiplication of *jātaka*s on temple murals as modern attempts to revitalize Buddhism in northern Thailand:

> It is our argument . . . that among the young particularly, a modern materialist conviction that a living being has only one life to live would badly undermine belief in the entire religion. . . . Therefore, the defense of the religion against such danger, through the symbolic "drama" of the murals, stresses the importance of rebirth over great periods of time. One can easily recognize the rebirth there. . . .
> (Ferguson and Johannsen 1976: 602)

Commenting on one of the most popular sets of murals, the last ten lives of the Buddha-to-be, they write, "It is quite evident that the [*jātaka* murals'] stress upon giving of food, robes, monasteries . . . affirms this ritual and cultural value in the face of modern attitudes that involve relatively less support" (ibid.).

12. In a recent essay on the enduring power of Catholic tradition, the sociologist Andrew W. Greely focuses upon two themes that connect with the dual emphases in this volume: satisfying sacramental ritualism and the rich story narratives. He writes:

> It may seem that I am reducing religion to childishness—to stories and images and rituals and communities. In fact, it is in the poetic, the metaphorical, the experiential dimension of the personality that religion finds both its origins and raw power. Because we are reflective creatures we must also reflect on our religious experiences and stories; it is in the (lifelong) interlude of reflection that propositional religion and religious authority become important, indeed indispensable. But then the religiously mature person returns to the imagery, having criticized it, analyzed it, questioned it, to commit the self once more in sophisticated and reflective maturity to the story. (Greely 1994: 40)

13. If we follow the insight of the Nepalese tradition, I would also add that most living Newar Buddhist art has a connection with family ritual practice: sculptures and paintings, and *caitya*s and *stūpa*s have been created for merit-making ritual and are pivotal to the regular continuation of local Buddhist practice.

14. See the passage quoted at the start of this chapter.

15. See Samuel Beal (1970: 21–22).

16. Intellectuals interested in finding Buddhism free of elitist bias might consider the experience of the psychologist and Harvard professor William James who had an awakening about the necessity of staying open to "the folk" to understand the broader sweep of history. The quote beginning this chapter follows from his travels in rural America. As Lawrence W. Levine relates,

> One hundred years ago, William James wrote of being in the mountains of North Carolina and seeing what at first appeared to be pure squalor: settlers had killed all the trees, planted their crops around the stumps, and erected rough cabins and crude fences, thus marring the landscape. "The forest," James observed, "had been destroyed; what had 'improved' it out of existence was hideous, a sort of ulcer, without a single element of artificial grace to make up for the loss of Nature's beauty. . . ." But greater acquaintance with the people of the area taught him his error.
>
> > When *they* looked on the hideous stumps, what they thought of was personal victory. The chips, the girdled trees and the vile split rails spoke of honest sweat, persistent toils and final reward. The cabin was a warrant of safety for self and wife and babes. In short, the clearing, which to me was a mere ugly picture on the retina, was to them a symbol redolent with moral memories and sang a very paen of duty, struggle, and success." (Levine 1996: 144–45).

He then wrote the words that begin this chapter.

Bibliography

Aalto, Pentti. "Prolegomena to an Edition of the *Pañcarakṣā*," *Studia Orientalis Fennica* 19 (12), 1954, 5–48.

———. *Qutut-Tu Pancarakṣā Kemeku Tabun Sakiyan Neretu Yeke Kolgen Sudur*. Weisbaden: Otto Harrassowitz, 1961.

Allen, Michael. "Buddhism Without Monks: The Vajrayana Religion of the Newars of the Kathmandu Valley," *South Asia* 3, 1973, 1–14.

Amore, Roy C. and Larry D. Shinn. *Lustful Maidens and Ascetic Kings*. New York: Oxford University Press, 1981.

Babb, Lawrence A. *The Divine Hierarchy: Popular Buddhism in Central India*. New York: Columbia University Press, 1975.

Bagchi, P. C. "The Eight Great *Caityas* and Their Cult," *Indian Historical Quarterly* 17, 1941, 223–35.

Bailey, H. W. "The Pradaksina-Sutra of Chang-Kuin," in L. Cousins et al., eds. *Buddhist Studies in Honour of I.B. Horner*, Dordrecht, Netherlands: Reidel, 1974, 15–18.

Bajracarya, Badri. *Dashakarma Pratiṣṭhā, Chāhāyeke Bidhi va Balimālā*. Kathmandu, Nepal: Malakara Printing Press, 1988.

Bajracarya, Madan Sena. "Nekūbājā: Chagūadhyayana," *Nepayā Lokabajā* 1990, 26–30.

Bajracharya, Purna Harsha. "Than Bahil, An Ancient Centre for Sanskrit Study," *Indologica Taurinensia* 7, 1979, 62–64.

Bareau, Andre. "Constellations et divinities protectrices des merchants dans le bouddhisme ancien," *Journal Asiatique* 247, 1959, 303–9.

———. "La Construction et le culte des stūpa d'apres les Vinayapiṭaka," *Bulletin de l'Ecole Francaise d'Extreme-Orient* 50, 1962, 229–74.

———. "Un Personage bien mysterieux: L'Epouse du Buddha," in L. A. Hercus et al., eds. *Indological and Buddhist Studies: Volume in Honour of Professor J.W. de Jong on his Sixtieth Birthday*. Canberra, Australia: Faculty of Asian Studies, 1982, 31–59.

Barnes, Nancy J. "The *Triskandha*, Practice in Three Parts: Study of an Early Mahāyāna Ritual," in N. K. Wagle and F. Watanabe, eds. *Studies on Buddhism in Honour of Professor A.K. Warder*. Toronto: University of Toronto, 1993, 1–10.

Basak, Radhagovinda, ed. *Mahāvastu Avadāna*. Calcutta: Sanskrit College, 1963.

Beal, Samuel, trans. *Si-Yu-Ki: Buddhist Records of the Western World*. New York: Paragon Book Reprint, 1970.

Beckwith, Christopher I. "Tibet and the Early Medieval Florissance in Eurasia: A Preliminary Note on the Economic History of the Tibetan Empire," *Central Asiatic Journal* 21, 1977, 91–112.

Bendall, Cecil. "The Mahamegha Sutra," *Journal of the Royal Asiatic Society* 1880, 286ff.

———and W. H. D. Rouse. *Siksa Samuccaya*. New Delhi, India: Motilal Banarsidass Reprint, 1971.

Bennett, Tony. "Texts in History: The Determination of Readings and Their Texts," in Derek Attridge et al., eds. *Post-structuralism and the Question of History*. Cambridge: Cambridge University Press, 1987, 63–81.

Bentor, Yael. "The Redactions of the *Adbhutadharmaparyāya* from Gilgit," *Journal of the International Association of Buddhist Studies* 11 (2), 1988, 21–52.

———. "On the Indian Origins of the Tibetan Practice of Depositing Relics and *Dhāraṇīs* in Stūpas and Images," *Journal of the American Oriental Society* 115 (2), 1995, 248–261.

Beresford, Brian C. *Āryaśūra's Aspiration* and *A Meditation on Compassion*. Dharamsala, India: Library of Tibetan Works and Archives, 1979.

Beyer, Stephan. *The Cult of Tara: Magic and Ritual in Tibet*. Berkeley: University of California Press, 1973.

Bharati, Agehananda. *The Tantric Tradition*. London: Rider, 1965.

Bhattacharyya, Benoytosh. *The Sadhanamala*. Baroda, India: Gaekwad's Oriental Series 41, 1968a.

———. *Indian Buddhist Iconography*. Calcutta, India: Firma K. L. Mukhopadhyay, 1968b.

Bhattacharyya, D. C. "The Five Protective Goddesses of Buddhism," in P. Pal, ed. *Aspects of Indian Art*. Leiden, Netherlands: E. J. Brill, 1972, 85–92.

———. "Iconography of the Pancarakṣā," in D. C. Bhattacharyya, *Studies in Buddhist Iconography*. New Delhi, India: Manohar, 1978, 78–100.

———. "The Vajrāvalī-nāma-mandalopāyikā of Abhayākaragupta," *Melanges Chinois and Bouddhiques* XX, 1981, 70–95.

Bista, Dor. "Nepalis in Tibet," in James Fisher, ed. *Himalayan Anthropology*. The Hague: Mouton, 1978, 187–204.

Blondeau, Anne-Marie. "The Life of the Child Padma `od-`bar: From the Theatre to the Painted Image," in Jamyang Norbu, ed. *ZLOS-GAR*. Dharamsala, India: Library of Tibetan Works and Archives, 1986, 20–44.

———. "La Vie de l'enfant Padma 'od-'bar: du texte a l'image," *Arts Asiatiques* 1003, 1988, 40–59.

Bloss, Lowell W. "The Buddha and the Nāga: A Study in Buddhist Folk Religiousity," *History of Religions* 13 (1), 1973, 36–53.

Bond, George D. "The Gradual Path as a Hermeneutical Approach to the *Dhamma*," in Donald S. Lopez, ed. *Buddhist Hermeneutics*. Honolulu: University of Hawaii Press, 1988, 29–45.

Bowen, John R. "The Forms Culture Takes: A State-of-the-Field Essay on the Anthropology of Southeast Asia," *Journal of Asian Studies* 54 (4), 1995, 1047–78.

Braarvig, Jens. "*Dhāraṇī* and *Pratibhāna*: Memory and Eloquence of the Bodhisattvas," *Journal of the International Association of Buddhist Studies* 8 (1), 1985, 17–29.

Brough, John. "Legends of Khotan and Nepal," *Bulletin of the School of Oriental and African Studies* 12, 1948, 333–39.

———. "The Language of the Buddhist Sanskrit Texts," *Bulletin of the School of African and Asian Studies* 16, 1954, 351–75.

Brown, D. Mackenzie. "Didactic Themes of Buddhist Political Thought in the Jātakas," *Journal of Oriental Literature* 1 (2), 1955, 3–7.

Brown, W. Norman. "Duty as Truth in Ancient India," *Proceedings of the American Philosophical Society* 116 (3), 1972, 252–68.

Bue, E. "The Newar Artists of the Nepal Valley. An Historical Account of Their Activities in Neighbouring Areas with Particular Reference to Tibet, I," *Oriental Art* 21 (3), 1985, 262–77.

———. "The Artists of the Nepal Valley, II," *Oriental Art* 21 (4), 1986, 409–20.

Burlingame, Eugene Watson. *Buddhist Legends: The Pali Text of the Dhammapada Commentary*. London: Pali Text Society, 1990. (Original edition 1921)

Burrow, T. *A Translation of the Kharosthi Documents from Chinese Turkestan*. London: Royal Asiatic Society, 1940.

Buswell, Robert E., ed. *Chinese Buddhist Apocrypha*. Honolulu: University of Hawaii Press, 1990.

Cabezon, Jose Ignacio. "Buddhist Studies as a Discipline and the Role of Theory," *Journal of the International Association of Buddhist Studies* 18 (2), 1995, 231–68.

Carolan, Trevor. "The Wild Mind of Gary Synder," *Shambala Sun* May 1996, 18–26.

Carrithers, Michael. "Jainism and Buddhism as Enduring Historical Streams," *Journal of the Anthropological Society of Oxford* 21 (2), 1990, 141–63.

Chakravarti, Shyamalkanti. "Three Dated Nepalese *Paṭas* in the Indian Museum," *Indian Museum Bulletin* 4 (2), 1969, 124–33.

Coedes, George. *The Indianized States of Southeast Asia*. Honolulu: University of Hawaii Press, 1971.

Collins, Steven. *Selfless Persons: Imagery and Thought in Theravada Buddhism*. Cambridge: Cambridge University Press, 1982.

Conze, Edward. *Astasahasrika Prajnaparamita*. Rome: ISMEO, 1962.

Cowell, E. B., ed. *The Jātaka* (6 Vols.). London: Routledge and Kegan Paul Reprint, 1957.

———and others. *Buddhist Mahāyāna Texts*. New York: Dover reprint, 1969.

Crites, Stephen, "Angels We Have Heard," in James B. Wiggins, ed. *Religion as Story*. New York: Harper, 1975, 23–63.

Curtin, Philip. *Cross-Cultural Trade in World History*. Cambridge: Cambridge University Press, 1984.

Czuma, Stanislaw J. *Kushan Sculpture: Images from Early India*. Cleveland: Cleveland Museum of Art, 1985.

Dallapiccola, Anna, ed. *The Stupa: Its Religious, Historical, and Architectural Significance*. Wiesbaden: Franz Steiner Verlag, 1980.

Dargyay, Eva K. "Merit-Making and Ritual Aspects in the Religious Life of Zanskar (West Tibet)," in Ronald W. Neufeldt, ed. *Karma and*

Rebirth. Albany: SUNY Press, 1986, 179–89.

———. "Buddhism in Adaptation: Ancestor Gods and Their Tantric Counterparts in the Religious Life of Zanskar," *History of Religions* 28, 1988, 123–34.

Das, Sukumar R. "Hindu Calendar," *Indian Historical Quarterly* 4, 1928, 483–511.

Dasgupta, Shashibhusan. *Obscure Religious Cults*. Calcutta: Firma K. L. Mukhopadhyay reprint, 1969.

———. *An Introduction to Tantric Buddhism*. Berkeley: Shambala, 1974.

Davidson, Ronald M. "Litany of Names of Mañjusrī: Text and Translation of the Mañjushrī Ṇāmasaṃgīti," *Melanges Chinois et Bouddhiques* 20, 1981, 1–69.

———. "An Introduction to the Standards of Scriptural Authenticity in Indian Buddhism," in Robert A. Buswell, ed. *Chinese Buddhist Apocrypha*. Honolulu: University of Hawaii Press, 1990, 291–325.

Dayal, Har. *The Bodhisattva Doctrine in Buddhist Sanskrit Literature*. London: Routledge and Kegan Paul, 1932.

De, Gokuldas. *Significance and Importance of Jatakas*. Calcutta: Calcutta University Press, 1951.

Decleer, Hubert. "Atisha's Journey to Sumatra," in Donald S. Lopez Jr., ed. *Buddhism in Practice*. Princeton: Princeton University Press, 1995, 532–40.

Dehejia, Vidya. *Early Buddhist Rock Temples: A Chronology*. Ithaca: Cornell University Press, 1972.

Desai, Devangana. "The Social Milieu of Indian Terracottas 600 BC-600 AD," in Amy Poster, ed. *From Indian Earth*, New York: Brooklyn Museum, 1986, 29–42.

DeVisser, M. W. "The Goddess Mahamayuri in China and Japan," in *German Scholars on India*. Bombay: Nachiketa Publications, 1976, 193–209.

Diamond, Jared. *Guns, Germs, and Steel: The Fates of Human Societies*. New York: W. W. Norton, 1997.

Diskul, M. C. Subhadradis, ed. *The Art of Srivijaya*. New York: Oxford University Press, 1980.

Dowman, Keith. *The Legend of the Great Stupa*. Kathmandu, Nepal: Diamond Sow Publications, 1978.

———. "A Buddhist Guide to the Power Places of the Kathmandu Valley," *Kailash* 8, 3–4, 1982, 183–291.

Dupont, Pierre. *La Version Mone du Narada-Jataka*. Saigon: Ecole Francaise d'Extreme Orient, 1954.

Duroiselle, Charles. "Pictorial Representations of Jatakas in Burma," *Archaeological Survey of India Report* 1912–13, 87–119.

Dutt, Nalinaksha. "Popular Buddhism," *Indian Historical Quarterly* 21 (4), 1945b, 245–70.

———. "The Place of the Laity in Early Buddhism," *Indian Historical Quarterly*, 21 (3), 1945a, 163–183.

———. *Mahayana Buddhism*. Delhi, India: Motilal Banarsidass, 1977.

Dutt, Sukumar. *Buddhist Monks and Monasteries of India*. London: Allen and Unwin, 1962.

Eckel, Malcolm David. "The Ghost at the Table: On the Study of Buddhism and the Study of Religion," *Journal of the American Academy of Religion* 62 (4), 1994, 1085–1110.

Edgerton, Franklin. *Buddhist Hybrid Sanskrit Doctionary*. New Haven: Yale University Press, 1953.

Emmerick, R. E. *The Book of Zambasta: A Khotanese Poem on Buddhism*. London: Oxford University Press, 1968.

Evans-Wentz, W. Y. *Tibet's Great Yogi Milarepa*. New York: Oxford University Press, 1969.

Falk, Nancy. "To Gaze on the Sacred Traces," *History of Religions* 16, 1977, 281–93.

Ferguson, John P. and Christina B. Johannsen. "Modern Buddhist Murals in Northern Thailand: A Study of Religious Symbols and Meaning," *American Ethnologist* 3 (4), 1976, 645–69.

Fontein, Jan. "Notes on the Jatakas and Avadanas of Barabudur," in Luis O. Gomez and Hiram W. Woodward, eds. *Barabudur*. Berkeley: Buddhist Studies Series, 1981.

———. *The Sculpture of Indonesia*. New York: Harry N. Abrams, 1990.

Foucher, Alfred. *Etude sur l'iconographie bouddhique de l'Inde*. Paris: Ernest Leroux, 1900.

Freemantle, Francesca and Chogyam Trungpa. *The Tibetan Book of the Dead*. Boston: Shambala Press, 1987.

Furer-Haimendorf, Christoph von. *Himalayan Traders*. New York: St. Martin's Press, 1975.

Geertz, Clifford, "Religion as a Cultural System," in Michael Banton, ed. *Anthropological Approaches to the Study of Religion*. London: Tarstock Publishers, 1966.

Gellner, David N. "Max Weber, Capitalism and the Religion of India," *Sociology* 16 (4), 1982, 526–43.

———. "Language, Caste, Religion and Territory: Newar Identity Ancient and Modern," *European Journal of Sociology* 27, 1986, 102–48.

———. "The Newar Buddhist Monastery: An Anthropological and Historical Typology," in N. Gutschow and A. Michaels, eds. *The Heritage of the Kathmandu Valley*. Sankt Augustin: VGH Wissenschaftsverlag, 1987, 364–414.

———. "Monastic Initiation in Newar Buddhism," in R. F. Gombrich, ed. *Oxford University Papers on India* 2 (1), 1988, 42–112.

———. "Monkhood and Priesthood in Newar Buddhism," *Purushārtha* 12, 1989, 165–91.

———. "Introduction: What Is the Anthropology of Buddhism About?" *Journal of the Anthropological Society of Oxford* 21 (1), 1990, 95–112.

———. "Hinduism, Tribalism and the Position of Women: The Problem of Newar Identity," *Man* (N.S.) 26 (1), 1991a, 105–25.

———. "Ritualized Devotion, Altruism, and Meditation: The Offering of the *Guru Maṇḍala* in Newar Buddhism," *Indo-Iranian Journal* 34, 1991b, 161–97.

———. *Monk, Householder and Tantric Priest: Newar Buddhism and Its Hierarchy of Ritual*. Cambridge: Cambridge University Press, 1992.

———. "Priests, Healers, Mediums, and Witches: The Context of Possession in the Kathmandu Valley, Nepal," *Man* 29 (1), 1994, 27–48.

———and Declan Quigley, eds. *Contested Hierarchies: A Collaborative Ethnography of Caste among the Newars of the Kathmandu Valley, Nepal*. Oxford: Oxford University Press, 1995.

Gernet, Jacques. *Buddhism in Chinese Society: An Economic History from the Fifth to the Tenth Centuries*. New York: Columbia University Press, 1995.

Getty, Alice. *The Gods of Northern Buddhism*. New York: Dover reprint, 1988.

Gokhale, Balkrishna Govind. "The Early Buddhist Elite," *Journal of Indian History* 43, 1965, 391–402.

———. "The Merchant in Ancient India," *Journal of the American Oriental Society* 97, 1977, 125–130.

Gombo, Ugen, "Belief in Karma and Its Social Ramification in Samsara," in Barbara N. Aziz and Matthew Kapstein, eds. *Soundings in Tibetan Civilization*. New Delhi: Manohar, 1985, 233–44.

Gombrich, Richard F. *Precept and Practice: Traditional Buddhism in the Rural Highlands of Ceylon*. Oxford: Oxford University Press, 1971.

———. "The Vessantara Jātaka, the Rāmāyaṇa and the Dasaratha Jātaka," *Journal of the American Oriental Society* 105 (3), 1985, 427–37.

Gombrich, Richard F. *Theraveda Buddhism*. New York: Routledge and Kegan Paul, 1988.

——— and Gananath Obeyesekere. *Buddhism Transformed: Religious Change in Sri Lanka*. Princeton: Princeton University Press, 1988.

Gomez, Luis O. "Buddhist Views of Language," in Mircea Eliade, ed. *The Encyclopedia of Religion*, Volume 8. New York: Macmilla, 1987, 446–451.

Gomez, Luis O. "A Mahāyāna Liturgy," in Donald S. Lopez Jr., ed. *Buddhism in Practice*. Princeton: Princeton University Press, 1995a, 183–96.

———. "Unspoken Paradigms: Meanderings through the Metaphors of a Field," *Journal of the International Association of Buddhist Studies* 18 (2), 1995b, 183–230.

Greenwold, Stephen M. "Buddhist Brahmins," *Archives Europeennes de Sociologie* 15, 1974, 483–503.

———. "The Role of the Priest in Newar Society," in James Fisher, ed. *Himalayan Anthropology*. The Hague, Netherlands: Mouton, 1978, 483–503.

Greely, Andrew W. "Because of the Stories," *New York Times Magazine*, July 10, 1994, 38–41.

Griswold, A. B. "The Holy Land Transported: Replicas of the Mahabodhi Shrine in Siam and Elsewhere," *Paranavitana Felicitation Volume*. Colombo, Sri Lanka: M. D. Gunasena, 1965, 173–221.

Groslier, Bernard. *Angkor: Hommes et Pierres*. Paris: Arthaud, 1968.

Grunwedel, Albert. *Altbuddhistische Kultstatten in Chinesisch-Turkistan*. Berlin: Durck und Verlag von Georg Reimer, 1912.

Gupta, Sanjukta. "Mantra," in Mircea Eliade, ed. *The Encyclopaedia of Religion* 9, 1987, 176–77.

Gutschow, Niels. *The Nepalese Caitya*. Stattgart: Edition Axel Menges, 1997.

Gyorgy, Kara. *Az Ot Oltalom Konyve: Pancarakṣā Ayusi Atdolgozott Forditas`a (Mongol Nyelvemlektar VIII)* Budapest: Elte Belso-Azsiai Intezet, 1965.

Kolver, Bernhard. "Stages in the Evolution of a World Picture," *Numen* 32 (2), 1985, 131–68.

Hallisey, Charles. "The Advice to Layman Tuṇdila," in Donald S. Lopez Jr. ed. *Sourcebook on Buddhist Religion*. Princeton: Princeton University Press, 1995a, 302–13.

———. "Roads Taken and Not Taken in the Study of Theravada Buddhism," in Donald S. Lopez Jr., ed. *Curators of the Buddha: The Study of Buddhism under Colonialism*. Chicago: University of Chicago Press, 1995b, 31–61.

——— and Anne Hansen. "Narrative, Sub-Ethics, and the Moral Life: Some Evidence from Theravada Buddhism," *Journal of Religious Ethics* 24 (2), 1996, 305–25.

Hare, E. M., trans. *The Book of Gradual Sayings, Vol. 3*. Oxford: Pali Text Society, 1988.

Harvey, P. "The Symbolism of the Early Stupa," *Journal of the International Asociation of Buddhist Studies* 7, 1984, 67–93.

Heitzman, James. "Early Buddhism, Trade and Empire," in Kenneth A. R. Kennedy and Gregory L. Possehl, eds. *Studies in the Archaeology and Paleoanthropology of South Asia*. New Delhi, India: Oxford and IBH Publishing, 1984, 121–37.

Heller, Amy. *Tibetan Collection* Volume 3 (2d ed.). Newark: Newark Museum, 1986.

Hirakawa, Akira. "The Rise of Mahāyāna Buddhism and Its Relationship to the Worship of Stupas" in *Memoirs of the Research Department of the Tokyo Bunko* 22, 1963, 57–106.

Hodgson, Brian H. *Essays on the Languages, Literature, and Religion of Nepal and Tibet*. New Delhi, India: Manjusri, 1972 (Original edition 1874).

Hoffman, Frank J. "*Evam Me Sutam:* Oral Traditions in Nikaya Buddhism," in Jeffrey R. Timm, ed. *Texts in Context*. Albany: SUNY Press, 1992, 195–219.

Holt, John Clifford. *Buddha in the Crown: Avalokiteshvara in the Buddhist Traditions of Sri Lanka*. New York: Oxford University Press, 1991.

———. *The Religious World of Kirti Sri: Buddhism, Art, and Politics in Late Medieval Sri Lanka*. New York: Oxford University Press, 1996.

Hunter, William Wilson. *The Life of Brian Houghton Hodgson*. 1896, reprint. New Delhi, India: Asian Educational Services, 1991.

Hurvitz, Leon. *The Lotus Blossom of the True Law*. New York: Columbia University Press, 1976.

Hutt, Michael James. *Himalayan Voices: An Introduction to Modern Nepali Literature*. Berkeley: University of California Press, 1991.

Huxley, Andrew. "Studying Theravada Legal Literature," *Journal of the International Association of Buddhist Studies* 20 (1), 1997, 63–91.

Iltis, Linda. *The Svastani Vrata: Newar Women and Ritual in Nepal*. Ann Arbor, Mich.: University Microfilms International, 1985.

Iwamoto, Y. *Bukkyo Setsuwa Kenkyu Josetsu*. Kyoto, Japan: Hozokan, 1967, 247–94.

Jackson, Roger R. "Matching Concepts: Deconstructive and Foundationalist Tendencies in Buddhist Thought," *Journal of the American Academy of Religion* 57 (3), 1989, 561–89.

Jaini, Padmanabh S. "The Story of Sudhana and Monoharā: An Analysis of the Texts and the Borobudur Reliefs," *Bulletin of the School of Oriental and African Studies* 29, 1966, 533–58.

Jest, Corneille. "The Newar Merchant Community in Tibet: An Interface of Newar and Tibetan Cultures," in Gerard Toffin, ed. *Nepal, Past and Present*. Paris: CNRS, 1992, 159–68.

Jones, J. J. *The Mahavastu* (3 Vols.). London: Luzac, 1949–56.

de Jong, J. W. "The Magic Wall of the Fortress of the Ogresses: Apropos of *asiyati* (Mahāvastu III, 86.3)," in Gregory Schopen, ed. *Buddhist Studies by J.W. de Jong*. The Hague, Netherlands: Mouton, 1981, 293–96.

———. "The Study of Buddhism, Problems and Perspectives," in Gregory Schopen, ed. *Buddist Studies by J.W. de Jong.* The Hague, Netherlands: Mouton, 1981, 15–28.

Jorgensen, Hans. *Vicitrakarnikavadanoddhrta: A Collection of Buddhist Legends*. London: Royal Asiatic Society, 1931.

Kane, P. V. *History of the Dharma Sastra*. Poona, India: Bhandarkar Oriental Research Institute, 1974.

Kalamandapa. *Buddhist Ritual Dance*. Kathmenda: Institute of Classical Nepalese Performing Arts, 1986.

Keyes, Charles F. "Buddhist Pilgrimage Centers and the Twelve-Year Cycle: Northern Thai Moral Orders in Space and Time," *History of Religions* 15, 1975, 71–89.

———. "Merit-Transference in the Kammic Theory of Popular Theravāda Buddism," in Charles F. Keyes and E. Valentine Daniel, eds. *Karma: An Anthropological Inquiry.* Berkeley: University of California Press, 1983, 261-286.

Kloppenberg, Ria. "Theravada Buddhism in Nepal," *Kailash* 5 (4), 1977, 301–22.

Kolver, Bernhard. "Stages in the Evolution of a World Picture," *Numen* 32 (2), 1985, 131–68.

Kosambi, D. D. *Ancient India*. New York: Meridian, 1964.

Krairiksh, Piriya. *Buddhist Folk Tales Depicted at Chula Pathon Cedi*. Bangkok, Thailand: Prachandra Press, 1974.

———. "*Semas* with Scenes from the Mahānipāta-Jātakas in the National Museum at Khon Kaen," in *Art and Archaeology in Thailand*. Bangkok, Thailand: Fine Arts Department, 1974.

Kreijger, Hugo E. *Kathmandu Valley Painting: The Jucker Collection*. Boston: Shambala, 1999.

Ku, Cheng-mei. "A Ritual of Mahāyāna Vinaya: Self-Sacrifice," in David Kalupahana, ed. *Buddhist Thought and Ritual*. New York: Paragon, 1991, 159–71.

Lai, Whalen. "*Avadana-vada* and the Pure Land Faith," *Pacific World* 1989, 1–7.

Lamb, Alastair. "Mahayana Buddhist Votive Tablets in Perlis," *Journal of the Malaysian Branch of the Royal Asiatic Society* 37, 1964, 47–59.

Lamotte, Etienne. "The Buddha, His Teachings, and His Sangha," in Heinz Bechert and Richard Gombrich, eds. *The World of Buddhism*. New York: Facts on File, 1984, 41–58.

———. *History of Indian Buddhism: From the Origins to the Saka Era*. Louvain, Belgium: Institut Orientaliste, 1988.

Law, B. C. "Some Observations on the Jatakas," *Journal of the Royal Asiatic Society* 1939, 241–51.

Legge, James, trans., *A Record of Buddhist Kingdoms*. Oxford: Clarendon Press, 1886.

Lehman, F. K. "Doctrine, Practice, and Belief in Theravada Buddhism," *Journal of Asian Studies* 31 (2), 1971, 372–80.

Leoshko, Janice. "An Eleventh Century Jambhala Mandala of the Pala Period," *Orientations* 27 (7), 1996, 35–37.

Lester, Robert C. *Buddhism*. New York: Harper, 1987.

Levi, Sylvain. *Le Nepal* (3 Vols.). Paris: Leroux, 1905–8.

———. "Les Elements de Formation du *Divyāvadāna*," *T'oung Pao* 8, 1907, 105–22.

———. "Le Catalogue des *yakṣa* dans la *Mahāmāyūrī*," *Journal Asiatique* 1915, 19–38.

———. "Les 'merchants de mer' et leur role dans le bouddhisme primitif," *Bulletin de l'Association Francaise de Amis de l'Orient*, October 1929, 19–39.

Levine, Lawrence W. *The Opening of the American Mind: Canons, Culture, and History*. Boston: Beacon, 1996.

Levy, Robert I. *Mesocosm: Hinduism and the Organization of a Traditional Newar City in Nepal*. Berkeley: University of California Press, 1990.

Lewis, Todd T. *The Tulādhars of Kathmandu: A Study of Buddhist Tradition in a Newar Merchant Community*. Ann Arbor, Mich.: University Microfilms International, 1984.

———. "Mahāyāna *Vratas* in Newar Buddhism," *The Journal of the International Association of Buddhist Studies* 12 (1), 1989a, 109–38.

———. "Childhood and Newar Tradition: Chittadhar Hridaya's *Jhi Maca*," *Asian Folklore Studies* 48, 1989b, 195–210.

———. "Newars and Tibetans in the Kathmandu Valley: Ethnic Boundaries and Religious History," *Journal of Asian and African Studies* 38, 1989c, 31–57.

———. "Newar-Tibetan Trade and the Domestication of the *Siṃhalasārthabāhu Avadāna*," *History of Religions* 33 (2), 1993a, 135–60.

———. "Himalayan Frontier Trade: Newar Diaspora Merchants and Buddhism," in Charles Ramble and Martin Brauen, eds. *Anthropology of Tibet and the Himalayas*. Zurich: Volkerkundemuseum, 1993b, 165–78.

———. "Contributions to the Study of Popular Buddhism: The Newar Buddhist Festival of *Guṃlā Dharma*," *Journal of the International Association of Buddhist Studies* 16 (2), 1993c, 7–52.

———. "The *Nepāl Jana Jīvan Kriyā Paddhati*, A Modern Newar Guide for Vajrayāna Life-Cycle Rites," *Indo-Iranian Journal* 37, 1994a, 1–46.

———. "Contributions to the History of Buddhist Ritualism: A Mahāyāna *Avadāna* on *Caitya* Veneration from the Kathmandu Valley," *Journal of Asian History* 28 (1), 1994b, 1–38.

———. "The Himalayan Frontier in Comparative Perspective: Considerations Regarding Buddhism and Hinduism in Diaspora," *Himalayan Research Bulletin* 14 (1–2), 1994c, 25–46.

———. The Newar Buddhist Samyaka Festival: A Photo Essay," *Religious Studies News*, May 1994d, 2–10.

———. "Buddhist Merchants in Kathmandu: The Asan Tol Market and Urāy Social Organization," in David Gellner and Declan Quigley, eds. *Contested Hierarchies: A Collaborative Ethnography of Caste among the Newars of the Kathmandu Valley, Nepal*. Oxford: Oxford University Press, 1995a, 38–79.

———. "The Power of Mantra: A Story of the Five Protectors," in Donald S. Lopez Jr., ed. *Religions of India in Practice*. Princeton: Princeton University Press, 1995b, 227–35.

———. "The Story of the Horn-Blowing," in Donald S. Lopez Jr., ed. *Buddhism in Practice*. Princeton: Princeton University Press, 1995c, 328–35.

———. "The Tale of Siṃhala the Caravan Leader," in Donald S. Lopez Jr., ed. *Buddhism in Practice*. Princeton: Princeton University Press, 1995d, 151–69.

———. "*Sukhāvatī* Traditions in Newar Buddhism," *South Asia Research* 16 (1), 1996a, 1–30.

———. "Notes on the Uray and the Modernization of Newar Buddhism," *Contributions to Nepalese Studies* 23 (1), 1996b, 109–117.

———. "Patterns of Religious Belief in a Buddhist Merchant Community, Nepal," *Asian Folklore Studies* 55 (2), 1996c, 237–70.

———. "A Chronology of Newar-Tibetan Relations in the Kathmandu Valley," in Sigfried Lienhard, ed. *Change and Continuity: Studies in the Nepalese Culture of the Kathmandu Valley*. Torino, Italy: Edizioni Dell'orso, 1996d, 149–66.

———. "The Anthropological Study of Buddhist Communities: Historical Precedents and Ethnographic Paradigms," in Steven Glazier, ed. *Shamanism, Altered States, Healing: Essays in the Anthropology of Religion*. Westport, Conn.: Greenwood Press, 1997a, 319–67.

———. "Growing Up Newar Buddhist: Chittadhar Hridaya's *Jhī Macā* and Its Context," in Al Pach and Debra Skinner, eds. *Selves in Time and Place: Identities, Experience, and History in Nepal*. Boulder: Rowman and Littlefield Press, 1998, 301–318.

———. "The Use of Visual Media in the Study of Religious Belief and Practice" [with Christine Greenway] in Steven Glazier, ed. *Anthropology of Religion: A Handbook of Method and Theory*. Westport, Conn.: Greenwood Press, Forthcoming 2000.

——— and L. Jamspal. "Newars and Tibetans in the Kathmandu Valley: Three New Translations from Tibetan Sources," *Journal of Asian and African Studies* 36, 1988, 187–211.

——— and Daya Ratna Shakya, "Contributions to the History of Nepal: Eastern Newar Diaspora Settlements," *Contributions to Nepalese Studies* 15, 1, 1988, 25–65.

Lienhard, Siegfried. *Manicudavadanoddhrita*. Stockholm: Almquist and Wiksell, 1963.

———. "Nepal: The Survival of Indian Buddhism in a Himalayan Kingdom," in Heinz Bechert and Richard Gombrich, eds. *The World of Buddhism*. New York: Facts on File, 1984a, 108–14.

———. *The Songs of Nepal*. Honolulu: University of Hawaii Press, 1984b.

———. *Die Abenteuer des Kaufmanns Simhala*. Berlin: Museums fur Indische Kunst, 1985.

———. "A Nepalese Painted Scroll Illustrating the *Siṃhalāvadāna*," in Berhnard Kolver and S. Lienhard, eds. *Nepalica*. Sankt Augustin: VGH Wissenschaftsverlag, 1987, 51–53.

———. *Nepalese Manuscripts. Part 1. Nevari and Sanskrit*. Stuttgart, Germany: Franz Steiner Verlag, 1988.

———. "Avalokitesvara in the Wick of the Night Lamp," *Indo-Iranian Journal* 36, 1993, 93–104.

Lingat, Robert. "Vinaya et Droit Laique," *Bulletin de l'Ecole francaise d'Extreme-Orient* 37, 1937, 415–77.

Liu, Xinru. *Ancient India and Ancient China*. New Delhi, India: Oxford University Press, 1988.

Locke, John K. "Newar Buddhist Initiation Rites," *Contributions to Nepalese Studies* 2, 1975, 1–23.

———. *Karunamaya*. Kathmandu, Nepal: Sahiyogi, 1980.

———. *Buddhist Monasteries of Nepal*. Kathmandu, Nepal: Sahiyogi, 1985.

———. "The Vajrayana Buddhism in the Kathmandu Valley," in John K. Locke, ed. *The Buddhist Heritage of Nepal*. Kathmandu, Nepal: Dharmodaya Sabha, 1986, 43–72.

———. "Uposadha Vrata of Amoghapasa Lokesvara in Nepal," *L'Ethnographie* 83, 1987, 159–89.

Lopez, Donald S. Jr. "Introduction," in Donald S. Lopez Jr., ed. *Buddhism in Practice*. Princeton: Princeton University Press, 1995a, 3–36.

———. "Introduction," in Donald S. Lopez Jr., ed. *Curators of the Buddha: The Study of Buddhism under Colonialism*. Chicago: University of Chicago Press, 1995b, 1–29.

Luce, G. H. "The 550 Jatakas in Old Burma," *Artibus Asiae* 19, 1956, 291–307.

Macdonald, A. W. and Anne Vergati Stahl. *Newar Art: Nepalese Art During the Malla Period*. Warminster, England: Aris and Phillips, 1979.

MacQueen, Graeme. "The Conflict Bewteen External and Internal Mastery:

An Analysis of the Khantivadi Jataka," *History of Religions* 20 (2), 1981, 242–52.

Mair, Victor H. *Painting and Performance: Chinese Picture Recitation and Its Indian Genesis*. Honolulu: University of Hawaii Press, 1997.

Malandra, Geri H. *Unfolding a Mandala: The Buddhist Cave Temples at Ellora*. Albany: SUNY Press, 1993.

Malla, Kamal Prakash. *Classical Newari Literature*. Kathmandu, Nepal: Nepal Study Centre, 1981.

Mallmann, Marie-Therese. *Introduction a l'iconographie du Tantrisme Bouddhique*. Paris: Centre de Recherches sur l'Asie Centrale et la Haute Asie, 1975.

Manandhar, Thakur Lal. *Newari-English Dictionary*. Delhi, India: Agam Kala Prakashan, 1986.

Marriot, McKim. "Little Communities in an Indigenous Civilization," in M. Marriot, ed. *Village India: Studies in the Little Community*. Chicago: University of Chicago Press, 1955, 171–222.

Masquelier, Adeline. "Encounter with a Road Siren: Machines, Bodies and Commodities in the Imagination of a Mawri Healer," *Visual Anthropology Review* 8 (1), 1992, 56–69.

Matsunaga, Yukei. "A History of Tantric Buddhism in India with Reference to Chinese Translations," in Leslie S. Kawamura and Keith Scott, eds. *Buddhist Thought and Asian Civilizations*. Emeryville Illinois, 1977, 167–81.

McNeill, William H. *Plagues and Peoples*. New York: Anchor, 1977.

Meech-Pekarik, Julia. "The Flying White Horse: Transmission of the Valahassa Jataka Imagery from India to Japan," *Artibus Asiae* 43, 1981, 111–28.

Mevissen, Gerd J. R. "Transmission of Iconographic Traditions: *Paṇcarakṣā* Heading North," in Catherine Jarrige, ed. *South Asian Archaeology 1989*, 415–24.

———. "Studies in *Paṇcarakṣā* Manuscript Painting," *Berliner indologische Studien* 4/5, 1991/2, 351-382.

———. "The Indian Connection: Images of Deified Spells in the Arts of Northern Buddhism, Part I," *Silk Road Art and Archaeology* 1, 1990, 227-246.

———. "The Indian Connection: Images of Deified Spells in the Arts of Northern Buddhism, Part II," *Silk Road Art and Archaeology* 2, 1991, 351-382.

Miller, Robert J. "The Buddhist Monastic Economy: The *Jisa* Mechanism," *Comparative Studies in Society and History* 3, 1962, 427–38.

Mitra, Rajendralala. *The Sanskrit Buddhist Literature of Nepal*. Calcutta: Sanskrit Pustak Bhandar reprint, 1971.

Monier-Williams, Sir Monier. *A Sanskrit-English Dictionary*. (2d ed.). London: Oxford University Press, 1956.

Mumford, Stan R. *Himalayan Dialogue*. Madison: University of Wisconsin Press, 1989.

Mus, Paul. "Thousand-Armed Kannon: A Mystery or a Problem?" *Indogaku Bukkyogaku Kenkyo* 11 (1), 1964, 438–70.

Mya, U. *Votive Tablets of Burma*. Rangoon, Burma: 1961.

Nakamura, Kyoto Motomochi. *Miraculous Stories from the Japanese Buddhist Tradition: The Nihon Ryoiki of the Monk Kyokai*. Cambridge: Harvard University Press, 1973.

Nattier, Jan. *Once Upon a Future Time: Studies in a Buddhist Prophecy of Decline*. Berkeley: Asian Humanities, 1991.

———. "Visible and Invisible," *Tricycle: The Buddhist Review* Fall 1995, 42–49.

Novak, Charles M. *Catalogue of Selected Buddhist Manuscripts in the Asha Saphu Kuthi*. Kathmandu, Nepal: Jore Ganesh Press, 1986.

Obeyesekere, Gananath. "The Buddhist Pantheon in Ceylon and Its Extensions," in Manning Nash, ed. *Theravada Buddhism: Anthropological Studies*. New Haven: Yale University Press, 1964, 1–26.

———. "Theodicy, Sin, and Salvation in a Sociology of Buddhism," in Edmund Leach, ed. *Dialectic in Practical Religion*. Cambridge: Cambridge University Papers in Anthropology 5, 1968, 7–40.

———. "Buddhism and Conscience: An Exploratory Essay," *Daedalus* 120 (3), 1991, 219–39.

Obeyesekere, Ranjini. *Jewels of the Doctrine: Stories of the Saddharma Ratnavaliya by Dharmasena Thera*. Albany: SUNY Press, 1991.

O'Connor, Stanley J. "Buddhist Votive Tablets and Caves in Peninsular Thailand," in M. C. Subhadradis Diskul, ed. *Art and Archaeology in Thailand*. Bangkok, Thailand: Fine Arts Department, 1974, 67–84.

———. "A Metal Mould for the Manufacture of Clay Buddhist Votive Stupas," *Journal of the Malaysia Branch of the Royal Asiatic Society* 48 (2), 1975, 60–63.

O'Flaherty, Wendy Doniger. "Impermanence and Eternity in Indian Art and Myth," in Carla M. Borden, ed. *Contemporary Indian Tradition*. Washington: Smithsonian Institution Press, 1989.

Orzech, Charles D. "Puns on the Humane King: Analogy and Application in an East Asian Apocryphon," *Journal of the American Oriental Society* 109 (1), 1989, 17–24.

Overmyer, Daniel L. "Dualism and Conflict in Chinese Popular Religion," in Frank E. Reynolds and Theodore M. Lugwig, eds. *Transitions and Transformations in the History of Religions*. Leiden, Netherlands: E. J. Brill, 1980, 153–84.

Owens, Bruce. "The Politics of Divinity in the Kathmandu Valley: The Festival of Bunga Dya/Rato Matsyendranath." Columbia University: Ph.D. Dissertation, 1989.

———. "Blood and Bodhisattvas: Sacrifice among the Newar Buddhists of Nepal," in Charles Ramble and Martin Brauen, eds. *Anthropology of Tibet and the Himalayas*. Zurich: Ethnological Museum of the University of Zurich, 1993, 258–69.

———. "Human Agency and Divine Power: Transforming Images and Recreating Gods among the Newar," *History of Religions* 35, 1995, 201–40.

Pal, Pratapaditya. *The Art of Licchavi Nepal*. Bombay, India: Marg Publications, 1974.

———. Pal, Pratapaditya. *Arts of Nepal*. Leiden, Netherlands: E. J. Brill, 1974.

———. *Nepal: Where the Gods Are Young*. New York: Asia House, 1975.

———. "The Bhīmaratha Rite and Nepali Art," *Oriental Art* 23 (2), 1977, 176–89.

Parimoo, Ratan, "Vidhurapandita-Jataka—From Bharhut and Ajanta—A Study of Narrative, Semiological and Stylistic Aspects," in Ratan Parimoo et al, eds. *The Art of Ajanta: New Perspectives* (2 Vols.). New Delhi, India: Books and Books, 1991.

Paul, Diana Y. *Women in Buddhism: Images of the Feminine in the Mahāyāna Tradition*. Berkeley: University of California Press, 1985.

Pelikan, Jaroslav. *The Vindication of Tradition*. New Haven: Yale University Press, 1984.

Petech, Luciano. *The Medieval History of Nepal*. (2nd ed.). Serie Orientale Roma, 54, 1984.

Pezzali, Amalia. "The Spiritual Progress to Reach Nirvāṇa According to

Vasubandhu," in *Premier Colloque Etienne Lamotte*. Louvain, Belgium: Publications de L'Institute Orientaliste, 1993, 124–29.

Poussin, L. de La Vallee. "Staupikam," *Harvard Journal of Asiatic Studies* 2, 1937, 276–89.

Prebish, Charles S. *Buddhist Monastic Discipline: The Sanskrit Pratimoksa Sutras of the Mahasamghikas and Mulasarvastivadins* University Park: Pennsylvania State University Press, 1975a.

———, ed. *Buddhism: A Modern Perspective*. University Park: Pennsylvania State University Press, 1975b.

Prothero, Stephen. "Henry Steel Olcott and 'Protestant Buddhism'," *Journal of the American Academy of Religion* 52 (2), 1995, 281–302.

Prusek, Jaroslav. "The Narrators of Buddhist Scriptures and Religious Tales in the Sung Period," *Archiv Orientalni* 10, 1938, 375–89.

Przyluski, J. "The Harmika and the Origin of Buddhist Stupas," *The Indian Historical Quarterly* 11 (2), 1935, 199–210.

Pye, Michael. *Skillful Means: A Concept in Mahayana Buddhism*. London: Duckworth, 1978.

Rajapatirana, Tissa. "*Suvarṇavarṇāvadāna*: Translated and Edited Together with Its Tibetan Translation and the *Lakṣacaityasamutpatti*," Australian National University: Ph.D. Dissertation, 1974.

Ramanujan, A. K. "Who Needs Folklore? The Relevance of Oral Traditions to South Asian Studies," *South Asia Occasional Papers (University of Hawaii)* 1, 1990, 12.

Ray, Himanshu P. *Monastery and Guild: Commerce under the Satavahanas*. Delhi, India: Oxford University Press, 1986.

Ray, Reginald A. *Buddhist Saints in India: A Study of Buddhist Values and Orientations*. New York: Oxford University Press, 1994.

Reader, Ian. "Social Action and Personal Benefits in Contemporary Japanese Buddhism," *Buddhist-Christian Studies* 15, 1995, 3–17.

Reader, Ian and Tanabe, George J. *Practically Religious: Worldly Benefits and the Common Religion of Japan*. Honolulu: University of Hawaii Press, 1998.

Reynolds, Vernon and Tanner, Ralph. *The Social Ecology of Religion*, (*2d ed.*). New York: Oxford University Press, 1995.

Rhys-Davids, Caroline F. "Notes on Early Economic Conditions in Northern India," *Journal of the Royal Asiatic Society* 53, 1901, 859–888.

Rhys-Davids, Thomas W. *The Questions of King Milinda*. New York: Dover reprint, 1963.

———. *Buddhist Suttas*. New York: Dover reprint, 1969.

Riccardi, Theodore. "Buddhism in Ancient and Early Medieval Nepal", in A. K. Narain, ed. *Studies in the History of Buddhism*. New Delhi, India: B. R. Publishing, 1980, 265–81.

Richman, Paula. *Women, Branch Stories, and Religious Rhetoric in a Tamil Buddhist Text*. Syracuse: Syracuse University Press, 1988.

Rimpoche, Tenga. "The Benefits of Building a Stupa," *Vajradhatu Sun*, Fall 1990, 23–25.

Robinson, Richard H., trans. *Chinese Buddhist Verse*. London: John Murray, 1954.

———. "The Ethic of the Householder Bodhisattva," *Bharati* 9 (2), 1966, 25–56.

Roerich, G. N. *The Blue Annals of gZhon-nu-dpal*. Volume 2. Calcutta, 1953.

Rose, Leo E. "Secularization of a Hindu Polity: The Case of Nepal," in Donald E. Smith, ed. *Religion and Political Development*. Boston: Little Brown, 1970, 31–48.

Rosen, Elizabeth S. "Buddhist Architecture and Lay Patronage at Nagarjunakonda," in Anna Dallapiccola, ed. *The Stupa: Its Religious, Historical, and Architectural Significance*. Wiesbaden, Germany: Franz Steiner Verlag, 1980, 112–26.

Rubin, David. *Nepali Visions, Nepali Dreams The Poetry of Laxmiprasad Devkota*. New York: Columbia University Press, 1980.

Ruegg, David Seyfort. "Some Observations on the Present and Future of Buddhist Studies," *Journal of the International Association of Buddhist Studies* 15 (1), 1995, 104–17.

Samuel, Geoffrey. *Civilized Shamans: Buddhism in Tibetan Societies*. Washington: Smithsonian Institution Press, 1993.

Schank, Roger C. *Tell Me a Story*. New York: Scribner, 1990.

Scherrer-Schaub, Cristina Anna. "Some *Dhāraṇī* Written on Paper Functioning as Dharmakaya Relics: A Tentative Approach to PT 350," in Per Kvaerne, ed. *Tibetan Studies, Vol. 2*. Oslo, 1994, 711–27.

Schopen, Gregory. "The Phrase '*sa pṛthivīprades`as` caityabhūto bhavet*' in the *Vajracchedikā*: Notes on the Cult of the Book in Mahāyāna," *Indo-Iranian Journal* 17, 1975, 147–81.

———. "*Sukhāvatī* as a Generalized Religious Goal in Sanskrit Mahāyāna Sūtra Literature," *Indo-Iranian Journal* 19, 1977, 177–210.

———. "Mahāyāna in Indian Inscriptions," *Indo-Iranian Journal* 21, 1979, 1–19.

———. "Filial Piety and the Monk in the Practice of Indian Buddhism: A Question of, 'Sinicization' Viewed from the Other Side," *T'oung Pao* 70, 1984, 110–26.

———. "Two Problems in the History of Indian Buddhism: The Layman/Monk Distinction and the Doctrines of the Transference of Merit," *Studienzur Indologie und Iranistik* 10, 1985a, 9–47.

———. "The Bodhigarbhālankāralakṣa and Vimaloṣṇīṣa Dhāraṇīs in Indian Inscriptions: Two Sources for the Practice of Buddhism in Medieval India," *Wiener Zeitschrift fur die Kunde Sudasiens und Archiv fur indische Philosophie* 29, 1985b, 119–49.

———. "Burial '*ad sanctos*' and the Physical Presence of the Buddha in Early Indian Buddhism: A Study in the Archaeology of Religions, *Religion* 17, 1987a, 193–225.

———. "The Inscription on the Kushan Image of Amitabha and the Character of the Early Mahāyāna in India," *Journal of the International Association of Buddhist Studies* 10 (2), 1987b, 99–134.

———. "On Monks, Nuns and 'Vulgar' Practices: The Introduction of the Image Cult into Indian Buddhism," *Artibus Asiae* 49 (1/2), 1988–89, 153–68.

———. "The Stupa Cult and the Extant Pali Vinaya," *Journal of the Pali Text Society* 13, 1989a, 83–100.

———. "A Verse from the *Bhadracarīpraṇidhāna* in a 10th Century Inscription found at Nalanda," *Journal of the International Association of Buddhist Studies* 12 (1), 1989b, 149–57.

———. "An Old Inscription from Amaravati and the Cult of the Local Monastic Dead in Indian Buddhist Monasteries," *The Journal of the International Association of Buddhist Studies* 14 (2), 1991a, 281–329.

———. "The Ritual Obligations and Donor Roles of Monks in the Pali Vinaya," *Journal of the Pali Text Society* 16, 1991b, 1–21.

———. "Monks and the Relic Cult in the *Mahaparinibbanasutta*: An Old Misunderstanding in Regard to Monastic Buddhism," in G. Schopen and K. Shinohara, eds. *From Benares to Beijing: Essays on Buddhism and Chinese Religion in Honor of Jan Yun-hua*. Oakville, Canada 1991c, 187–201.

———. "Archaeology and Protestant Presuppositions in the Study of Indian Buddhism," *History of Religions* 31 (1), 1991d, 1–23.

———. "On Avoiding Ghosts and Social Censure: Monastic Funerals in the Mulasarvastivada-Vinaya," *Journal of Indian Philosophy* 20, 1992, 1–39.

———. “Stupa and Tirtha: Tibetan Mortuary Practices and an Unrecognized Form of Burial *Ad Sanctos* at Buddhist Sites in India,” in T. Skorupski, ed. *Buddhist Forum II: Papers in Honour of D.S. Ruegg*. Tring, England: The Institute of Buddhist Studies, 1993a.

———. “Burial Rights and Bones of Contention: More on Monastic Funerals and Relics in the *Mūasarvāstivāda-Vinaya*,” *Journal of Indian Philosophy* 21, 1993b, 31–81.

———. “The Monastic Ownership of Servants or Slaves: Local and Legal Factors in the Redactional History of Two *Vinayas*,” *Journal of the International Association of Buddhist Studies* 17 (2), 1994a, 145–74.

———. “Doing Business for the Lord: Lending on Interest and Written Loan Contracts in the Mulasarvastivadin-Vinaya,” *Journal of the American Oriental Society* 114 (4), 1994b, 527–54.

———. “The Lay Ownership of Monasteries and the Role of the Monk in the Mulasarvastivadin Monasticism,” *Journal of the International Association of Buddhist Studies* 19 (1), 1996, 81–126.

Seckel, Dietrich. *The Art of Buddhism*. New York: Crown, 1964.

Shaku, Soyen. “Sutra of Forty-two Chapters,” in D. T. Suzuki, trans. *Sermons of a Buddhist Abbot*. New York: Samuel Weiser, Inc., 1971, 3–21.

Shastri, Hara Prasad, ed. *The Vrihat Svayambhu Puranam*. Calcutta: Asiatic Society of Bengal, 1894.

Shih, Heng-ching, trans. *The Sutra on Upasaka Precepts*. Berkeley: Numata Center for Buddhist Translation and Research, 1994.

Shih, Hsio-yen. “Readings and Re-Readings of Narrative in Dunhuang Murals,” *Artibus Asiae* 53 (1–2), 1993, 59–88.

Shils, Edward. *Tradition*. Chicago: University of Chicago Press, 1981.

Shakya, Hemaraj. *Srī Svayambhū Mahācaitya*. Kathmandu, Nepal: Vikas Mandal, 1977.

———. *Samyak Mahādāna Guthi*. Kathmandu, Nepal: Samkata Press, 1980.

Sharkey, Gregory S. J. “Daily Ritual in Newar Buddhist Shrines.” Oxford: Oxford University: D. Phil Thesis, 1994.

Shih, Hsio-yen. “Readings and Re-Readings of Narrative in Dunhuang Murals,” *Artibus Asiae* 53, 1993, 59–88

Shukla, N. S. “The Qualities of an Ācārya on the Basis of the *Ācāryakriyasamuccaya* of Jagaddarpaṇa,” in R. C. Pandeva, ed. *Buddhist Studies in India*. New Delhi, India: Manohar, 1975, 126–29.

Silva, Lily de. “Ministering to the Sick and Counseling the Terminally Ill,” in N. K. Wagle and F. Watanabe, eds. *Studies on Buddhism in Honour of Professor A.K. Warder*. Toronto: University of Toronto, 1993, 29–39.

Sircar, D. C. *The Sakti Cult and Tara*. Calcutta: University of Calcutta, 1967.

Sizemore, Russell F. and Donald K. Swearer, *Ethics, Wealth, and Salvation: A Study in Buddhist Social Ethics*. Columbia: University of South Carolina Press, 1991.

Skilling, Peter. "The Rakṣā Literature of the Srāvakayāna," *Journal of the Pali Text Society* 16, 1992, 109–82.

Skorupski, Tadeuz, *The Sarvadurgatiparisodhana Tantra*. Delhi, India: Motilal Banarsidass, 1983.

———. "Observations on the Nature of Buddhist Rituals Described in the *Kriyāsaṃgraha*," 1996, manuscript.

Slusser, Mary. *Nepal Mandala*. Princeton: Princeton University Press, 1982.

———. "On a Sixteenth-Century Pictorial Pilgrim's Guide from Nepal," *Archives of Asian Art* 38, 1985, 6–36.

Snellgrove, David L. *Buddhist Himalaya*. Oxford: Cassirer, 1957.

———. "The Notion of Divine Kingship in Tantric Buddhism," *Studies in the History of Religions* 4, 1959, 204–18.

———. "The Sākyamuni's Final Nirvāṇa," *Bulletin of the School of Oriental and African Studies* 36, 1973, 399–411.

———. *Indo-Tibetan Buddhism*. Boulder: Shambala Press, 1987.

——— and Tadeusz Skorupski. *The Cultural Heritage of Ladakh* Vol. 1. New Delhi, India: Vikas, 1977.

Snodgrass, A. *The Symbolism of the Stupa*. Ithaca: Cornell University Press, 1985.

Southwold, Martin. "Buddhism and the Definition of Religion," *Man* 13, 1978, 362–75.

———. "Religious Belief," *Man* 14, 1979, 628–44.

———. *Buddhism in Life: The Anthropological Study of Religion and the Sinhalese Practice of Buddhism*. Manchester, England: Manchester University Press, 1983.

———. "The Concept of Nirvana in Village Buddhism," in Richard Burghart and Audrey Cantille, eds. *Indian Religion*. New York: St. Martin's, 1985, 15–50.

Spencer, Robert F. "Ethical Expressions in a Burmese Jātaka," *Journal of American Folklore* 79, 1966, 278–301.

Speyer, J. S. *The Jatakamala*. New Delhi, India: Motilal Banarsidass, 1971.

Spiro, Melford E. "The Internalization of a Burmese Gender Ideology," in Spiro, *Anthropological Other or Burmese Brother?: Studies in Cultur-*

al Analysis. New Brunswick, New Jersey: Transaction Publishers, 1992, 223–46.

Sponberg, Alan "Attitudes toward Women and the Feminine in Early Buddhism," in Jose Egnacio Cabezon, ed. *Buddhism, Sexuality, Gender.* Albany: SUNY Press, 1992, 3–36.

Stablein, William. "A Medical-Cultural System among the Tibetan and Newar Buddhists: Ceremonial Medicine," *Kailash* 1 (3), 1973, 193–203.

———. "The Mahākāla Tantra: A Theory of Ritual Blessings and Tantric Medicine." Columbia University: Ph.D. Dissertation, 1976a.

———. "Mahākāla the Neo-Shaman: Master of the Ritual," in John Hitchcock and R. Jones, eds. *Spirit Possession in the Nepal Himalayas*. Warminster: Aris and Phillips, 1976b, 361–75.

———. "A Descriptive Analysis of the Content of Nepalese Buddhist Pujas as a Medical-Cultural System, with References to Tibetan Parallels," in Agehananda Bharati, ed. *The Realm of the Extrahuman: Ideas and Actions*. The Hague, Netherlands: Mouton, 1976c, 403–11.

Strickmann, Michel. "The Consecration Sutra: A Buddhist Book of Spells," in Robert Buswell Jr., ed. *Chinese Buddhist Apocrypha*. Honolulu: University of Hawaii Press, 1990, 75–118.

Strong, John S. "The Transforming Gift: An Analysis of Devotional Acts of Offering in Buddhist *Avadāna* Literature," *History of Religions* 18 (3), 1979, 221–37.

———. *The Legend of King Asoka*. Princeton: Princeton University Press, 1983.

———. *The Legend and Cult of Upagupta*. Princeton: Princeton University Press, 1992.

———. *The Experience of Buddhism*. Belmont, Calif.: Wadsworth, 1995.

Sudarshan, Bhikshu. *Simhalasārthabāha va Kabir Kumar Bākhan*. Kathmanda, Nepal: Cvasapasa, 1967.

Sukatno, Hadiyati Endang. "Stupikas and Votive Tablets Found in Indonesia," *Proceedings of the 1983 SPAFA Consultative Workshop on Archaeological and Environmental Studies on Srivijaya*. Bangkok, Thailand: SPAFA, 1984.

Taddei, Maurizio. "Inscribed Clay Tablets and Miniature Stupas from Ghazni," *East and West* 20, 1970, 70–84.

Takaoka, Hidenobu, ed. *A Microfilm Catalogue of the Buddhist Manuscripts in Nepal*. Nagoya, Japan: Buddhist Library, 1981.

Takakusu, J. *A Record of the Buddhist Religion*. New Delhi: Munshiram Manoharlal, 1982.

Tambiah, Stanley J. "The Magical Power of Words," *Man* 3, 1968, 175–208.

———. "Literacy in a Buddhist Village in North-east Thailand," in J. Goody, ed. *Literacy in Traditional Societies*. Cambridge: Cambridge University Press, 1968, 86–131.

———. "Buddhism and This-Worldly Activity," *Modern Asian Studies* 7 (1), 1973, 1–20.

———. *Buddhist Saints of the Forest and the Cult of Amulets*. Cambridge: Cambridge University Press, 1984.

Tatelman, Joel. "'The Trials of Yaśodharā': The Legend of the Buddha's Wife in the *Bhadrakalpāvadāna*," *Buddhist literature* 1, 1999, 176-261.

Templeman, David. *The Origin of the Tara Tantra by Jo-nan Taranatha*. Dharamsala, India: Library of Tibetan Works and Archives, 1981.

Tewari, Ramesh Chandra. "Socio-Cultural Aspects of Theravada Buddhism in Nepal," *Journal of the International Association of Buddhist Studies* 6 (2), 1983, 67–93.

Thera, Narada. *Everyman's Ethics*. Kandy, Sri Lanka: Buddhist Publication Society, 1966.

Thomas, Edward J. *The History of Buddhist Thought*. London: Routledge and Kegan Paul, 1933.

Thurman, Robert A. F. *The Holy Teaching of Vimalakirti: A Mahāyāna Scripture*. University Park: University of Pennsylvania Press, 1976.

Toffin, Gerard. "Etudes sur les Newars de la Vallee Kathmandou: Guthi, Funerailles et Castes," *L'Ethnographie* 2, 1975a, 206–25.

———. "L'Indra Jatra à Pyangaon," *L'Ethnographie* 1, 1978, 109–37.

———. *Société et religion chez les Néwar du Népal*. Paris: CNRS, 1984.

———. "Mythical and Symbolic Origins of the City: The Case of the Kathmandu Valley," *Diogenes* 152, 1990, 101–23.

———. *Le Palais et le Temple: La fonction royale dans la vallée du Nepal*. Paris: CNRS, 1993.

Tucci, Guiseppe. "The Sea and Land Routes of a Buddhist Sadhu in the Sixteenth Century," *Indian Historical Quarterly* 7 (4), 1931, 683–702.

———. *Stupa: Art, Architectonics and Symbolism (Indo-Tibetica I)* English translation in *Sata-Pitaka Series* #347, Lokesh Chandra, ed. New Delhi, India: Aditya Prakashan, 1988.

Turner, Ralph Lilley. *A Comparative and Etymological Dictionary of the Nepali Language*. London: Routledge and Kegan Paul, 1931.

Uprety, Prem. *Nepal-Tibet Relations, 1850–1930*. Kathmandu, Nepal: Puja Nara, 1980.

Vaidya, Janak Lal and Prem Bahadar Kamsakar. *A Descriptive Catalog of Selected Manuscripts Preserved at the Asa Sapha Kuthi*. Kathmandu: Cvasapasa Press, 1991.

Vajracarya, Adivajra. *Pañcarakṣā Pāṭha Sūtra*. Kathmandu, Nepal: Pracanda Mahalaksmi Press, 1993.

Vajracarya, Divya Vajra. *Dharmasamgraha Kosa*. Kathmandu, Nepal: Madan Printing Press, 1979.

———. *Pañca Raksā Kathāsāra*. Kathmandu, Nepal: Jana Kalyana Press, 1980.

Vajracarya, Naresh Man. *Gurumandalārcana*. Kathmandu, Nepal: 1989.

Vajracarya, Ratna Kaji. *Yeṃ Deyä Bauddha Pūjā Kriyāyā Halaṃjvalaṃ*. Kathmandu, Nepal: Sankata Printing Press, 1981.

———. *Buddhist Ritual Dance*. Kathmandu, Nepal: Kala-mandapa, 1986.

Van Kooji, Karel Rijk. "The Iconography of the Buddhist Wood-carvings in a Newar Monastery in Kathmandu (Chusya-Baha)," *Journal of the Nepal Research Centre* 1 (Humanities), 1977, 39–82.

Veith, Ilza and Atsumi Minami. "A Buddhist Prayer Against Sickness," *History of Religions* 5 (2), 1966, 239–49.

Vidyabhusan, Satis Chandra Acharyya. "The Story of Mahakashyapa," *Journal of the Buddhist Text and Anthropological Society* 6 (1–2), 1895, 16–19.

Vitali, Roberto. *Early Temples of Central Tibet*. London: Serindia Publications, 1990.

Waddell, Augustine, "Note on Some Ajanta Paintings," *The Indian Antiquary* 22, 1893, 1–13.

Wadley, Susan S. "*Vrats*: Transformers of Destiny," in Charles F. Keyes and E. Valentine Daniel, eds. *Karma: An Anthropological Inquiry*. Berkeley: University of California Press, 1983, 147–62.

Wangu, Madhu Bazaz. "Hermeneutics of a Kashmiri *Mahātmya* Text in Context," in Jeffrey R. Timm, ed. *Texts in Context*. Albany: SUNY Press, 1992, 147–68.

Warren, Henry Clarke. *Buddhism in Translations*. Cambridge: Harvard University Press, 1922.

Wayman, Alex. "Buddhism," *Historia Religionum* 2, 1971, 372–464.

———. "The Significance of Mantras, from the Veda Down to Buddhist Tantric Practice," *The Adyar Library Bulletin* 39, 1975, 65–89.

———. "The Sarvarahasyatantra," *Acta Indologica* 6, 1984, 521–69.

———. "Esoteric Buddhism," in Mircea Eliade, ed. *The Encyclopaedia of Religion*. Vol. 2. New York: Macmillan, 1987, 473–82.

Whitaker, K. P. K. "A Buddhist Spell," *Asia Major* 10 (1), 1963, 9–22.

Wijayaratna, Mohan. *Buddhist Monastic Life*. Cambridge: Cambridge University Press, 1990.

Willis, Janice Dean.: *On Knowing Reality: The Tattvartha Chapter of Asanga's Bodhisattvabhumi*. New York: Columbia University Press, 1979.

Williams, Paul. *Mahāyāna Buddhism: The Doctrinal Foundations* New York: Routledge, 1989.

Willson, Martin. *In Praise of Tara*. Boston: Wisdom, 1996.

Wiltshire, Martin. "The 'Suicide Problem' in the Pali Canon," *Journal of the International Association of Buddhist Studies* 6 (2), 1983, 124–40.

Winternitz, Maurice. *A History of Indian Literature*. Calcutta: University of Calcutta Press, 1933.

Woodward, F. L., trans. *The Book of the Gradual Sayings*. Vol. 2. Oxford: Pali Text Society, 1992.

Wright, Arthur F. *Buddhism in Chinese History*. Palo Alto, Calif.: Stanford University Press, 1959.

Wright, Daniel. *History of Nepal*. New Delhi: Asian Educational Services, 1990 (Original edition 1877).

Yu, Chun-fang. "A Sutra Promoting the White-Robed Guanyin as Giver of Sons," in Donald S. Lopez, ed. *Religions of China in Practice*. Princeton: Princeton University Press, 1996, 97–105.

Yun-Hua, Jan. "Buddhist Self-Immolation in Medieval China," *History of Religions* 4 (2), 1965, 243–68.

———. "The Power of Recitation: An Unstudied Aspect of Chinese Buddhism," *Studi Storico Religiosi* 1 (2), 1977, 289–99.

Zurcher, Erik. *The Buddhist Conquest of China*. Leiden, Netherlands: E. J. Brill, 1972.

Zysk, Keneth G. *Asceticism and Healing in Ancient India: Medicine in the Buddhist Monastery*. New York: Oxford University Press, 1991.

Index